INDUSTRIAL ARCHAEOLOGY

Kenneth Hudson's early career was spent teaching in schools and in the Extra Mural Department of the University of Bristol. In 1954 he joined the BBC as a producer and industrial correspondent, leaving in 1966 to become Senior Lecturer, University of Bath. Since 1972 he has been a free-lance writer working from Bath, and has travelled extensively in Europe and America lecturing on industrial archaeology. In 1973 he became a consultant to UNESCO, working as general editor and researcher for their forthcoming report *Museums for the 1980s*. Editor of the quarterly journal *Industrial Archaeology* from 1964-69, he has recently become a member of the judging panel for the Museum of the Year award.

HUDSON, Kenneth. Industrial archaeology: a new introduction. 3d. ed., rev. and reset. John Baker (dist. by Humanities), 1977 (c1976). 240p ill bibl index. 12.50 ISBN 0-212-97014-3

CHOICE   JUNE '77

History of Science &

Technology

Once skeptically viewed by historians as artifactual or, even worse, as antiquarian in orientation, industrial archaeology seems to be coming of age. This latest edition of a highly articulate exposition of industrial archaeology extends current thinking to encompass people as well as machines and structures. The social role of technology and the historical circumstances that gave rise to the Industrial Revolution receive a greater share of attention then previously; the third edition's contextual analysis of technology will surely appeal to a broader range of scholars. Hudson describes machines, products, and processes with such an enticingly palpable sense that even the old and familiar in technology take on new life. His work is free of muddy descriptions or explanations that so frequently dull the works of armchair scholars. No mere abstractions but solid field experience guide his descriptions. Numerous illustrations and drawings further enhance the text. Although this work addresses the archaeology of the Industrial Revolution as it occurred in England alone, it does establish a useful pattern for similar enterprises in other countries. It therefore offers something of value to American readers beyond those specializing in British history or the Industrial Revolution. The author's achievement may also inspire many Americans by realizing what is possible in preserving their own industrial heritage. Recommended for undergraduate and graduate libraries.

INDUSTRIAL ARCHAEOLOGY

a new introduction

KENNETH HUDSON

John Baker
London

Distributed in the U.S.A. by
Humanities Press
Atlantic Highlands, N. J.

First published 1963
Second, revised edition 1966
Third, revised and reset edition 1976
John Baker (Publishers) Ltd
35 Bedford Row, London WC1R 4JH
© 1976 John Baker (Publishers) Ltd

ISBN 0 212 97014 3

Printed in Great Britain by
BAS Printers Limited, Wallop, Hampshire

Contents

Illustrations

Photographs

Foreword

In 1961 the late John Baker, one of the most enterprising figures in British post-war publishing, invited me to write a book on Industrial Archaeology, a subject or pastime which in that period of innocence very few people had ever heard of. In 1963 this pioneering work appeared, with the active support of the Council for British Archaeology, and the advice and help of a number of people whose names are remembered with gratitude in the Acknowledgments of the present book. Mr. Baker did very well with his enlightened and public-spirited suggestion. A new edition of *Industrial Archaeology: an Introduction* appeared in 1966, and with this, too, long since exhausted, the present publishers, who had acquired the rights in the book, have decided to embark on a completely rewritten version.

The original book, I said in 1963, 'does not set out to be an encyclopaedia of Industrial Archaeology. Its aim is the more modest one of attempting to draw attention to the surviving memorials of our industrial past and to help to create a public opinion which is sufficiently well informed to approve of money being spent on recording and preserving tangible evidence of some of the most remarkable achievements of a country which was, in its time, the leading industrial nation in the world.' My aim has changed only to the extent of understanding that one must never cease to emphasise that workers are as important as machines and buildings. Industrial Archaeology, in other words, is essentially a humane study.

In the following pages I have done my best to illustrate this and to show why I believe that the Industrial Archaeologist is never likely to be short of battles to fight. A high proportion of the work carried out during the past dozen years has been on the initiative of local groups, whose membership is invariably very mixed, educationally, socially and professionally. Wherever possible, I have chosen my examples from the research done by these groups, of which there are now eighty or so dotted unevenly over Britain. To have done otherwise would have been both ungrateful and unfair. As things have turned out, the close co-operation between the academics and the weekend Industrial Archaeologists has been one of the most remarkable and most British features of a post-war phenomenon which one hopes will continue for a long time.

During the ten years of its existence, from 1964 to 1974, the quarterly which began as *The Journal of Industrial Archaeology* and ended as *Industrial Archaeology* gave a very wide range of people an opportunity to publish the results of their fieldwork and researches. Since its regretted death, no adequate substitute has so far appeared, but the abundant references to it in the present work indicate the invaluable part it played during a creative and important period.

1976   Kenneth Hudson

Acknowledgments

In preparing the first edition of this book, I was greatly helped by a number of specialists, whose names I should like to record with gratitude once again: They were: Frank Atkinson; J. Baker; N. W. Bertenshaw; C. R. Clinker; Norman Davy; W. K. V. Gale; E. R. R. Green, Charles Hadfield; R. S. Haggar; John Higgs; W. G. Hoskins; E. L. Kelting; Peter Mathias; Arthur Raistrick; W. A. Seaby; B. Spiller; F. B. Stitt; A. Stowers; A. J. Taylor; Rex Wailes and P. N. Wilson. These twenty-one pioneers were the frontline troops of Industrial Archaeology in 1963 and several of them are fortunately still in that position now, in 1976.

Since 1963, local groups of enthusiasts have been established all over the country, academic interest has grown to an extent which it would have been impossible to forecast twelve years ago, a national journal has been founded, dozens of books written, and information has poured in from all sides. In the process, what might be called the philosophy of Industrial Archaeology has undergone a series of modifications. The new information and the new philosophy are the reasons for rewriting the present book, and it is a pleasure to have this opportunity of thanking the people who have pushed and encouraged me to rethink my ideas. A number of them live abroad, which is a token of the encouraging fact that Industrial Archaeology has shown itself to possess a high degree of export potential.

Of my overseas friends and colleagues, I should like to single out especially Georges van den Abeelen, of Brussels; Marcel Evrard, of Le Creusot; Jerzy Jaziuk, of Warsaw; Anders Jespersen, of Copenhagen; Thomas W. Leavitt, of the Merrimack Valley Textile Museum, Massachusetts, U.S.A.; Jiri Majer and Jiri Vondra, of Prague; Marie Nisser, of Uppsala; Sigvard Strandh, of Stockholm; Paul Stumes, of Ottawa; Robert M. Vogel, of Washington, and Otfried Wagenbreth, of Freiberg.

Among those in Britain who have helped me towards a better understanding of what Industrial Archaeology is all about, and on whose friendship I relied on constantly, I am particularly indebted to Neil Cossons, of Ironbridge; Michael Rix, of Wolverhampton; Frank Atkinson, of Beamish, once again; Donald Cross, of Salisbury; Ray Sutcliffe, of the BBC's History and Archaeology Unit; Richard Storey, formerly of the National Register of Archives; and L. T. C. Rolt, kindest and most omniscient of men, whose death in 1974 has robbed Industrial Archaeology of one of its main sources of strength, respect and humanity.

Caution

This essay is a foray into the debatable borderland between history, technology and economics. Anyone who sets up as a middleman is likely to provoke the traditional mistrust of brokers and bodgers.

H. J. Habakkuk
*American and British Technology
in the Nineteenth Century*

1

What is
Industrial Archaeology?

The term 'Industrial Archaeology' was almost certainly invented early in the 1950s by Mr. Donald Dudley, later Professor of Latin in the University of Birmingham and at that time Director of its Extra-Mural Department.

Mr. Dudley did no more than throw this very useful phrase into conversation. Its first appearance in print appears to have occurred in the autumn of 1955, in an article written by Mr. Michael Rix for *The Amateur Historian*. In this article Mr. Rix implied, rather than stated, a definition of the new term. 'Great Britain,' he said, 'as the birthplace of the Industrial Revolution is full of monuments left by this remarkable series of events. Any other country would have set up machinery for the scheduling and preservation of these memorials that symbolise the movement which is changing the face of the globe, but we are so oblivious of our national heritage that, apart from a few museum pieces, the majority of these landmarks are neglected or unwittingly destroyed.'

Mr. Rix went on to instance the kind of monuments he had in mind – eighteenth and early nineteenth century factories, 'the steam engines and locomotives that made possible the provision of power, the first metal-framed buildings, cast-iron aqueducts and bridges, the pioneering attempts at railways, locks and canals'. All these things, he believes, 'represent a fascinating interlocking field of study, whole tracts of which are still virtually unexplored'.

Since Mr. Rix gave the phrase 'Industrial Archaeology' to the world in this way it has been much disliked and strongly criticised, although nobody has yet been able to suggest a more acceptable alternative. To the objectors, 'Industrial Archaeology' is an impossible mongrel, the ugly offspring of two parents who should never have been allowed to breed. 'Industry', they say, is by common agreement, a recent growth, a phenomenon no more than two hundred years old. 'Archaeology', also by common agreement, deals with the more distant past.

15

How then, they demand, is it reasonable or decent to speak of industry and archaeology in the same breath?

The main cause of the difficulty is the regrettable, but not unalterable, fact that during the past fifty years the word archaeology has been quietly taken over and narrowed in meaning by the most active and most spectacular section of archaeologists, the excavators, and more especially by those concerned with pre-history, with the result that nowadays some of them appear to be getting very close to the position of claiming patent rights on it. Archaeology, they rightly claim, is concerned with things that are old. Certainly, one may reply, but how old is old? Everything has its birth and its old age and each industry has to be seen and studied against its own time-scale. In the case of the petroleum industry, for instance, the old and rare monuments date from the second half of the nine-teenth century. For atomic energy and for a number of plastics and synthetic fibres it is the 1940s that we have to consider. For iron bridges it is the middle of the eighteenth century. It is pointless and ridiculous to try to establish an arbi-trary date which can be used to divide the old from the recent, the archaeo-logically approved from the archaeologically disreputable.

In this respect our grandfathers thought and wrote in a more tolerant age. In 1878, for example, the *Transactions of the Cumberland and Westmorland Antiquarian and Archaeological Society* included a very useful and well-documented paper called 'The Archaeology of the West Cumberland Coal Trade'. The author, Mr. Isaac Fletcher, was an astronomer by profession and sufficiently eminent and scholarly to have become a Fellow of the Royal Society. He was writing in a period when it was still possible for an astronomer to write about economics, about history and about technology without being laughed at as a charlatan and when the word archaeology could still be used without difficulty or offence in the broad sense of a study of the past based on tangible remains. Mr. Fletcher's paper covered only the eighteenth and nineteenth centuries and it drew its facts from manuscripts, from personal visits to mines, from drawings of old machinery and from conversations with men who had spent a lifetime in the industry. 'I have had an opportunity,' he tells us, 'of examining a number of the weekly pay bills for the year 1709, still preserved in Whitehaven Castle, which throw much light on the state of mining operations at that period', and he reports on the 1795 Heslop winding engine at Low Wreak Pit in the same personal, observant way: 'She is at work to this day, and is well worth seeing by all who are interested in the archaeology of the steam engine. She is the last of her race and I believe it is the intention of her noble owner, after the exhaustion of Low Wreak Pit, that she shall be carefully preserved either at the South Kensington Museum or else-where.'[1]

It is impossible to know whether Mr. Fletcher would have felt inclined to describe himself as an archaeologist. What is quite clear is that he saw no reason

[1] This Heslop winding engine has been exhibited in the Science Museum, South Kensington since the Earl of Lonsdale presented it in 1878.

why he should not refer to 'the archaeology of the coal trade' or to 'the archaeology of the steam engine', and in this sense he is the ancestor of Mr. Dudley and
Mr. Rix.

'The history of the coal trade' or 'the history of the steam engine' would not
have had quite the same meaning or the same flavour. 'Archaeology' was the
right word for describing the investigations of a practical, inquisitive man who
saw the necessity of collecting a great deal of his own evidence on the spot, the
man who was as happy out in the field as behind a desk or in a library. 'History'
might well have suggested a more book-centred, more sedentary approach.

But since 1878, as we have already noticed, the word 'archaeology' has narrowed its meaning very considerably, mainly as a result of being appropriated by
scholars whose principal evidence is normally to be found buried under several
feet of soil and rubbish. This process has gone so far that in the minds of most
people now living, archaeology is almost a synonym for the excavation of prehistoric remains. This is a great pity for two reasons, first, because it deprives
students of later periods of civilisation of a very useful word and, second, because
it denies the essential continuity of both scholarship and civilisation.

No one has protested against this state of affairs more strongly and more wisely
than the founder and editor of *Antiquity*, the late O. G. S. Crawford.[2] 'Archaeology,' he writes, 'is merely the past tense of anthropology. It is concerned with
"past phases of human culture".' And the basis of culture, he insists, is technology.
A good archaeologist must be interested in every aspect of the culture he has
chosen to study – its technology, its social organisation, its political system.
Otherwise, he cannot interpret what he finds, he cannot talk sense.

It is impossible, in Crawford's opinion, to draw a time-line across the subject,
to declare, in effect, that 'archaeology ends here'. 'We are allowed,' he says, 'to
use archaeological technique in dealing with a well-documented "historical"
period like the Dark Ages, or one that is less well documented, such as ancient
Egypt or Mesopotamia. Future archaeologists will perhaps excavate the ruined
factories of the nineteenth and twentieth centuries, when the radiation effects of
atom bombs have died away. These technological matters will then be legitimate.
Why are they not so when they are so much better known?'

Crawford's campaign to widen and liberalise the meaning of archaeology
coincided with a very similar battle on behalf of local history, in which one of the
leading figures has been Professor W. G. Hoskins, who, like Crawford, sees no
point at all in the mere discovery and accumulation of facts. One has to have an
attitude to the facts in order to perceive any sense and cohesion in them. Discovering and recording evidence is a sterile activity, unless one has some idea as
to what it is evidence of. On the one hand, says Hoskins, we have an abundance
of local historians who are 'preoccupied with facts and correspondingly unaware
of problems' and, on the other, we are faced with a group of people who refuse

---

[2] Particularly in his *Archaeology in the Field*, 1953.

to submit their theories to the test of field work. 'Some of the best documented local histories,' he notes, 'betray not the slightest sign that the author has looked over the hedges of his chosen place, or walked its boundaries, or explored its streets, or noticed its buildings and what they mean in terms of the history he is trying to write.'[3]

Isaac Fletcher, whose paper on the West Cumberland Coal Trade was referred to earlier, appears to meet the requirements of both Dr. Crawford and Professor Hoskins. He was certainly a local historian who, in Hoskins' phrase, was not afraid to get his feet wet, and whose interest in the theme of technological progress allowed him to sift and discipline his facts. And he was equally an archaeologist who discovered much of his information in the only place where it existed, in the field. So far as he was concerned, any evidence was valuable, provided it could 'shed light on mining operations'. Whether his field of activity is best described as archaeology or local history or industrial history is surely beside the point. What matters is that he went to a lot of trouble to get his facts right and to link them together in a meaningful, and therefore interesting way. He belonged to an age in which it was comparatively easy and reputable for one man to develop interests which straddled several academic principles, to move, for example, from engineering to economic history and from economic history to geology and geography, in order to produce an intelligible and rounded study of the subject in hand.

Nowadays, this is much more difficult to achieve. A necessarily hybrid subject, such as industrial archaeology, is bound to be regarded with great suspicion, if not outright hostility, by those specialists who prefer to see firm and clear dividing lines between different fields of study. The label 'Industrial Archaeology' has come under equally heavy fire from economists, historians and archaeologists, partly for reasons of sheer conservatism, partly from resentment against an upstart and partly because of serious and genuine doubts that industrial archaeology can be made into a satisfactory academic discipline.

Mr. Rix, as we have seen, appears to have committed himself to saying that 'industrial archaeology is the study of early remains produced by the Industrial Revolution'. Quite a number of people who are professionally concerned with industrial archaeology would find this definition too constricting. 'The Industrial Revolution' is not a precise term and for this reason many historians have become rather chary of using it. There are those who distinguish between the first and second stages of the Industrial Revolution, the first, beginning in the sixteenth century and characterised by the increased use of coal and iron and by the increasing concentration of workers, first into workshops and then into factories, and the second, the period of electricity, scientific method and man-made materials, which began about 1850 and is still in progress. Others again, quarrel about the real meaning of 'Industrial' and either deny that anything truly 'industrial' occurred before the second half of the eighteenth century or make a distinction, not always easy to defend, between an industry and a rural craft.

[3] *Local History in England*, 1959, p. 3.

'We in the Welsh Folk Museum,' declared its then Curator, 'are concerned with rural crafts, whereas industry is dealt with by the Department of Industry in the National Museum of Wales. The small woollen mills, the rural tannery, the blacksmith's shop, etc., are examples of rural crafts in our sense. The rural woollen mill was never a factory employing a labour team from outside; it was generally a family affair with possibly one or two assistants. I cannot believe that these rural crafts have any relevance for any form of archaeology.'[4] This fairly rigid division between an industry – a manufacturing unit employing outside workers – and a craft – a manufacturing unit employing almost exclusively family labour – has a great deal to commend it and it is no doubt useful administratively, as a means of preventing the Welsh Folk Museum and the National Museum of Wales from treading on one another's toes, but a thoroughgoing attempt to observe it would almost certainly produce craft archaeology, technological archaeology, architectural archaeology and other not very helpful sub-categories of industrial archaeology.

One not infrequently hears and sees industrial archaeology described, if not actually defined, as 'the study of industrial monuments', but this is not very helpful, because there appears to be a good deal of disagreement as to what constitutes an industrial monument. An unofficial attempt made early in 1962, in self-defence, by a senior member of the Inspectorate of Ancient Monuments at the Ministry of Works produced this explanation. 'An industrial monument is any building or other fixed structure, especially of the period of the Industrial Revolution, which either alone or associated with primary plant for equipment, illustrates the beginning and development of industrial and technical processes, including means of communication.' The Council for British Archaeology and Research Committee on Industrial Archaeology has accepted a slightly modified version of this, according to which an industrial monument is 'any building or other fixed structure – especially of the period of the Industrial Revolution – which either alone or in association with plant or equipment, illustrates or is significantly associated with the beginnings and evolution of industrial and technical processes. These may be concerned with either production or communications.'

This definition, which must have nearly the force and authority of Canon Law, would certainly cover the select list of outstandingly important industrial monuments given in the Annual Reports for 1957 and 1961 of the Ancient Monuments Board for England – the Abbeydale Works at Sheffield, the Stretham engine and scoopwheel near Ely, the cottages at Wortley Forge near Sheffield, the tidemill at Woodbridge, the Cornish pumping engines and the Abraham Darby blast-furnace at Coalbrookdale. It would very probably bring into the canon such things as textile mills, together with any machinery that might still be in place, rope-walks, tanneries, bridges, toll-houses, railway stations and viaducts, canal locks and windmills. It would not include machinery and equipment transferred to museums.

[4] Dr. Iowerth Peate, in a letter to the author, 22nd October 1962.

Pearce's warehouse, Welshback, Bristol. Built in the Bristol Florentine style, *c.*1870

If a personal definition may be allowed, industrial archaeology is the discovery, recording and study of the physical remains of yesterday's industries and communications. But each decade will interpret 'study' in its own way, with its own ideas as to what is to be looked for and what details should be recorded. During the past twenty years industrial archaeology in Britain has passed through two stages of development and redefinition and is now entering a third. The process may be described as follows:–

Stage 1

A small and curiously assorted body of pioneers devoted a great deal of time and energy to stirring up the public conscience about the rapid disappearance of buildings and machinery which document the history of British industry and technology, especially in the nineteenth century. In books, articles, lectures, broadcasts and letters to the press, these enthusiasts and crusaders tried to convince disbelieving and tightfisted bureaucrats, uncomprehending industrialists and cynical, if not actually hostile academics that mills, steam engines and canal locks were of as much historical and cultural importance as castles, cathedrals and eighteenth century furniture.

These evangelists gradually learnt patience in countering accusations that they were sentimental fanatics and enemies of progress. By about 1960 considerable progress had been made and Stage 1 was shading into Stage 2.

Stage 2

This had three characteristic features – the creation all over Britain of amateur groups pursuing industrial archaeology as a hobby, the beginnings of a rudimentary National Register of Industrial Monuments, and the belated growth of academic interest in the subject.

If Britain has made a special contribution to industrial archaeology, as I believe it has, it has been in the form of these amateur groups and societies. The tradition of harnessing the energy of non-professionals in this way has already been established by certain outstanding local historians, including Dr. W. G. Hoskins, and by the Council of British Archaeology in what might be called excavation-archaeology. By the early 1950s it was accepted by many, if not most, British archaeologists and social historians that people working in their spare time could obtain a great deal of information, which might subsequently be digested and published by professional scholars and writers. The psychological gap between amateurs and professionals was certainly much narrower in 1955 than it had been twenty years earlier.

In the field of industrial archaeology this was particularly important, because this heavily industrialised country contained an abundance of nineteenth and early twentieth century material which was being rapidly and ignorantly swept away during the years of rebuilding and modernisation which followed the war. Without the expertise and specialised knowledge of local people, it would have been quite impossible to discover and record this great mass of historic buildings, machinery and equipment before it was demolished and bulldozed away.

One should not, however, paint too rosy a picture of what happened, or of what is still happening. In Britain, as elsewhere, amateur organisations are started and kept going by devoted people, prepared to give up many hours each week to creating enthusiasm, maintaining morale and carrying out correspondence and other frequently tedious paper-work. Such individuals are rare, an unfortunate truth which is evidenced by the very unequal distribution of industrial archaeology groups over the country as a whole, and by the way in which once thriving societies fade away if the key figure dies, becomes ill or, more often, moves from the district.

The National Survey of Industrial Monuments, now based at the University of Bath, is itself a reflection of both the strength and the weakness of local industrial archaeology groups and societies – strength, because a large proportion of the thousands of record cards completed and sent in to the Survey have come from such people, and weakness, because the quality of the cards is very uneven and many parts of England, Wales and Scotland are poorly covered.

The real importance of these spare-time industrial archaeologists may, however, have been political, rather than academic. Their influence has made itself felt partly in the bulletins, newsletters, meetings and visits which have formed a continuous and cumulative pressure on public education and public opinion, and partly as a result of many of those involved being exceptionally lively-minded and energetic people who take a leading part in the running of the political, industrial and educational life of the areas where they live.

An interesting reflexion of this has been the not always well-publicised fact that, in those cases where an industrial monument has been saved, restored and preserved, the necessary support and finance has nearly always come from local, not national, sources. The amount of money provided from central funds has been very small, something which is not, perhaps, well-known outside Britain, which is often regarded by starry-eyed and frustrated foreigners as an industrial archaeologists' paradise.

One should mention three other important developments which took place within Stage 2. The first was the founding of the *Journal of Industrial Archaeology*, later called, more simply *Industrial Archaeology*, which for more than ten years functioned as a strange, and perhaps typically British, bridge between the amateurs and the academics, with the academics providing most of the weighty articles and the amateurs filling up, quarter by quarter, the pages allocated to Notes and News. If the mixture came to acquire a somewhat old-fashioned flavour, it performed a useful and probably indispensable function during the key period when the subject was in the process of acquiring academic respectability and of losing its image of quaintness and crankiness.

The second, and also markedly British, characteristic of this particular decade was the growth of an astonishing plethora of adult education courses in industrial archaeology. The universities and the local education authorities soon came to realise that industrial archaeology had become fashionable and that considerable numbers of people could be attracted to evening courses, weekend courses and summer schools. An interesting and significant graph could be plotted, showing the annual increase in the numbers of people attending industrial archaeology courses and lectures between, say, 1955 and 1970. Since 1970 there has been, one suspects, some falling-off in attendance. There are signs that the market has become saturated and that the usual consumer-resistance has set in. It may well be, too, that the modern breed of amateur industrial archaeologist prefers to do things, rather than listen to presentations of other people's experiences and scholarship.

And the third point to bear in mind is the remarkable spawning of books about industrial archaeology which began about 1960 and shows little sign of disappearing. One British publisher especially, David & Charles, showed great enterprise in this matter. This young and extremely successful firm sensed the emerging British interest in industrial archaeology more quickly and more surely than anyone else. A study of their annual catalogues over the past ten years shows how much the subject owes to their encouragement and commercial vision. If their books now seem somewhat stereotyped and, like *Industrial Archaeology*, slightly old-fashioned, it is mainly because they created a prosperous market for themselves and because, like Henry Ford, they find it difficult to believe that the new generation wants something different from its predecessor. David & Charles' industrial archaeology books are the Model T Ford of the publishing world, the symbol and in some ways the crown of Stage 2 of the progress of British industrial archaeology. For Stage 3, their commercial flair will undoubtedly produce another recipe.

Stage 3

This is the moment when an increasing number of people begin to take stock of what has been achieved during Stage 1 and Stage 2 and to ask what it all means. What is it all for? How much industrial archaeology do we need? Having beaten off the enemies of preservation and won glorious victories in saving that old water-mill, this old gas-works and that old steam-engine for posterity, what is the true nature of such triumphs?

Accumulating pieces of industrial archaeology is not unlike collecting stamps or coins or matchbox labels. For some people, the mere act of collection is sufficient. It becomes absorbing in itself, and a passion which began at the age of fourteen is still a passion at sixty. But for others, mere acquisition for acquisition's sake is likely to pall, whether the collection consists of birds' eggs or of items for the National Survey of Industrial Monuments. The bits and pieces must add up to something, they must contribute to the understanding of a wider field.

It is not difficult, in the case of industrial archaeology, to suggest what this wider field may be. There can be, of course, a highly specialised interest. The engineer or the architectural historian or the economic historian is perfectly capable of

Fleshers at C. and J. Pittard's leather dressing works, Yeovil, 1935

finding complete satisfaction within what an outside observer might consider a very restricted band of intellectual territory. To the specialist himself, however, the room available may seem more than ample for anything his mind needs.

The more ordinary intelligent citizen is unlikely to react in quite this way. He finds, or he can be induced to find, industrial archaeology interesting because in some way it brings the past alive, and we have learnt, during the past fifteen years or so, that far more people can have their historical imagination stimulated by an old iron-works or a canal or a Victorian kitchen than by coming to grips with the details of the Battle of Waterloo or the Treaty of Versailles.

If one is concerned, as I am, more with arousing the interest, or neutralising the hostility, of the average intelligent citizen than with providing fodder for the ambitions of academics, one looks round for suitable means of communication. If one is reasonably honest, one is likely to admit that such a wish to proselytise is rooted in three motives:–

(a) Vanity. One would like as many other people as possible to share and value one's own interests.

(b) Social justice. Preservation costs a lot of money, most of which comes from the pockets of taxpayers. One has a duty to try to interest the taxpayer in the objects on which his money is spent. Best of all, it is pleasant if he can be pursuaded that his money has been well spent.

(c) A perhaps antiquated belief that it is good and useful to develop[s] knowledge and awareness of the past.

Of all our means of communication, television appears to me to have the greatest chance of succeeding with the greatest number of people. The BBC's History and Archaeology Unit has given a great deal of attention to the problems of finding a large viewing audience for industrial archaeology and by now its highly skilled producers certainly know more about this than any other television people anywhere in the world. They have organised television competitions for industrial archaeology groups, they have filmed the work these groups have been doing, they have compared the advantages of filming individual sites and groups of related sites, they have worked out the subtle balance of people and things which makes for the most effective television. There is no magic about it. All one needs is administrative goodwill, capable producers with a missionary urge and, of course, money. Given these things, an audience of several millions is perfectly possible. It can be done anywhere. The British have no patent rights.

But, and one has to emphasise this, popularisation is not welcome in all quarters. In industrial archaeology, as in wine-drinking, art-history and foreign travel, there are powerful vested interests and a well-protected élite which prefers to keep knowledge and pleasure to itself.

2

The Value and Urgency
of Industrial Archaeology

Society has to change and develop and it is neither realistic nor desirable to try to preserve more than a very tiny proportion of our surviving stock of obsolete industrial buildings and equipment. There is not, and there never will be enough money, labour and land available to allow more than a small selection of even the most important items to be saved for posterity to look at. What is possible on a much bigger scale, however, is to aim at photographing, measuring and describing in detail every really significant old building and piece of machinery before the demolition gangs and scrap-metal merchants get near it, and to press for comprehensive lists of what remains in each locality to be drawn up and published so that proper recording can be achieved in good time, and so that conservation can be a matter of deliberate, discriminating choice, not of panic.

Most destruction of valuable and interesting material occurs as a result of sheer ignorance, in cases where contractors or owners have no idea of the importance of what is being bulldozed or altered or thrown away. The business firm only too often fails to realise the historical value of the documents or photographs it is sending for pulping. The scrap-merchant clears away the old beam engine in much the same spirit as he would a wrecked motor-car.

There is, though, a second type of destruction which is knowledgeable and wilful. It is ordered by people who are fully aware of what they are doing but who have come to what they believe to be the responsible and public-spirited decision that the march of progress demands that the old should be replaced by the new and the sooner the better.

It may well be true to say that the only way in which both kinds of destruction can be prevented or sufficiently delayed is to develop a public conscience in the matter and to educate at least the more influential members of the community – town councillors, managing directors, architects – up to the point at which they automatically, as a part of their normal routine, commission, file and index a set of

26

photographs before removing any evidence of the past. It is difficult to carry out this educational process sufficiently quickly, however, with the result that well-informed and public-spirited people are continually involved in exhausting and unnecessary battles with officialdom. And since those who wish to get rid of relics of the past almost invariably present the issue in terms of a progressive policy being obstructed by die-hards and cranks, the preservationists usually get a bad press. The jobs-or-sentiment argument is familiar, although in planning and development the crimes and idiocies of the past twenty-five years have brought about a refreshingly widespread realisation that not everything new is good.

The more valuable the site upon which an old building stands, the more nearly impossible it is to prevent demolition from taking place. A notorious example of this was the fate of Philip Hardwick's famous Doric arch in the forecourt of Euston Station. This gateway, with its two flanking lodges, was eventually demolished in 1962, despite a long and vigorously conducted campaign to save it. In a final appeal to the Prime Minister,[1] the Ancient Monuments Society described the portico as 'a simple but inspiring piece of architecture which deserves preservation as a symbol of the Railway Age.' The Society noted, with regret, that the railway authorities appeared to believe that 'Hardwick's portico, however appropriate in the year 1835, is not an appropriate symbol for the new railway age that they hope to inaugurate' and its letter to Mr. Macmillan – a former railway director – went on: 'There has never been any real contradiction between the old and the new in good architectural styles. Keen as we are to preserve the monuments of past ages we do not regard this as incompatible with the development of contemporary structures in an idiom suitable to our own age. The blending of the old and the new at Euston would, in our view, have been entirely fitting.'[2]

The letter to Mr. Macmillan unfortunately had no more success than earlier appeals to the British Transport Commission itself. The Commission had a site worth a great deal of money, it intended to build a new railway station on it and since, no doubt rightly, it felt it was in the railway, not the museum, business, the portico had to go.

It did, in fact, ask for tenders for the job of moving the arch to another site, but the Society made some quiet investigations of its own and discovered that, although the lowest quotation the Transport Commission received was £190,000, another and equally reputable firm of contractors, which for some reason was not asked to tender, was prepared to demolish, transport and re-erect the offending structure for the much more reasonable figure of £90,000. This revelation came too late to change the decision, however, and Hardwick's portico disappeared rapidly and finally. It is worth recording, however, that the campaign to save

[1] Some very restrained details of this campaign are given in the Society's Annual Report for 1962, pp. 25–27. In the end, a distinguished three-man delegation, which included Sir William Holford and Sir John Summerson, went to see Mr. Macmillan personally, but met with small sympathy.

[2] The philistine attitude to industrial archaeology is discussed by Kenneth Hudson, 'The Taming of Industrial Archaeology', *Museums Journal*, Vol. 65, No. 1, June 1965.

Portico and offices at Curzon Street, Birmingham, the former terminus of the London-Birmingham railway

Hardwick's second arch, at the Birmingham end of the line, was successful. The Curzon Street arch still stands, although the station to which it belonged was demolished in the late 1960s, to be replaced by a modern freight depot.

Looking back now on the Euston Arch controversy, it is difficult to avoid the conclusion that the Ancient Monuments Society was quite correct in its view that the Transport Commission had come to regard the past as a thorough nuisance and wanted to do everything possible to rid the railways of their nineteenth century associations.

The most significant and disturbing aspect of the controversy was the Transport Commission's apparent belief that history stood in the way of commercial success. The Euston portico, one might say, created the wrong image of the railways. It suggested to the public that travelling by train was a nineteenth century, out of date, way of getting from place to place. It recalled steam, dirt and discomfort, instead of the much more desirable associations of electric or diesel power, cleanliness and smooth riding.

It is worth pointing out, perhaps, that neither the Transport Commission nor anybody else, so far as I know, ever carried out any research to discover if the assumptions were correct. In the absence of such research it seems equally possible that the portico carried a public image of reliability, punctuality, politeness and cheapness, stolid Victorian qualities which a great many people recalled with understandable nostalgia and which had largely vanished by 1960.

It is to be hoped that conferences on Industrial Archaeology, of which there are now many, will one day include contributions by psychologists. An understanding of why people in authority sometimes appear so unreasonably anxious to get rid of historical items might often be a helpful first step in a campaign to preserve an old building or an old piece of machinery. The fashionable lust for destruction, the pride at being called a vandal, calls for a long period of psychological treatment, but unfortunately there are no prospects yet of such treatment being made available to delinquent town councillors, cabinet ministers or company directors.

The present administration may feel that a particular heirloom perpetuates the idea of the importance of the founder of the firm or of the older generation of directors, and that anything which symbolises or suggests the former power and prestige of outmoded ideas is much better out of the way. Or it may be considered that the business is in urgent need of new designs and new conceptions and that reminders of the past are a barrier to forward-thinking.

Occasionally a gap in a company museum may be caused by the removal of what the management believes to have been a bad product and a bad advertisement. A wish to live down past mistakes is understandable, particularly if those mistakes belong to the recent past, but today's blunders very quickly become yesterday's oddities and few people are likely to blame a firm for what it was doing twenty years ago.

People's motives in sweeping away remnants of the past are usually very mixed. One of the first acts of a certain West Country textile manufacturer, after succeeding to the control of the family business a few years ago, was to have a well-preserved old beam-engine dismantled and removed from the premises.[3] Publicly, he announced that this step had been taken because the space was urgently needed. In private conversation, he admitted that he was anxious and determined to shake off reminders of his father's rule and that no reminder was more powerful than this previously cherished beam-engine. As it happened, the engine was not sold for scrap, because an American collector was only too happy to buy it at a bargain price, and it was crated and on its way across the Atlantic before the local

---

[3] A similar engine, belonging to a silk factory at Taunton, met with a happier fate. Mr. E. L. Kelting, Engineer to the Somerset River Board and a keen local historian, successfully campaigned for funds to get the engine moved to the County Museum, where it is now preserved, although in a rather tomb-like and meaningless fashion.

museum was aware of its departure from the site where it had been installed a century ago. A rather similar story concerns the new Chairman of a Regional Gas Board, who showed no inclination to keep in the Board's possession a remarkable collection of early meters, cookers, geysers and other old gas equipment, painstakingly built up by his predecessor and very compactly and harmlessly set out in a small room in a back-street storage building. Officially, 'the space was needed'. The collection's true crime, however, was that it might be capable of encouraging the Board's employees, and possibly the public, to have backward-looking, rather than forward-looking thoughts about gas. Most of the items fortunately found a new home with a museum in Birmingham.

Industrial relics usually disappear for hard-headed reasons, or, at any rate, for what the authorities concerned believe to be hard-headed reasons. James Bunning's demolished Coal Exchange, in Lower Thames Street, London, was an excellent case in point. Completed in 1849, two years before the Crystal Palace, it was an early and exceptionally interesting example of a public building which incorporated a large proportion of prefabrication in cast iron. It happened to be in the way of a proposed road-widening scheme and, despite appeals, the well-intentioned Ministry of Housing and the City Corporation succumbed to pressure from the Ministry of Transport and decided that it would be too expensive to change the line of the new road, even by a few feet, and demolition accordingly started early in 1962.

Operations were temporarily halted, while a campaign was waged to preserve the rotunda, with its huge dome and three tiers of galleries, on some other site. There was a possibility that the City of Melbourne might acquire these relics and ship them to Australia for re-erection as part of the city's new cultural centre, at that time under construction. But the negotiations all came to nothing and in the autumn this statement appeared: 'The Court of Common Council of the City of London was told yesterday that the City Architect had been instructed to resume demolition of the Coal Exchange rotunda. The announcement was greeted with applause and there was no discussion.'[4]

It is only fair to point out that Bunning's Coal Exchange, like Hardwick's portico, was carefully photographed and recorded before it was destroyed. It is, in fact, extremely unlikely that any industrial monument as well known as this would disappear without being properly recorded, although, as we have seen, the importance of a monument does not appear to increase its chances of being preserved if it is unfortunate enough to be situated in the centre of a large city.

But industrial history cannot be written or illustrated only in terms of its outstanding monuments, any more than of its most remarkable engineers or entrepreneurs. The most essential and most easily neglected task at the present time is to discover, list and describe the less distinguished relics of past industries – the smaller works, the rapidly disappearing family workshops, the toll-houses, the mills, the machinery, the pits, the workers' cottages. This is the sector of Industrial

[4] *The Times*, 19th October, 1962.

Tinplate Works (now closed), Redbrook, Forest of Dean. The dark-coloured blocks in the wall are copper-slag, evidence of a previous era of metal-working on the site

Archaeology where the greatest amount of disaster is likely to occur, mainly because local people are unaware of what exists and what is important in their own district.

One or two examples will illustrate the point. In December 1961, the tinplate works at Redbrook, in the Forest of Dean, closed down. It was the last place in Britain to make tinplate by the traditional hand method and it was interesting for another reason – Redbrook had a history of metal-working that went back to at least Roman times. It is not impossible that some of the men making tinplate there in 1961 had a family connexion both with Redbrook and with metals that had continued unbroken for several hundred years.

I myself visited the works in the month before it closed, in order to make a television film. The film was completed and with reasonable luck, the wonderful skill of these teams of men and women who turned iron billets into paper-thin tinplate has been preserved for future generations to marvel at. But what, through pressure of time, was not done was to take still photographs of the machinery in use, of the various processes, and of the lay-out and equipment of the works. Enquiries made later revealed that the directors of the firm had nothing, nor had any of their former employees, nor had any museum, nor had the local newspaper. All that was available was a series of pictures of the exterior of the buildings and of such interesting, but minor, details of the surroundings as blocks of copper slag built into the walls, evidence that other metals than iron had once been worked here.[5]

Valuable material may be almost under one's nose and yet contrive successfully to hide itself. A cloth manufacturer and a leading authority on the history of the Wiltshire textile industry, Mr. Kenneth Ponting, once revealed that he was staggered to learn of the visit of the head of the Textile Section of the Science Museum to Trowbridge to inspect an early slubbing machine and a cutting machine in a mill a stone's throw from Mr. Ponting's own premises. Mr. Ponting, although familiar with the other factory, knew nothing of the machines.

It is so easy to ignore the task of collecting evidence until the chance to do so has gone for ever. In 1960, an old-established brewery in Somerset was bought by a larger concern, who shortly afterwards were themselves taken over by an even bigger one. It was an interesting group of nineteenth century buildings, put up over a much earlier range of cellars which may possibly have some connexion with the woollen trade. Shortly after it ceased to be a brewery, it was bought by a local man who gutted it and converted it into a plant for the production of broiler chickens. When I heard of the change of use, and of the removal of the old brewing equipment, I asked the former managing director if he had any photographs of the interior of the buildings in their brewing days. He happened to be a man of keen historical interests, but neither he nor any of his colleagues had thought to take photographs of their own business, nor had any attempt been made to collect the memories of veteran workers, which would have been a valuable source of information for future historians. Consequently, what had been working only two years previously had passed out of existence undocumented.

Take-over bids and mergers of companies make this sort of misfortune increasingly common. In these days, family businesses are vanishing on a considerable scale and the large groups and combines which absorb them rarely show much interest in the survivals of the old days of a concern they have bought to modernise or shut down. When the news comes that a business is to close or be taken over, the first person to be on the spot ought to be the industrial archaeologist, with his notebook, camera, and tape-recorder, because the bonfires and the clearances and the demolitions usually occur very soon after the sale.

Destruction of valuable historical evidence is just as likely to take place with the enterprise that is thriving and growing as with the old-fashioned firm that is

[5]According to one authority, Rhys Jenkins, in *Transactions of the Newcomen Society*, Vol. 24 (1943–45), Redbrook was the site of 'the birth of revived English copper-smelting in 1688'.

bought up or closed down when the proprietor dies or retires. A few years ago I was visiting a large and flourishing business on the outskirts of Southampton that makes domestic radiators. This has developed since the war from a one-man business in a shed to an industrial leader worth many millions of pounds. During my tour, the firm's founder and present managing director proudly showed me the original radiator and a primitive piece of machinery that had been used to make it. Three years later I wrote to ask if I might have a photograph of these relics. I received this sad reply: 'I am sorry to tell you that the original radiator has been scrapped and there are no photographs available. We are so busy planning ahead that we tend to forget the past.'

In another instance I was interested to obtain a photograph of the very humble beginnings of what is now one of the biggest manufacturers of plastic floor and roofing tiles in Europe. The firm had been established in 1923 and in this case the letter I had in answer to my enquiry said this: 'So far as I know there is no photograph of the first shop, but I will look through all the old photographs that we have. I think, however, to save you possible future disappointment that I should make it clear that none of the buildings have what can, by any stretch of the imagination, be described as archaeological interest; there is, in fact, nothing earlier than 1923.'

Further investigation showed that the original tile-shop was now the core of a large factory. It was no longer a separate building, although its original roof remained. An aerial photograph was the only way in which the beginnings of this new industry could be seen. Nothing at all survived of the early machinery and there were no photographs of things as they were in the twenties. Here was a new industry whose beginnings had been swept away after thirty years by the sheer impetus of growth. The fact that its history only went back to 1923 is immaterial. The students of 2023 are quite likely to criticise this firm's management for its obsession with growth and development, just as we now reproach the coal-owners for destroying so many of their old records before they handed over the industry to the National Coal Board.

It is unfortunate that so many firms appear to be able to live only in the present and the future. Despite unceasing propaganda from the Business Archives Council, and sporadic support from the Confederation of British Industries, they destroy their own past almost as willingly and innocently as they empty their wastepaper baskets. Machinery is declared obsolete and replaced, buildings are torn down, documents burnt, with no record at all kept of what is being thrown away. What is old is inefficient and shameful. So it goes, unwept, as a token of the firm's progressive habits. Occasionally, an item or two may be presented to a museum and, even more occasionally, something may survive the holocaust because a director with eccentric or antiquarian tastes manages to defy the torrent of modernism. But this is becoming exceptional and, as a result, the history of many firms is eventually going to be difficult to write and even more difficult to illustrate.

Having said that, it is only fair to mention that some concerns have tackled the difficult and expensive problem of preservation in a most efficient and

C. and J. Clark, shoemakers, Street, Somerset. The factory and Cyrus Clark's house, *c*.1845. From a painting on glass by Edwin Dodge

The same view of Clark's factory today. The gabled buildings to the left of the central gateway are the original factory. The windows are a twentieth century modification

praiseworthy fashion. Three examples which come immediately to mind are English China Clays, in St. Austell; Pilkington Brothers, the glass-makers, of St. Helen's; and C. and J. Clark, shoe-manufacturers, of Street, in Somerset. Each of these has its own museum, on which a great deal of money has been spent, and its own carefully maintained archive of photographs, documents and printed material relating to the business and the industry. The National Coal Board has, from its earliest days, followed a most enlightened and public-spirited archives policy and so, despite the upheavals caused by merging BOAC and BEA, has British Airways. For all the hard things that industrial archaeologists may say about it from time to time, often with complete justice, British industry is well above the European average in its willingness to preserve the evidence of the past. A championship table including all the countries in Europe, East and West of the Iron Curtain would probably show Britain in fourth place, after Sweden, West Germany and the Netherlands, with France and Italy tying for the bottom position.

Nowadays, Coalbrookdale means, to anyone interested in industrial archaeology, the Ironbridge Gorge Museum Trust, the most remarkable and extensive open-air industrial museum in the world. It should not be forgotten, however, that long before the Trust came into being, Allied Ironfounders, who operated a steelworks at Coalbrookdale, carried out a major excavation and rehabilitation of the site of Abraham Darby's ironworks there. In the foreword to Dr. Raistrick's pamphlet history of the Coalbrookdale Company, published in 1959 on the occasion of its 250th anniversary, the Chairman of that company and of Allied Ironfounders put their signatures to a statement that could serve as a model for any company. 'The 250th Anniversary,' it says, 'marking as it does the passing of more than eight generations, cannot but give pause for reflexion on the progress that has been wrought over that period. Few industries can look back on a greater change than has occurred in the iron industry, and this metamorphosis had its birthplace at Coalbrookdale 250 years ago.

'To mark our gratitude for this long record, and our pride in the products of the works, Allied Ironfounders have made possible the preservation of the Darby Old Furnace 1777 and the display of some of the Company's records and achievements, and we hope that these will prove to be of interest and an inspiration to many in future years.'

It not infrequently happens, alas, that a firm, anxious to see a piece of historically interesting equipment preserved, is often unable to find a museum willing or able to accept it. Writing about a horse-mill at Pockthorpe, near Norwich, in an early Newcomen Society paper,[6] H. O. Clark said: 'It is a pity that such a fine mill could not have been preserved, but of course interest in the archaeology of engineering has only awakened within recent years. The writer knows that the owners would have been only too pleased to have presented it to any institution willing to preserve it. Each Member of this Society should make it his business to

[6] 'Notes on Horse-Mills', Vol. 8, 1927–28.

Early nineteenth century fulling-stocks at Cam, Gloucestershire

know of the existence of all such relics in his district and see that none is destroyed without a chance of its being acquired by some institution, preferably a local one.'

Each year produces a fresh crop of these can-anyone-offer-a-good-home cases. In November 1971, Stuart Smith, of the Sunderland Museum, reported[7] that, as a result of the Museum's successful appeal on behalf of the Ryhope pumping engines, 'we have been offered several pieces of equipment which we unfortunately cannot accept'. All, like the Ryhope engines, belonged to local water boards, who would have been happy to give their obsolete equipment away. The Conway Water Board had two throw-pumps, powered by gas-engines of 1906 and 1914; the Ely, Mildenhall and Newmarket Water Board was offering a 110 h.p. Hawthorn Davey triple expansion engine, and the Dorset Water Board did not know what to do with a rather smaller Hawthorn Davey engine, of 70 h.p.

[7] *Industrial Archaeology*, November 1971.

In one sense, the more successful industrial archaeologists are, the more problems they create for themselves. The publicity given to the beam-engines at Ryhope drew the attention of other owners to the fact, surprising to many of them, that they had interesting material in their care. Not wishing to be considered irresponsible vandals, but embarrassed by the continued presence of this obsolete equipment on their premises, they approached the only specialists in the good-homes-for-old-machinery business they knew, the Sunderland Museum, and they may well have been surprised to hear that Sunderland was in no position to solve their problem for them. It has been suggested many times during the past twenty years that what we need very badly are perhaps four large warehouses distributed over the country – one in Scotland, one in the North of England, one in the Midlands and one in the South – where historical material – machinery documents and all types of big and small equipment – could be stored temporarily, until suitable museum accommodation could be found for it. Such rescue depots might be run either by the Department of the Environment or by regional groups of museums. They would meet a very real need and prevent at least some of the disasters with which we have become all too familiar in recent years.

As matters stand, the public-spirited manufacturers often find themselves in the unfortunate predicament of wanting to save items from destruction, but of failing to discover anyone to take custody of what they can no longer keep. Survival consequently depends to a great extent on chance, rather than merit. In 1963, for instance, the Gloucestershire textile firm of Hunt and Winterbotham, of Cam, decided to complete the modernisation of their fulling-house. This demanded the removal of a set of wooden fulling-stocks built for them in 1815 by William Kilburn of Leeds. It so happened that the Curator of Stroud Museum, Lionel Walrond, had a particular interest in the history of the woollen industry. He was therefore able to advise the Company on the dismantling and storage of the stocks until a permanent place could be found for them in a museum.[8] Had he not been on the spot, and known to the management, it is extremely probable that these very rare items of textile machinery would have disappeared unwept and in all likelihood unrecorded as well, a fate which befell a similar set of fulling-stocks at Wallbridge Mills, Stroud, a few years earlier. These were broken up following a sale of machinery in 1958. They had never been either measured or photographed.

The Cam stocks eventually came to rest in the Stroud Museum. They were exceptionally fortunate. In 1971 W. Branch Johnson, the leading authority on the industrial archaeology of Hertfordshire, found himself faced with a similar problem. Webb and Co., an old-established firm of leather-dressers at Hertford, had a battery of five fulling stocks for disposal. These were of approximately the same age as the Cam stocks and very probably by the same maker. The City Museum, St. Albans, took one set, but it proved impossible to find anyone who would be

---

[8] These fulling stocks were described by Mr. Walrond in Vol. 1, No. 1, May 1964 of the *Journal of Industrial Archaeology*.

Maltings, Ship Lane, Ely. Exterior

interested in the others and, despite their rarity and historical importance, they were broken up.

In general, however, buildings present a more serious problem than machinery. Every year, in its Annual Report, the Victorian Society laments the demolition of this office block or department store or that cotton mill, with the occasional victory over developers to give heart to those who are trying to preserve a few of the best examples of our ancestors' achievements. But, with the best will in the world, no one with a direct interest in industry or commerce can set aside the fact that most nineteenth century buildings need to have a lot of money spent on them it they are to meet today's demands. Working spaces are either too small or too large, pillars and thick party walls make it difficult to install modern machinery and working systems, passages and staircases are too numerous and too narrow, and windows inadequate. It is all very well to stir up a campaign to preserve St. Pancras Station for use as offices or an hotel, but the plain truth is that its attractions, like those of the Houses of Parliament, are entirely from the outside and that, as a place to work and live in, it is difficult to imagine anything more inconvenient or more dismal.

This is not, of course, true of every old industrial building. Maltings and breweries, for instance, can be very pleasantly converted to other purposes – the task has been excellently carried out at Ely, Snape and Oxford, to name only three places – and a number of watermills and small textile factories have proved very satisfactory for housing. But what is one to do with the retort-house of a Victorian gasworks, or a group of old blast-furnaces?

The climate is gradually changing, however, and both architects and their clients are beginning to discover that some old buildings at least can be excellent propositions in a period when the cost of new buildings has become prohibitive. What has been done in Liverpool, Bristol and at St. Katharine's Dock in London to give nineteenth century warehouses a new lease of life as flats, studios, offices and teaching accommodation is an encouraging indication of what can be done when there is sufficient determination and imagination.

It is even possible for miracles to happen. At Shepton Mallet in Somerset, for instance, the great viaducts carrying the Somerset and Dorset Railway round the edge of the town seemed doomed to neglect, decay and eventual collapse when the line closed ten years ago, even though they were officially listed as historic monuments. Once the track was up, British Rail was certainly not going to spend anything on maintenance and preservation. One stretch of these dramatic viaducts formed the boundary of the factory headquarters of the new Lords of Shepton Mallet, the Showering family, with their Babycham fortune available to buy the viaduct and use it as a back-cloth to the works and the offices. Handsome lakes and gardens were laid out and the top of the viaduct converted into the biggest window box in Britain, the Hanging Gardens of Shepton Mallet. So long as Babycham continues to be drunk, the viaduct is safe.

Examples such as this illustrate the whimsy which controls the fortunes of industrial monuments. This one finds a patron, a fairy godfather, that one, equally deserving, does not. Shepton Mallet Viaduct survives, somewhat down-graded perhaps, and the fine tidemill, Wootton Old Mill, in the Isle of Wight, has gone. Strenuous and imaginative efforts on the part of the County Planning Officer and other local people had failed to discover any use to which this attractive group of buildings might be put. They were in poor condition and had been standing empty for many years. Nobody wanted to live in them or to convert them to any industrial purpose. The only alternative to pulling them down was to allow them to stand and rot. In the circumstances, the decision to demolish was

Maltings, Ship Lane, Ely. Part of interior. The maltings have now been converted into a public hall for the town

probably the right one, but in this case, as in many others, it would be quite wrong to suppose that either the authorities or the owner were happy about the action that was taken. It is in the nature of buildings, as of people, to grow old and die. The process can be delayed, but not indefinitely, and it is very expensive and demands skilled manpower that is in short supply. For every industrial monument and every piece of old machinery that slips through the demolition-net and survives, 10,000 will have to be content with photographs, notes and drawings as a record for posterity.

3

The Approach

According to the person involved, industrial archaeology, like archaeology in general, can be regarded either as an academic subject or an agreeable hobby. It can be either a tough discipline or a gentle pleasure, a means of adding to the world's store of knowledge or a route to increasing one's own personal awareness of the past, an excuse for tourism or a well-organised historical laboratory. It would be unreasonable to expect the university lecturer in pursuit of promotion or a higher degree to look for quite the same details or to find quite the same satisfaction as, say, the schoolmaster or the railway enthusiast. The approach must to some extent condition both the achievement and the form in which the results of investigations are eventually written up. Cross-fertilisation between one variety of industrial archaeologist and another is not infrequent. The present author, who, despite working for twelve years at two universities, has always considered himself a populariser rather than an academic, was surprised to find a quotation from the first edition of *Industrial Archaeology* selected as a question for a final degree paper in Economic History at the University of Leeds in 1965.

Perhaps the best way of illustrating the great variety of useful contributions which different kinds of people of different generations can make to industrial archaeology is to consider a few individual cases in detail, beginning with some of those who helped to establish and popularise industrial archaeology in the early 1960s and moving forward to a new generation with somewhat different ideas.

Rex Wailes and windmills

Mr. Wailes was trained as a civil engineer and spent most of his working life in the family business. He became interested in windmills in the early 1920s and had to live through the sadness of watching English windmills going out of use very rapidly, so rapidly in fact that, whereas 350 were still working in 1919, this number had been reduced to fifty in 1946 and to twenty-one in 1954.[1] When, in that year, Mr. Wailes published his great book on windmills, he felt able to make the confident forecast that in another ten or twenty years 'the only windmills remaining will be derelicts, converted into houses, or preserved through the efforts of private persons, societies, local authorities and the Ministry of Works'.

It would be no exaggeration to say that Mr. Wailes began to study windmills at the eleventh hour, when a fair number of elderly men who had built them, repaired them and worked with them were still alive and able to give him the practical details he needed to supplement his own observations. Historians of the future will owe him an enormous debt for his painstaking work in photographing and making measured drawings of hundreds of mills from Lincolnshire to Somerset and from Kent to North Wales, and perhaps even more for the technical conversations he had with such experts as Mr. John Russell of Cranbrook, 'miller, millwright and engineer', and with the veterans still alive in the Twenties and Thirties who had earned their living at the mills which were then becoming abandoned and derelict.

Mr. Wailes was an ideal observer. He had the engineering knowledge that made it possible for him to understand exactly how the mills were constructed and how they worked, the historical sense that enabled him to fit the English windmills into their place in the development of technology, and the interest in people that never allowed him to forget that these industrial monuments that occupied so much of his spare time were once the centre of the lives of real men and women.

Mr. Wailes, the historian, was able to note that, although the English windmill had its origins on the Continent, it developed in its own way, so that eventually it was English nineteenth century practice which spread to North-West Europe.[2] And Mr. Wailes, the engineer, was in a position to give the reason for this – that the advanced techniques of the nineteenth century English iron-founders allowed the millwrights to improve the engineering of the mills to a point where the Continent was left far behind. 'It was the skill in making accurate castings,' he tells us, 'both large and small, which made possible the invention of the fantail, with its small gears, the patent sail with its numerous small castings, and the much larger shafts and gears inside the mill itself.'[3]

And the more Mr. Wailes learnt about the mechanism and the design of eighteenth and nineteenth century mills the more he came to admire the skill of the men responsible for creating them. The millwrights were the early engineers and some of the best known of the engineers started their careers as millwrights. Among them were John Smeaton and Sir William Cubitt. 'The work of the millwrights in the mills that survive is part of the history of mechanical engineering,'

---

[1] *The English Windmill*, 1954, p. 180.

[2] Ibid, p. xxii.

Mr. Wailes reminds us, 'a history that has been as sadly neglected as it is fascinating.'[4]

Mr. Wailes, the social historian, added another dimension to his work by accumulating such significant human details as the fact that at Eastfield Mill, near Hickling, on the Broads, a certain Mr. and Mrs. Gibbs brought up their twenty-one children in the mill. 'They did have four floors and it was a brick tower mill, but as a home it must have been rather like the nest of a long-tailed tit.'[5]

And it was yet another Mr. Wailes, the observer with a talent for communicating his feelings about what he saw, who produced the many fine descriptions of mills at work and mills in the landscape which give flavour to his writings and tell the reader why he found all this trudging round the flatlands of England so rewarding. When he writes of 'the scene from the Acle "New Road" to Yarmouth from which, in the mid-twenties, nearly a score of mills could be seen in working order at all points of the compass,'[6] it is with a warmth and affection and nostalgia that reminds us that Industrial Archaeology at its best is not merely a matter of lists and committees and museums and protests.

Rex Wailes was refreshingly frank about his motives. On the one hand, he admits to having enjoyed himself, but on the other he has been fully aware of the public usefulness of his work. 'We must make haste to record and preserve while yet we can', he says. The effort is 'for the benefit of those who follow us as well as for the interest to ourselves'. The 'interest to ourselves' that Mr. Wailes speaks of can have its tense moments during the search for evidence that one can hardly believe to be still available, but which is essential if gaps in the survey are to be filled. In his own case, with all the surviving mills photographed, the problem was to somehow discover old photographs of mills which had disappeared. 'I have myself actually retrieved mill photographs from the scrap heap,' he assures us, 'and from the waste-paper basket.'

His books and articles on windmills provide an admirable proof, if proof were needed, that pleasure and enthusiasm are no barriers to sound scholarship and that a period of forty years is none too long for carrying out a piece of research on this mammoth scale, and for writing up the results in a way that will be helpful to those of our descendants who may want to know exactly how these vanished windmills worked, and how they fitted into the English economy of fifty and a hundred years ago.

With his basic work on mills safely behind him, Rex Wailes began a new career as what might be fairly described as the world's first full-time industrial archaeologist when, in 1963, he was appointed by the Ministry of Public Buildings and Works to carry out a survey of the industrial monuments of Britain. After

[4] Ibid, p. xxiii.

[5] Ibid, p. 80.

[6] Ibid, p. 72.

toiling at this for seven years, and showing a strong and understandable tendency to prefer field-work to committees, he finally retired to the peace of rural Buckinghamshire, emerging at regular intervals to deliver papers at international conferences of experts on wind and watermills or, to give them their delightful professional name, molinologists.

Robert Clough and the lead smelting mills of the Yorkshire Dales

Mr. Clough is an architect. His superb book on these old smelting mills and 'their Architectural Character, Construction and Place in the European Tradition' was published in 1962, as a record of twenty years of painstaking work.

He began, like Mr. Wailes, with the buildings themselves, most of them in remote parts of the moors and many in an advanced stage of decay, as a consequence of having been abandoned for more than a century. But, also like Mr. Wailes, as he studied these old buildings and ruins of buildings, he found himself getting increasingly interested in the people who had built them and worked in them. It soon became obvious to him that there was little point in writing about the mills as dead monuments. A meaningful book about the buildings would have to include a great deal about the miners and their families, as well as about the old techniques of mining and smelting.

The magnificent book that Mr. Clough eventually wrote is of great value as a record of an industry that has vanished, but is equally rewarding if read as an account of the gradual broadening of the author's sympathies and interests, as part of an autobiography, in fact.

'As the survey was gradually completed,' Mr. Clough tells us, 'it became clear that a most unusual and interesting group of buildings was being recorded for the first time, buildings of honest form and simple character, basically unaffected by any past styles. However, I feel that the book is very much more than a record of stones and mortar; it is a record of a way of life illustrated by certain buildings which were necessary to make that way of life possible. I have endeavoured to look into the lives of these people, at all times somewhat aloof; people who lived, worked and died unnoticed in their remote surroundings. It is only by this understanding that one can fully appreciate the purpose of these buildings.'[7]

With this philosophy to support his efforts, Mr. Clough gives us a detailed history of the mines, a splendid series of drawings and photographs of the mine buildings and of the cottages where the workers and their families lived, an historical account of the technology involved and a study of the growth and decay of the mining economy.

The many quotations and illustrations from early Continental writers on lead mining, especially Georgius Agricola, make it possible to reconstruct and explain

[7] *The Lead Smelting Mills of the Yorkshire Dales*, p. xiii.

the beginnings of these old Yorkshire workings in a way that would have been impossible if the author had been content to remain mentally at home. There is something extraordinarily impressive about the links that are established between the isolated nineteenth century mining communities in Mr. Clough's 'lonely gills and barren moors' and their predecessors in Germany and Bohemia.

It is moving, too, to read of the mining families who migrated to Yorkshire from Derbyshire and Cornwall, in search of the more secure and better paid work made possible by the lead boom of the 1820s, as a result of the importation of foreign lead, especially from Spain. Mr. Clough has discovered some remarkable photographs of these miners, some taken as early as 1860, and their presence makes all the difference to the book. The men are of a piece with the buildings. Both, to use Mr. Clough's phrase, are 'of honest form and simple character'. Each helps to explain the other. The buildings mouldered away and collapsed, the men went abroad or into the coalfields. The moors relapsed into silence.

Nobody, I imagine, would want to quarrel with Mr. Clough's decision to write his book in this way. The results are too good. But the practical difficulties involved after one has committed oneself to what we might describe as an all-front approach are very great, and it is useful to realise this in order to understand and acknowledge the size of the achievement. Mr. Clough had to wrestle with the problems created by his determination to work to the highest possible standards.

'This, my first book,' he admits, 'has not been an easy one for me to write, nor has it been an easy one to illustrate and produce. At times I wondered whether I should finally be able to retain my broad yet detailed approach and high standards of production, but took courage in the fact that so little of industrial and architectural history has been properly recorded by treatment as a single entity . . . As an architect and antiquary, I soon realised that merely to record these buildings in a series of measured surveys with descriptive text was an archaic approach to my subject and one which would tell less than half the story behind the buildings concerned; it would, in fact, omit the most important unit of all, namely the people of varied fortune who sponsored these ventures and the ordinary dalesfolk who lived their lives in and around these buildings.'[8]

Perhaps the most significant result of Mr. Clough's determination to publish his work in the way he was convinced it ought to be published was the fact that the book eventually cost £4, an enormous sum for a book in 1962, and had to be privately produced. It was financed by previous subscription and the list of subscribers at the end of the volume is encouraging evidence of the number and variety of people in Great Britain who believed in the early 1960s that industrial archaeology, under whatever name, was worth supporting.

The Ffestiniog enthusiasts

The Ffestiniog Railway is thirteen miles long. It runs over a narrow-gauge track

[8] Ibid, p. 144.

from Blaenau Ffestiniog to Portmadoc and it was opened in 1836 as a horse-drawn tramway for taking slate from the quarries down to Portmadoc for shipment. Steam engines replaced horses in 1863 and for twenty years the line was a commercial success. At its peak, it carried 150,000 tons of freight and 160,000 passengers a year. One of the first bogie coaches in the world ran over its lines, in 1872, and as late as 1885 the Company was building locomotives in its own workshops at Boston Lodge.

After 1910 Portmadoc was very little used as a port and consequently during the 1920s and 1930s the railway went from bad to worse. No passengers were carried after the outbreak of war in 1939 and the last freight train ran in 1946. The rolling stock, much of it of considerable historic interest, was left to rot and rust where it stood and trees and bushes soon covered the track.

In 1951 a group of enthusiasts met in Bristol to see if it might be possible to re-open the railway as an amateur venture. Three years later Mr. A. F. Pegler, a solicitor, took over control of the old railway company, by buying the shares. A new board of directors was appointed and the Ffestiniog Railway Society Ltd. was formed to organise volunteers and funds to get the railway into working condition again. In the following twelve months the track was dug out and re-sleepered where necessary, the old 1863 engine, *Prince*, was restored and a pioneering train was worked through from Portmadoc to Blaenau Ffestiniog, although for a long while the line was only open to passenger traffic for a short section.

Between 1955 and 1961 large-scale amateur efforts got further lengths of the line into order, the coaches and locomotives rebuilt and painted, an internal telephone system installed, bridges restored and stations refurbished. There was still much to be done before the whole 13 miles of line could be restored to the standard necessary for passenger services, but the work was gradually accomplished and the Ffestiniog Railway has now become a very remarkable working museum of transport history, a triumph of confidence and imagination.

Apart from the line itself, which had completely disappeared under earth and vegetation for long stretches and is now revealed as an impressive piece of railway engineering, with some formidable gradients, the collection of locomotives, carriages, wagons and track equipment assembled from a number of sources has an interest that extends beyond Wales. An ex-Lynton and Barnstaple Railway coach, for instance, was discovered marooned in the middle of a field in North Devon, the track over which it ran to reach its last resting place having long since ceased to lead anywhere. This coach, the last survivor of the Lynton and Barnstaple rolling stock, was taken to Portmadoc, rebuilt and restored to useful work.

Two other nineteenth century coaches from another disused railway had been sold to farmers as henhouses. These, too, were completely overhauled and put into service on the Ffestiniog Railway.

Perhaps the most important item to be restored was the first bogie coach to be built anywhere in Europe. It dates from 1872 and it was in very bad condition after spending many years in a derelict condition in the open. As it now appears, it gives visitors an excellent impression of what it was like to ride in a

mid-Victorian railway carriage, pulled by a mid-Victorian engine, which might
be *Prince*, built in 1863, or *Taliesin*, which dates from 1876.

Many people smile at such pieces of amateur enterprise as the restoration of
the Ffestiniog Railway. Such an attitude seems very unenlightened, since by
means of the railway, the several excellently illustrated publications describing
it, and the little museum at Portmadoc, many details of railway history which
would otherwise have disappeared have been preserved and recorded. It would
be good to see a similar amount of organised energy and public spirit directed
towards saving and reconditioning the remains of other industries.

J. P. M. Pannell and the Taylors of Southampton

Mr. Pannell, Engineer to the Southampton Harbour Board until his retirement
in 1964,[9] and previously a railway engineer, was always interested in history,
especially in anything connected with the history of his own profession of civil
engineering. In the course of his work he came across many significant reminders
of the past, dredged up, dug up and washed up in Southampton Water and along
the Rivers Test and Itchen.

Among the more curious of these relics were a number of lengths of stout
timber studded with large headed nails. Mr. Pannell was able to identify these
as having formed part of the piles of the Royal Pier, dating from the 1830s. The
original piles, placed in position in 1833, were eaten away by marine borers within
five years and when they were renewed they were protected by scupper nails.
'The method of protection,' says Mr. Pannell, 'was to drive short wrought iron
nails having large heads so closely spaced that the heads, when rusted, would provide a continuous iron layer over the wood. The length of timber to be protected
would be about ten feet and this required about 7000 nails, probably the week's
output of a woman nail maker somewhere in the Black Country.'[10]

The Southampton area is rich in material belonging to the history of dockyard
and port equipment. Mr. Pannell took a special interest in the once important
local industry of blockmaking and in the pioneers of mass-production methods in
this, or indeed any other field, the Taylors of Southampton, who made mechanical equipment for the Navy between 1760 and 1810.

At that time, a 74-gun ship needed 1400 blocks, for handling the sails and guns.
With the traditional hand-tools – axe, saw and auger – it was difficult to supply
the quantity of blocks needed and the quality was extremely unsatisfactory. No
two blocks were alike and they often failed.

During the 1750s, the Taylors built machine prototypes under conditions of
great secrecy in a cellar in Westgate Street. These machines for the accurate sawing, boring and turning of the components for ships' blocks were fundamental

[9] He died three years later. One of the fruits of his retirement was his *Techniques of Industrial
Archaeology*, published in 1966.

[10] *Civil Engineering, a History*, 1963, p. 163.

inventions, 'the first plant for the mass production of goods to a high standard of quality'.[11]

Mr. Pannell patiently pieced together the whole story of how these blocks came to be adopted by the Navy in 1770, of Walter Taylor's achievement in making half a million or more of them during the five years before the Battle of Trafalgar, of the development of Taylor's machines by Brunel, Sir Samuel Bentham and finally Henry Maudslay. In Maudslay's hands, the Taylors' inventions became 'the recognisable ancestors of a great range of machine tools and production techniques used today'.[12]

A large proportion of the evidence was gathered from eighteenth century books and manuscripts. But Mr. Pannell went to great pains to discover whatever remained of the workshops and products of the Taylors' business. He identified the ruins of the building in Westgate Street where the prototype machines were built, and the foundations of the mill at Weston. He came across examples of Taylor's sheaves still preserved at Portsmouth Dockyard and of his elm water-pipes at the Tudor House Museum in Southampton, and noted a portrait of the second Walter Taylor, painted about 1784, in which the block-maker is holding a circular saw, very appropriately, since he invented it.

Mr. Pannell, one of that rare and valuable breed of historically-minded engineers, devoted much of his spare time for nearly fifteen years to working on the Taylors. The detailed results of his researches are to be found excellently and attractively written up in a professional journal, the *Proceedings of the Institution of Mechanical Engineers*, where they are likely to be a good deal more use as an inspiration to other engineers than if they had appeared in an historical or archaeological publication. The illustrations to his paper are an important part of the story he had to tell, since so much evidence on the ground has disappeared during the past century. But, because of the number and quality of the illustrations, the cost of producing the paper must necessarily have been high, and Mr. Pannell was in an excellent position to persuade his own not impoverished professional organisation to meet the expense, as an enlightened piece of patronage.

Robin Atthill and the poetry of industrial archaeology

A recently retired public schoolmaster, Robin Atthill has written only about Somerset and Dorset, where he spent his childhood and most of his working life. The area he knows best is Mendip, the part of Somerset bounded roughly by Weston-super-Mare, Wells, Frome and Bath. He has written about it in one of the best and most deservedly successful of all books on local history and topography,

---

[11] Pannell: *Proceedings of the Institution of Mechanical Engineers*, 1955, Vol. 169, No. 46. By an odd coincidence, Mr. H. W. Dickinson was working on the Taylors at the same time as Mr. Pannell. His paper, 'The Taylors of Southampton, Their Ships' Blocks, Circular Saw and Ships' Pumps' was published in *Trans. Newcomen Society*, Vol. 29 (1955).

[12] Ibid.

Old Mendip, and in his railway classic, *The Somerset and Dorset Railway*. 'When Michael Rix gave the phrase "industrial archaeology" to the world,' he remembered,[13] 'I found myself in very much the same predicament as Molière's Monsieur Jourdain when he learned to his amazement that he had been speaking "prose" all his life. Of course industrial archaeology was what I had been committed to for about forty years.'

In 1918, when he was six, he had been 'nosing about in the flues of the abandoned lead-mines at Charterhouse-on-Mendip'. In the 1920s he was 'gazing awe-struck at "Headgears gaunt on grass-grown pit-banks"[14] in the Somerset coalfield', and 'regularly bicycled over to Stratford Mill on the river Chew to order corn for my father's hens, little thinking that within my lifetime it would have been dismantled piece by piece and re-erected under the aegis of the Bristol Museum as an industrial monument in the grounds of Blaise Castle'.

His own aim has been plainly stated in *Old Mendip*. 'From the landscape and its buildings,' he writes, 'from written records and from the lips of its inhabitants, both past and present, I have tried to recover something of an older Mendip which is still everywhere visible to those who have eyes to see.' Mendip is, of course, an old industrial area. Its quarries and iron-works were important in the nineteenth century[15] and there have been many others. Paper-making, lead-mining, coal-mining and cloth-making are just a few of them. Mr. Atthill has been walking over this district for more than fifty years, but he still finds himself asking questions about the origin and purpose of mysterious lanes and hedges and buildings. In the rural landscape, each clue leads to another, until the whole pattern of the past emerges. Near the main road from Bath to Weston-super-Mare, he found the ruins of Sherborne paper mill. These, he feels, 'have charm even in decay, with a façade centred upon a surprising little classical doorway, with a delicately moulded architrave. Local tradition says that the mill was later used as a button factory, Elihu Tucker being recorded as a button dealer in the Litton census returns of 1851. Only three houses survive in what was once a thriving and prosperous hamlet. A network of lanes led to the mill from almost every direction, some now used mainly for farming purposes, others abandoned and long since choked with undergrowth, serving no useful purpose in the local economy; only the double hedges and the deeply trodden trackways between high red banks show how much traffic the lanes once carried.'[16]

This is the poet's eye turned on to industrial archaeology, the eye of a man whose imagination is quickened by small details and who feels ghosts everywhere. A century ago Fussells of Mells was a household name in the iron industry, making hand-forged spades, shovels and edge-tools, but the firm failed to keep

[13] *Industrial Archaeology*, November 1972, p. 433.

[14] The quotation is from W. H. Auden. Atthill has noted Isherwood's comment that Auden 'loved industrial ruins, a disused factory or an abandoned mill'.

[15] The roadstone quarries today are among the most important in Britain.

[16] *Old Mendip*, pp. 63–64.

pace with the scale and techniques of factories in the Midlands and the North and in 1894 it went bankrupt. Now, even in their own villages, the Fussells have become almost completely forgotten. 'In parish registers,' Mr. Atthill tells us, 'on page after page, one may read their names, generation after generation, in faded ink on yellowing paper; their graves are levelled out in the graveyards besides the churches where they worshipped; the houses which they built for themselves and their heirs have passed into alien hands; and the Mendip streams wash against the crumbling walls of their once noisy and prosperous factories.'[17] The story of the Fussells has had to be pieced together from trade catalogues, parish registers, family memories and gossip, and climbing over and around ruins. Archaeology has contributed a great deal to the recreation of this remarkable family, but, in Mr. Atthill's hands, it has been only one tool among several.

For him, the past is as real as the present. He lives his material. The Somerset and Dorset was not just a railway. It was a line on which 'everybody seemed to know everybody', an individual line with a family flavour to it. 'I have talked to Driver Cook of Radstock who joined the railway in 1893', he tells us, 'and to Frank Redman who served under the great Alfred Whitaker, Locomotive Superintendent at Highbridge from 1889 to 1911. Mention Edgar Smith or Tom Mogg, and faces light up; Alfred Dando, the signal boy at Foxcote on the night of the Radstock accident in 1876, is remembered as "a quiet spoken man who read his Bible every day" – this was from the late Ewart Gulliford who worked with Dando on the Somerset and Dorset between 1913 and 1916.'[18]

When Robin Atthill watched the last train going up Masbury summit on March 6, 1966, he reminded himself that 'this was the end – not merely the end of the Somerset and Dorset, but the end of the era of steam in the West Country'. His family had spanned the life of the railway. 'My father,' he recalled, 'had been born in the same year as the Somerset Central, the senior partner of the Somerset and Dorset; as a child he had travelled up from Glastonbury on excursions to the seaside at Burnham; now I had watched the line die, 111 years later.'[19]

Philip Welch, archaeologist-entrepreneur

In 1970 Philip Welch sold up his road-haulage business in the Midlands and retired to Cornwall, full of energy and anxious to do something useful. He soon found the opportunity he was looking for, in the form of a mile of valley near Redruth. Fifty years ago the Tolvarden valley had been busily producing tin, but when Mr. Welch came on the scene it was completely derelict. The ore-roaster was a semi-ruin, the round-tables were rotten and useless, the water-courses were silted up and only one set of Cornish stamps was still in position, but not working and in need of repair.

[17] *Old Mendip*, p. 93.

[18] *The Somerset and Dorset Railway*, p. 13.

[19] Ibid, p. 11.

Mr. Welch was interested in tin and in the traditional methods of working it, and he thought out an ingenious plan to get the old machinery working again. The idea, briefly, was to rebuild one of the derelict plants, as a commercial enterprise, and give the public a chance to watch the operations. His first difficulties were with the planning authorities, who took the curious and, as it seemed to Philip Welch, perverse view that the place for visitors to Cornwall was down on the beaches, not inland looking round an old tin works. With the help of friends at court, first the County and then Redruth were persuaded to change their minds and permission was given to proceed with what was conceived from the outset as a working, profitable, open-air museum.

The technical problems were considerable. To reconstruct the revolving round-tables, which are used to separate the tin-oxide from the arsenic and waste sand, it was necessary to re-learn a skill which was no longer practised. The boards forming the top of the table have to be carefully tapered and laid wet, a type of carpentry which is no longer particularly attractive. The shaking-tables, which continue the separation process, and the scoop-wheels, which keep the tin-slurry moving round the system, also had to be rebuilt and made to operate by men without first-hand experience of the tradition. Within two years, however, everything was, miraculously, as Mr. Welch felt, in working order. And no part of the £30,000 required had come from trusts or public funds. This was very much a piece of private enterprise.

The raw material cost practically nothing. Until the 1930s, there had been a flourishing tin-producing area on the outskirts of Redruth.[20] Ore was mined there, crushed and processed for smelting in South Wales. It was a wasteful business, with a considerable amount of tin left in the heaps of waste sand. With world prices so low, it was not commercially worthwhile to bother about it. To Philip Welch, however, such wastefulness was a godsend, and the old waste-heaps became his source of supply.

With tin once again being produced in the Tolvarden Valley, it was possible for the company, the Tolgus Tin Company, to turn its attention to catering for the visitors which were to be an important part of the enterprise. Large car-parks were laid out, despite the prediction of the local planning authority that nobody would come; a restaurant was built with a bookshop and souvenir section attached; and there was a visitor-orientation centre, to tell people what they were going to see before they started on their tour. During the summer Tolgus now reckons to get at least 1000 visitors a week, which represents good business. No tin goes from Tolgus to South Wales for smelting. It is turned into tiny ingots on the spot, and these are sold very easily and profitably in the Company shop. On this basis, the price Philip Welch gets for tin is a great deal higher than the mining companies have to be content with.

---

[20] During the past twenty years there has been a welcome revival in the fortunes of the Cornish tin industry. Large-scale production is now to be found at three pits.

It is not easy to find the right label for the friendly, very approachable Mr. Welch, who combines cost-consciousness with determination and optimism in a most refreshing way. Archaeologist-entrepreneur is probably the closest we are likely to find. He would deny that his aim is to educate people, although they certainly leave better informed than they came. 'Education', he feels, is a word that is guaranteed to make visitors suspicious, if not to frighten them away altogether. On the other hand, there is no doubt about his own enthusiams for the history of the tin industry, and of Cornwall, or about his wish to inspire a similar interest in other people. He is certain that a tin-works where nothing moved and nothing happened would attract hardly anyone. For him, the whole point of studying industrial archaeology is to acquire the knowledge needed to get buildings repaired and machinery working again. After watching ore being converted into tin and admiring the craftsmanship and ingenuity of the equipment, people are much more likely to buy the books, pamphlets and postcards which are ready-to-hand for them. They want to know more.

An average car-load of visitors to Tolgus Tin will spend, in one way or another, roughly £3, of which perhaps £1 will be profit, to be devoted to improving the property. Whether the production of tin is subsidising the visitors or the visitors are subsidising the production of tin seems to Philip Welch to be immaterial. Any enterprise, he believes, must somehow pay, and, in his view, an archaeological site or a museum is, and must be, an enterprise. This philosophy may well prove valuable in the years ahead, when public money of any kind is likely to be extremely difficult to find.

Philip Riden, scholar-archaeologist

Philip Riden is in his early twenties. After taking a first-class degree in modern history at St. Edmund Hall, Oxford, he is in the process of settling into an academic career. He was not the usual kind of undergraduate, or, for that matter, the usual kind of history undergraduate. President of the Oxford University Archaeological Society – the first 'industrial' President in the Society's 53 years – he had been interested in industrial archaeology since his schooldays. His main interest is in early railways and during his undergraduate days he relaxed by writing the official history of the Butterley Company, iron and steel manufacturers in his native Derbyshire from 1790 until 1947.

His approach is unswervingly archaeological. Facts are facts, to be observed and recorded objectively and scientifically. Like all scientists, he believes that the heart and the emotions must not get in the way of the activities of the head. The style of his reports has the terseness and the precision of the *Antiquaries Journal*. Writing of an early nineteenth century plateway serving the Cromford Canal, he notes that 'on the southern side of the basin a double line of stone sleeper blocks lying in situ has been discovered. The blocks are of local freestone, 1 ft. 4 in. square and about 8 in. deep, with a single spike hole $1\frac{1}{2}$ in. in diameter. They are laid at intervals of 3 ft. to a gauge between the spike holes of 4 ft. 8 in. One or two are laid diagonally.'[21] In the course of excavations he discovered two pieces of cast iron plate rail, one weighing 21 lbs. per yard and the other 33, the length of each complete rail being about 3 ft. 'It is satisfying,' he remarks, 'to have established from archaeological evidence, where that of documents is lacking, the pattern and length of rail in use on the system.' This is a scientist's satisfaction. Mr. Riden shows no interest in such complications and irrelevancies as the wages, living conditions and diseases of the men who operated the plate-way and the canal, nor in the effect of the Butterley Works on the area in which it was situated. To reveal such an interest would be unscholarly. His discipline is archaeology. People are the raw material of historians with different and equally clear-cut specialities.

It is a point of view which can be defended, if one does not agree with it. In another article[22] Mr. Riden laments a decline in the standard and status of industrial archaeology since the golden age of the early 1960s,[23] when 'the subject seemed to be moving towards academic respectability'. Agreeing with D. W. Crossley that 'industrial archaeology runs the risk of becoming a resting-place for the easily satisfied, the successors of those earlier antiquarians whose ill-directed enquiries have posed such problems for prehistoric archaeologists of recent decades', he speaks of industrial archaeology as being 'weak academically' and is surprised and sad to notice that 'mere journalists' compilations' have 'a large and enthusiastic readership'.

The conclusion he draws from this is that 'the hundreds of dedicated amateurs throughout the country, with enormous reserves of energy and enthusiasm, but limited skill and resources' should stop riding on 'old trams at the Crich Tramways Museum' and 'old trains at Ffestiniog', stop regarding industrial archaeology as a branch of local history and 'join their county archaeological societies and work within the framework of archaeology as a whole'. If they do this, but not otherwise, their work will be valuable to scholars.

As one reads what Mr. Riden has to say, the shape of a pyramid begins to form in one's mind, with a scholarly élite as the apex and large numbers of energetic, tram-riding, damn-academic-disciplines-and-subjects enthusiasts as the base. This, no doubt, is how some academics do see the situation, but it could be fairly pointed out that there is no crime in regarding industrial archaeology as a branch of local history or in wishing to spend one's leisure time enjoying oneself. On one point, however, Mr. Riden is absolutely correct: the scholars and the weekend industrial archaeologists need each other's help and encouragement and some kind of common language between the two is essential.

---

[21] *Industrial Archaeology*, February 1973, pp. 79–80.

[22] 'Post-post-medieval archaeology', *Antiquity*, XLVII, 1973.

[23] The present author finds this encouraging. The first issue of the *Journal of Industrial Archaeology*, which he edited, appeared in 1963, and *Industrial Archaeology: an Introduction* in the same year.

4

The Necessary
Minimum of History

'A background of social and economic history,' wrote Dr. R. A. Buchanan in 1965, 'is desirable and even necessary to the study of industrial archaeology.'[1] Without such a background, Dr. Buchanan believed, it is difficult, if not impossible to decide whether this or that building, this or that piece of machinery is significant or not. One has no criteria of value.

But, in Dr. Buchanan's opinion, there is another and more powerful reason for insisting that the industrial archaeologist without adequate historical equipment is like a runner with one leg. Industrial archaeology is both a social study and 'intimately related to several other fields of study', notably geography, architecture, engineering, local and general history and 'conventional archaeology'. On this view of the subject, he insisted, 'the study of industrial archaeology is enmeshed in a range of other social studies, it cannot be considered in isolation from these studies without serious detriment to its own value; and industrial archaeology serves in turn to illuminate these companion subjects. Among these subjects is the study of economic and social history.'

What, however, is 'study'? Clearly it does not mean in this context merely study for an examination. Most people who are interested in industrial archaeology are not preparing themselves for examinations. It might perhaps be wiser and more accurate to say, instead of the study of economic and social history, an informed interest in economic and social history. What could the guide-lines of this informed interest reasonably be said to be?

They would certainly include an awareness of the pace and pattern of urban development. 'Industrial capitalism, when it matured,' wrote W. G. East,[2] '–

---

[1] *Journal of Industrial Archaeology*, October 1965.

[2] In *An Historical Geography of England before 1800*, edited by H. C. Darby, revised edition, 1961, p. 465.

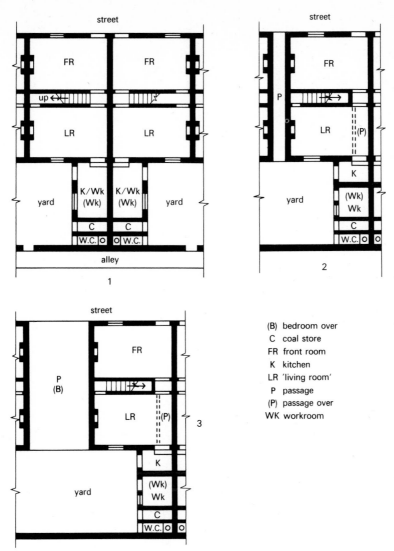

House-types connected with the Luton hat industry, *c.*1860–1900 (from *Industrial Archaeology*, February 1972)

and it matured after 1800 – produced changes on the map which were perhaps, unequalled in magnitude by any others subsequent to the Anglo-Saxon settlement.' These 'changes on the map' were, for the most part, vast concentrations of buildings covering what had been countryside only a very short time before.

During the whole of the eighteenth century the chief towns in Great Britain owed their importance not so much to their size as to the fact that they were economic centres for large areas. The typical pattern was of a town of 20–30,000 people serving a scatter of villages or smaller towns within a radius of about 40 miles from the metropolitan centre. The whole complex might be characterised by considerable industrial growth, but the industry concerned was basically rural rather than urban. There were fields and trees between the factories and workshops. As late as 1800 William Yates' map of Lancashire shows little genuinely urban development round Manchester and Salford. What on the other hand it does provide evidence of is a very slow thickening of the rural industrial settlements which were well scattered over Lancashire. John Turner's map of Yorkshire (1787) makes it clear that the West Riding had reached the same stage of industrialisation.

The localisation of industry, which seems normal today, was only just beginning in 1800. The woollen industry, for example, was very widespread, although a good deal of specialisation was noticeable in particular areas, mainly because some places had a much more ample water-supply than others. Broadcloths and serges needed fulling, which demanded large quantities of water, whereas the manufacture of blankets and flannels involved very little water. Consequently, broadcloths were made along the Cotswolds and in the valleys round Stroud, and serges at the foot of Dartmoor, all areas where there was a good head of water available. Worsteds, on the other hand, needed no fulling and could be produced without difficulty in Norfolk, where the supply of water was not so generous.

In the same way, the Yorkshire and East Lancashire textile industries depended on the fast-flowing streams of the Pennines, in the years before steam engines arrived to change the power situation. The reasons why cotton established itself in Lancashire are more complex – the suitability of the climate, a local labour force already skilled in working wool and flax, towns not hamstrung by the power and conservatism of ancient and well-entrenched guilds, ports near at hand for bringing in the raw cotton from overseas. But, with cotton, as with wool, the new carding and spinning machines had to have water power to drive them, before steam engines were installed to give manufacturers a greater choice of location.

The production of iron was as well distributed as that of cloth. In 1720 the total British output of pig iron was no greater than 17,000 tons and it was normal for an iron-works concerned with the finishing end of the trade to handle only a few hundred tons a year. These very small works, catering mostly for local customers, were situated all over the country and some of them miraculously survived into the twentieth century. Even in the eighteenth century, however, specialisation existed in a few districts. The fast-running streams and supplies of millstone grit gave the Sheffield and Rotherham areas, for instance, natural advantages for making steel cutlery.

The traveller through eighteenth century Britain moved from one largely self-sufficient area to another, each with its own pattern of industry and agriculture closely interwoven. Halfway through the century London was still the only really large urban community in the country.

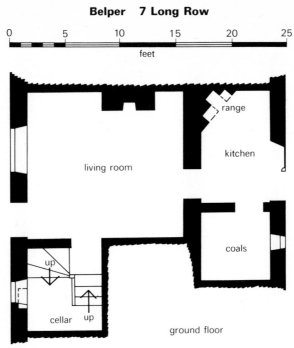

Ground-plan of industrial housing at Belper, Derbyshire

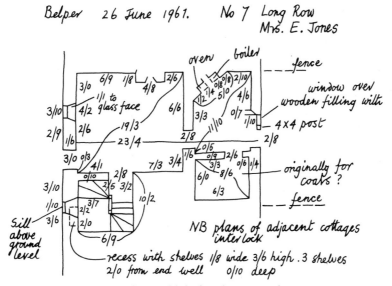

Sketch-plan and measurements from which the above was drawn

Housing at Belper, Derbyshire, *c*.1790

Next to it came Bristol, with 100,000 people, Norwich, with 50,000, Manchester, with 45,000 and Liverpool and Birmingham, with about 30,000 each.

The mostly thickly populated county was Middlesex, including London, where the density was 200 inhabitants to the square mile. Next came Gloucestershire, Warwickshire and Lancashire with 150 and then a much larger group with 100 – Somerset, Wiltshire, Worcestershire, Oxfordshire, Buckinghamshire, Kent, Hertfordshire, Suffolk, Northamptonshire, Durham, Bedfordshire, Leicestershire, Derbyshire, Staffordshire and the West Riding.

In 1700, outside the London area, the density of population had been determined mainly by the location of the woollen industry. In 1750 this was no longer true. Even before canals and turnpike roads and improved communications, the distribution of the population was changing rapidly, with textiles moving north and the areas where coal and iron were readily available beginning to be more thickly settled.

Between 1700 and 1800, the total population probably increased from about 6 million to about 9 million, an average of roughly 30,000 a year. But after that the growth was much more rapid. At the second census of 1811, the figure was 10 million, and in 1821[3] it was 12 million, a rate of increase five times as great as during the previous century. In the major industrial centres the change was even more striking. Manchester, in 1801, was a town of 90,000 people. In 1831 it had 237,000 and in 1861 400,000.

There has been a great deal of argument as to why this enormous increase occurred. There is no reason to suppose that the birth-rate suddenly soared. The main cause is likely to have been a remarkable fall in the death-rate, produced partly by improvements in sanitation and the water-supply and partly by the use of more skilled methods of midwifery. Infant mortality was halved between 1750 and 1830.

This unprecedented increase in the population was one of the two chief reasons for the rise in industrial and agricultural production during the eighteenth and nineteenth centuries. The basic needs of the extra millions had somehow to be met. The other and, in the case of the metal industries, probably more important reason, was war, always a prodigious consumer of iron and of the things made from it. And the eighteenth century was obligingly rich in wars.

We can use various commodities to show the growth in the size of the market. Raw cotton consumption, for instance, rose from 5 million pounds in 1781 to 124 million in 1810 and to 164 million in 1818. In 1790 the production of iron was 79,000 tons. Thirty years later, after the fillip given by the Napoleonic Wars, the figure was 400,000 tons.

As a market, the British people of 150 or 200 years ago would hardly have appeared promising to a modern manufacturer. From a commercial point of view, they had a discouragingly small amount of money to spend. In the 1760s and 1770s Arthur Young recorded the average industrial earnings as being between six shillings and eleven shillings a week, according to the area. The highest wages were to be found in the Western Counties and the lowest in East Anglia. Over the country as a whole, a family budget of £30 to £40 a year was normal. Even if we allow for the much higher spending power of a small, but steadily expanding, middle class and for the luxury market provided by a few thousand very rich people, it is surely true and remarkable that the great majority of the customers who ultimately financed the Industrial Revolution were humble and, by our standards, impoverished men and women who must have found it terribly difficult to maintain themselves on anything like a reasonable level. In these conditions, goods had to be cheap to sell at all, and it is not unreasonable to believe that the Industrial Revolution was inevitable not only because the manufacturers' potential customers were so numerous, but also because they were so poor.

---

[3] The more detailed census reports of 1831 give an excellent impression of the occupations and distribution of the British people at that time. There is no better way of feeling one's way into Britain at the time of the Industrial Revolution than spending a few hours browsing in the huge, pleasantly printed volumes.

It is just as necessary and illuminating to ask, 'why did this or that technological improvement happen?' as 'what technological improvements took place?'
The history of wool and iron is very usefully explored by means of 'why?'
questions.

Before about 1750, the manufacture of woollens and worsteds was much the
most important industry in Great Britain. It was carried out mainly in three
areas – the South West, parts of East Anglia and the West Riding. In the South,
the organisation and the capital were provided by wealthy merchant clothiers.
They bought the raw wool from the farmers, they passed it on to the spinners, they
sent the yarn to the weavers. Once the cloth was woven the merchants either had
it taken to other specialists for finishing or else undertook the bleaching and dyeing
themselves on their own premises. The spinning and weaving were easily done
in the workers' own houses, without the need for expensive equipment. The
finishing processes, even before the introduction of power-driven machinery,

The original spinning machine made by Sir Richard Arkwright in 1769 (Crown copyright; courtesy of the Science Museum, London)

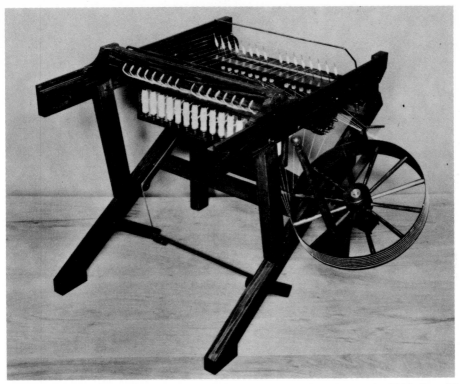

Reconstruction of the spinning jenny, patented by James Hargreaves in 1770, by which 16 threads could be spun simultaneously (Crown copyright; courtesy of the Science Museum, London)

were more efficiently and cheaply carried out in larger units, because a good supply of water and more elaborate buildings were essential.

The system in the West Riding was different. There, in the earlier part of the eighteenth century, the workshops were 'embryo factories without steam-power'.[4] The industry was in the hands of master-craftsmen, who bought their own wool, spun it, wove it, dyed it and eventually sold it. They employed assistants, they were in direct contact with the market and they controlled all the capital needed for converting raw wool into finished cloth. When steam-power became available, the Yorkshire clothiers were able to convert their workshops into factories with little difficulty and to push their Southern competitors out of the market. This, rather than 'because they were closer to the coalfields', seems to be the answer to the classic question, 'why did the woollen textile industry transfer its headquarters to the West Riding?'.

[4] G. D. Cole and R. Postgate: *The Common People* 1938, p. 64.

Crompton's mule. Replica of an early machine (Crown copyright; courtesy of the Science Museum, London)

The history of the Industrial Revolution suggests dozens of similar questions. Why, for instance, did so many years pass before Cartwright's power-loom, patented in 1785, became widely used and accepted? The short and conventional answer is 'the Luddites'. But this is really no answer at all, because it gives rise to another question, 'why were there no Luddites earlier in the century?' And the only satisfactory reply to this takes us back over three-quarters of a century of inventions.

In 1733 John Kay patented his famous flying-shuttle, the effect of which was to make it possible for the handloom weaver to increase his output up to a point where it was difficult to supply him with more yarn. Between 1738 and 1775 this led to a series of inventions by among others, Paul, Arkwright and Hargreaves, which went a long way towards mechanising the carding and spinning processes. In 1778, Samuel Crompton combined Arkwright's and Hargreaves' inventions into what became known as a spinning-mule. This machine made it possible and necessary to transfer the spinning process from the cottage to the factory, and, as a result, thousands of hand-spinners found themselves permanently out of work. Since, however, spinning was done by women and children and had always been regarded as an unskilled and part-time occupation, there was no doubt that a good deal of misery and privation was caused, as the family income was cut, but no machine wrecking.

Between 1770 and 1790, many spinning factories had been established, using water as their source of power, and in 1789 the first steam engine to drive spinning machinery was installed in Manchester. The application of power to spinning produced more yarn than the existing force of hand-loom weavers could cope with. The inevitable result was a great influx of weavers into Lancashire and Glasgow and a short period of high wages and prosperity for them. At this point Cartwright patented his power-loom. But, unlike the spinners, the weavers regarded themselves as skilled, they were the main breadwinners for their families and they were comparatively well organised. The consequence was a long period of active opposition to the new machine and of temporarily successful attempts to prevent its being used.

There are many useful ways of studying industrial and technological change. Our interest may be mainly philosophical, mainly political, mainly antiquarian, mainly scientific or mainly aesthetic.[5] We may prefer to focus our attention on an industry, a process, a firm or a district. But, whatever our particular approach may be, single-mindedness can be carried too far. The person carrying out research into, say, nail-making in the West Midlands is not likely to reach any very noteworthy conclusions unless he also knows a great deal about the sources from which the nail makers obtained their iron, about their markets for nails and about the general living and working conditions in the area. The student of the Welsh coal industry in the early nineteenth century or of Cornish china-clay in the early twentieth does well to learn as much as he can about the agricultural situation during the same period, in order to understand why it was necessary, or how it was possible, for many of the men to be half colliers and half small-holders. The economist has a duty to learn something about psychology and engineering and the social historian will miss a great deal of significance if he is ill-informed about popular literature or changes in building techniques.

As a method of self-defence, it is always useful to get a few fixed points and some simple, concrete facts clear in our mind before allowing ourselves to become hypnotised and quite possibly anaesthetised by detail and theory. Suppose, for instance, that we have discovered an interest in the architecture of the buildings in which industry and commerce have been carried on during the past two hundred years. Suppose we want to know what are the important features to look for, either in our own particular district or as we move about the country. In this case, the most profitable first step may not be to plod through a general history of architecture, which can easily prove an embarrassment at this stage. The better plan may be to look at J. M. Richards' *The Functional Tradition as shown in Early*

[5] As Miss Esther Moir points out in her interesting essay, 'The Industrial Revolution, A Romantic View' (*History Today*, September 1959), the motives of the late eighteenth century tourist in visiting mines and factories were 'at the same time economic and romantic, practical and aesthetic'. See also F. D. Klingender: *Art and the Industrial Revolution* (1947).

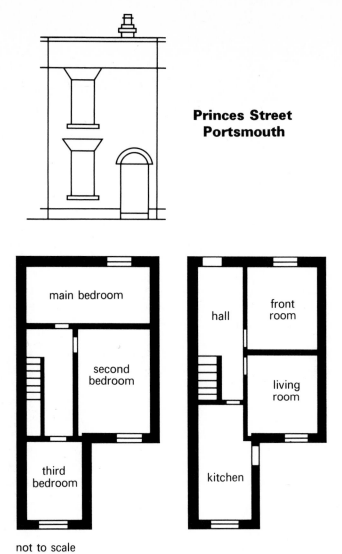

**Princes Street
Portsmouth**

not to scale

Working-class housing in Portsmouth, *c.* 1850 (from *Industrial Archaeology*, May 1973)

Industrial Buildings. In these splendidly illustrated seventy pages, we can pass with no waste of time or energy from warehouses to docks and from textile factories to breweries and finish our rapid survey equipped with the basic information for sifting out the significant buildings from the insignificant as we come across them, to build up our private and essentially practical architectural history, in fact.

Another method of making a beginning, which many people find helpful, is to turn to a book like Walter Godfrey's *History of Architecture in and around London*,[6] draw up a list of the non-domestic, non-ecclesiastical buildings he mentions and either go and see them, or, in cases where they have been demolished, study photographs or prints of them. A skeleton list, constructed in order to get our bearings, might look something like this:

1830 Covent Garden Market
1830 Hoare's Bank, Fleet Street
1831 Fishmongers' Hall, London Bridge
1838 Euston Station
1838 Nine Elms Station, Battersea
1843 Sun Assurance Office, Threadneedle Street
1847 The Corn Exchange
1852 King's Cross Railway Station
1852 Paddington Station Hotel
1879 Prudential, Holborn

Once real buildings have been seen and studied and their materials noted, it becomes fruitful to read about their place in the history of architecture and to make comparisons with less well-known and more modest buildings erected at the same time, with the kind of buildings, in fact, that one is likely to come across in the course of one's own investigations. But it is extremely discouraging to be faced in one's apprentice days with massive evidence of an expert's knowledge-ability and to try to evaluate dogmas and generalisations about objects one has personally never seen. The student of literature who reads volume after volume of dramatic criticism without going to the theatre is in a similarly impossible position.

The technique of starting with a skeleton and then gradually adding flesh to it is equally useful when one is trying to get to grips with the landmarks in the history of industry and technology. Part of our list of dates and events might read like this:

1709 Abraham Darby first used coke for smelting iron
1746 First cast-iron pipes laid by Chelsea Waterworks Company
1758 Bridgwater Canal
1767 Richard Reynolds installed iron tram rails at Coalbrookdale
1769 Watt's first steam engine. Arkwright's water frame
1774 John Smeaton re-discovered hydraulic cement
1778 First Watt steam engine installed in London for pumping water
1779 Crompton's Mule
1783/4 Henry Cort's patents for puddling and rolling iron. Watt's improved
        steam engine

[6] First published 1911. Reissued, much revised, 1962.

1785 Cartwright's first power-loom
1789 French Revolution
1796 First chain suspension bridge, built by Finley in America
1798 Malthus's *Essay on Population*
1801 First Census
1807 Slave Trade abolished
1811 Luddite troubles begin
1819 First Factory Act
1824 Aspdin's patent for Portland Cement
1825 Stockton and Darlington Railway opened
1826 Lancashire power-loom riots
1827 First successful filter bed constructed by James Simpson
1831 First angle-iron rolled

But, although a list of dates or a set of representative photographs can set the imagination working, remove a number of misconceptions and possibly serve as a reminder of the gaps in our knowledge, it is hardly possible to achieve much, if anything, within the field of industrial archaeology without a fairly solid understanding of the interrelated developments which gradually changed the economy of Great Britain from one which was based on agriculture and handicrafts to one characterised by concentrated urban communities and large-scale manufacturing units. This is probably best studied in the first place in terms of iron and coal. The great authority on the early history of coal mining, Professor J. U. Nef, came to the conclusion early in his researches that if one understood coal, one understood the Industrial Revolution. 'Even though the sources for a description of coal mining and the coal trade, in a narrow sense, were more than sufficient to occupy me,' he wrote, 'I was unable to confine myself to such a description. To study the history of this great industry is to become increasingly aware of its relation to other industries and, indeed, to the whole historical fabric of industrial civilisation.'[7]

The beginnings of the industry were humble enough. In a number of parts of Britain, outcrop coal, mostly of a bituminous type, was known and used locally in the Middle Ages, but except from the Tyne, where sea transport was possible, it was never sent away in quantities of more than a few hundred tons a year until well after 1500. This was not only because transport was poor. The bituminous coal was very unpleasant to burn in one's home – its smell and its smoke were notorious – and there was consequently good reason for not using it, so long as wood was available at a reasonable price.

Between 1560 and 1690, however, the production of coal increased almost as quickly as it did between 1775 and 1900, which is generally thought of as the period when the Coal Age really began. As Nef points out, there was hardly an

[7] *The Rise of the British Coal Industry*, 1932, Vol. 1, p. xi. See also Robert L. Galloway: *A History of Coal Mining in Great Britain*, 1882, Chapter Five.

important coalfield where production had risen less than ten-fold between 1590 and 1690. The growth was particularly spectacular in Wales, where shipments were thirty times bigger in 1690 than they had been in 1560. The Midlands, by contrast, developed a good deal more slowly, because, until the eighteenth century canals were built, they had little outlet by water. Round the Trent, on the other hand, progress was much faster.

Near the pits, coal was exceedingly cheap. In the early seventeenth century it cost less than two shillings a ton near Newcastle, although the price had risen to ten and fifteen shillings by the time the coal reached London. The difference in price was naturally reflected in the amount consumed. Nef quotes the case of a small tenant-farmer in South Durham who received a free supply of coal in exchange for granting a colliery owner a wayleave through his property. This comparatively humble man burnt twenty tons a year, nearly as much as was bought for a London mansion.

The use of coal developed much earlier in England than on the Continent. There were excellent reasons for this. Outcropping seams were well spread over the whole country, so that the distances between the pit and the consumer were not impossibly great. The fact that Britain was an island made transport of this bulky, heavy commodity much easier than in, say, France or Germany. The transfer of church property to lay owners after the Reformation produced a bigger investment in coal mining. Before then, the church had owned most of the mineral rights in Cumberland, Shropshire, Durham and Northumberland but had shown remarkably little interest in developing them.

The main reason, however, for the big increase in the use of coal was a serious timber crisis, which came much earlier in Britain than on the Continent. The demand for wood, both as a building material and as a domestic and industrial fuel, forced up the price to a point where coal became more economic, despite its high transport costs.

The really big consumers of wood were the glass makers and the iron smelters. With the techniques available in the sixteenth and seventeenth centuries, it took twelve loads of charcoal – the equivalent of eight young beech trees – to produce a ton of bar iron from the ore. And glassmaking unfortunately required just the sort of timber that the shipwrights needed. Without coal, therefore, British industry could not have continued to expand during the seventeenth century. The fact that it did expand is directly attributable to the ability of the mining areas to produce and ship more coal and to the willingness of merchants and landowners to provide the necessary capital. The result was, as Nef has pointed out, that by 1700 'some writers had a consciousness of Britain's industrial destiny which is too commonly supposed to have originated with Adam Smith'.[8]

Nowadays the visible evidence of these early coal workings is slight. Occasionally, excavations reveal a honeycomb of shallow pits below the surface of a field, each pit being wider at the bottom than at the top, and in other places there are

[8] Op. cit., Vol. 1, p. 188.

Free-miners at their non-nationalised drift coal mine near Cinderford, Forest of Dean

small mounds and depressions to show where the mines were sunk and the stone and earth dumped. The drift mines, which are still operated in the Forest of Dean, must use very similar techniques to those practised two or three hundred years ago, but for an understanding of pre-eighteenth century methods of pit-mining one has to resort to museum reconstructions and to contemporary drawings and descriptions.[9] The Whin Gin, for instance, a great wheel parallel to the ground, by means of which a horse drew coal up a shaft, was built largely of timber, and it is consequently rare to come across a survival example, whatever its condition.

During the seventeenth century and for much of the eighteenth as well, coal was a factor in industrial development only when it was available close to the point where it was to be used. The glass industry illustrates this very well. By 1700 it flourished at a number of centres – at Bristol, around Whitehaven, in Cumberland, at Dudley, Stourbridge and Birmingham in the Midlands, on the Tyne, and the Wear, in London, and in several towns in Lancashire. In the case of London, the coal was brought in relatively easily by sea, but in the other places the supply was conveniently close at hand.

The glass industry demanded a concentration of workers and considerable financial resources. Consequently, it seems to have been generally organised on a capitalistic basis from Jacobean times onwards. The most important figure in glass-making in the early seventeenth century, Sir Robert Mansell, spent more than £30,000 in obtaining satisfactory results from coal-firing, and his new furnaces at Newcastle-upon-Tyne cost him £2000. By 1700, the manufacture of glass, particularly of window-glass, had ceased to be possible for the small undertaking.

But, in terms of the early eighteenth century, a concern employing fifty people was large. The school-book picture of great mills and ironworks drawing in thousands of more or less willing workers from the surrounding country districts applies to some parts of Lancashire, Yorkshire and the Midlands during the period between about 1750 and 1850, but it is certainly not true of England as a whole.

As Professor A. H. Dodd has pointed out,[10] the phrase 'Industrial Revolution' has focussed attention on what he calls 'the highly unrepresentative Lancashire cotton and Yorkshire worsted industries'. This, he believes, 'inevitably lends colour to the legend of a rapid victory for steam power and big industry, accompanied by a hasty concentration of manufacturers on the coalfields and involving the summary demise of scattered trades and handicrafts. To counteract this impression, it is necessary to study other regions – especially regions which do not today form part of Industrial Britain, but which nevertheless shared in the wide diffusion of industrial enterprise, the general quickening of economic life,

---

[9] Some useful examples are to be found in Robert L. Galloway: *A History of Coal Mining in Great Britain*, 1882, although no sources are given for most of the information.

[10] *The Industrial Revolution in North Wales*, 2nd edition, 1951, VII. See also H. L. Beales, *History*, XIV, p. 125.

that constituted the first phase of the Industrial Revolution, before the era of concentration set in.'[11]

It is useful to make this distinction between areas, like North Wales and Somerset, which made considerable progress during this 'first phase of the Industrial Revolution' and others, like South Lancashire, which only came into their own during the second phase, 'the era of concentration'. 'First phase' areas are an excellent and much neglected field for the industrial archaeologist, with abandoned sites to be explored, derelict and much modified buildings to be identified, measured and photographed, decayed ports to be surveyed. Much of the material to be discovered here dates from long before the classic period of the Industrial Revolution. On the Flintshire coast, for instance, smelting had been extensively carried out since the Middle Ages, and when Sir Roger Mostyn, during the reign of Charles II, built a large furnace for smelting lead, with a water-wheel to work the bellows, he was doing no more than continue a long local tradition of extracting and working metal.

At least three seventeenth century forges, after reconstruction, continued producing iron until well into the nineteenth century. These were the Abenbury forge, the Pont y Blew forge, near Chirk, and the Mattrafal forge, in the heart of Montgomeryshire. This degree of continuity was exceptional. A more typical fate was that of John Wilkinson's once celebrated forge and foundry at Bersham. In 1801 this works produced, as an impressive token of its skill and organisation, an iron plate weighing $18\frac{1}{2}$ tons for the glass works at St. Helens. In 1812, the premises were sold. By 1830, they were in ruins. The village ceased to be industrial and, in Professor Dodd's words, 'the remains of the great cannon-factory must now be sought in the walls of farm buildings'.

Wilkinson's other works, at Brymbo, fared a good deal better. It operated until the 1950s, adapted to producing steel by the open-hearth process. There are many reminders, too, of the once thriving flannel and woollen industries – one or two rural mills still working and others only recently abandoned or converted to other uses, and the markets at Welshpool, Montgomery, Newtown, Llanid-loes, Oswestry and Shrewsbury.

In some areas – Central Wales, Wiltshire, Shropshire and Sussex are good examples – tombstones provide useful evidence of the district's former industrial glories. Quite a number of those belonging to the eighteenth and early nine-teenth century are industrial monuments in the most literal sense – monuments to the local industrialists who built up the prosperity of the town and who, in later generations, saw prosperity fade away, men like Charles Cole, the woollen manufacturer of Llanidloes, whose stone records his achievement and his stake in the community:

'By his active exertions he encouraged and extended the manufactures of the place, and by his liberality he provided employment for the industrious poor, to whom he was a kind and constant benefactor.'

[11] Ibid, VII.

Eighteenth century pin maker's forge, Folk Museum, Gloucester. The Museum was originally the pin-maker's workshop

or Humphrey Tugwell, of Bradford-on-Avon, 'who carried on an extensive manufactory in this town upwards of fifty years, with unblemish'd integrity' and died in 1775.

It is not only the historians of these areas of once flourishing industries who have found it necessary to remind us that, in its earlier stages, the Industrial Revolution was centred on villages and small towns, rather than on large urban communities. Professor Court has suggested that the Midlands themselves 'form a region where there never was an Industrial Revolution, in the sense of a general supersession of small industrial units by factories'.[12] Until the nineteenth century, he insists, the West Midlands were no more than 'an industrialised countryside', 'a strung-out web of iron-working villages, market-towns next door to collieries, heaths and wastes gradually and very slowly being covered by the cottages of nailers and other persons carrying on industrial occupations in rural surroundings'.[13]

Having used a phrase like 'rural surroundings', which for most people has strong agricultural associations, one is inevitably faced with the problem of

[12] W. H. B. Court: *The Rise of the Midland Industries*, Preface.
[13] Ibid, p. 22.

deciding how large a part agriculture continued to play in the lives of the people who lived in an 'industrialised countryside'. Before the arrival of the time when workers were concentrated into factories, the only way to meet the growing demand for the kind of product in which the Midlands specialised was to put more and more people to work in their homes, or in workshops built on to their homes. The very long hours these men and women needed to spend at their work in order to earn a tolerable living makes it certain that they, at any rate, can have had little time or energy left for agricultural pursuits of any kind. If the industrial workers were so numerous by comparison with the agricultural workers and with those engaged in the traditional rural crafts, it is debatable if we are justified in talking about a rural community at all. And, in Professor Court's opinion, even by the end of the Stuart period it is quite probable that a majority of the workers in the Midlands were employed in various forms of manufacture and not in agriculture.

As the fields and the heaths and the wastes became increasingly built over during the eighteenth and nineteenth centuries, the original interdependence of one trade on another persisted and even increased. The fact that the person who supplies you with raw material, or with components, or who carries out some kind of finishing process on an article you have just made, lives two streets away, instead of a quarter of a mile down the lane and across a field, makes no essential difference to the situation. The Midlands, like London and the Manchester area, have been for two centuries and more places of a great number of interlocking occupations. One trade grows or stagnates with another since, in Professor Court's words: 'Much of the business of a modern industrial district consists in taking in its own washing on a colossal scale'.[14] It is certainly true that a great part of the industrialisation of the Midlands in the seventeenth and eighteenth centuries was due to this process. One firm grew because another needed its services. Even today, some of the most indispensable concerns in a highly industrialised district are those employing fifty people or less, on very specialised work. The absence of this interlocking network of local specialists has been a great, and not always foreseen disadvantage to manufacturers who decide to leave one of the major industrial areas and to re-locate themselves in, say, Weston-super-Mare or Plymouth.

Much of the land in what are now the industrial areas was not built over, despite the demand for building sites, for the very good reason that it was covered by waste heaps, by huge stagnant lakes and by sheer devastation – the unpleasant, befouling by-products of industrialisation. The Black Country, for instance, was a pleasant, green landscape until the middle of the eighteenth century. The mountains of rubbish which changed its appearance were the result of primitive iron-smelting methods. The furnaces were charged with 8 tons of ore, 4 of limestone and 12 of coke – 24 tons of material altogether. This produced between 3 and 4 tons of iron every 12 hours. Of the remainder of the charge, 11 tons went away

[14] Ibid, p. 76.

to the atmosphere as gas and soot – a Black Country bonus – leaving 5 tons of slag to be dumped on the meadows of rural Staffordshire. During the past twenty years a great deal of reclamation work has been carried out in the Black Country. Huge areas of derelict land have been levelled and restored, for development as housing estates or playing-fields. As a result of this and of the rigorous policy of smoke control, the Black Country no longer deserves its title.

Chemical works destroyed the countryside as ruthlessly as iron and coal. One of the earliest of them was at Tipton. It was established by James Keir in the 1780s in order to supply alkali to the soap-makers. It went on to make soap itself and in the course of time added red and white lead to its products. Its waste materials either piled up round the works or were poured away to pollute the rivers and streams, much as they did later around Widnes and Wigan.

During one of the excursions organised in connection with the British Association's meeting in Manchester in 1962, members of the geography section visited the derelict areas of South Lancashire – subsidences, disused opencast workings, slag heaps, murky pools of stagnant water, where small children have been drowning themselves for more than a century, abandoned coal mines. The leader of the party, Mr. H. B. Rodgers, a lecturer in geography at Manchester University, referred in memorable terms to 'the ravaged landscape of South Wigan, where the noble masses of the Wigan Alps tower over man-made lakes thinly coated with coal-dust'.

Bagging china clay *c.* 1880

Bal-maidens scraping sand and straw off blocks of china clay, *c.* 1880

Cornwall, which must include nearly as much murdered countryside as Lancashire, has been more fortunate in its waste heaps, because, although they are extensive, they happen also to be clean and, in the view of some enthusiasts, even picturesque. It is certainly difficult to deny that quality to the white, man-made hills around St. Austell, the moon-landscape created by the waste sand from the china-clay industry. But these enormous heaps have sterilised millions of tons of valuable china-clay which lie untouched beneath them and millions of tons more in pits which cannot be worked any deeper because there is nowhere to dump the waste sand washed out of the clay. The high proportion of Cornish land covered with the waste heaps and the burrowings of two centuries of intensive mineral working is just as truly derelict as the dreary areas in Lancashire. But Cornwall, by the grace of Providence, did not include coal among its useful minerals, with the result that the landscape remains unblackened and 'un-industrialised'.

The industrial waste lands are gradually being obliterated now, as land becomes more valuable and as heavy equipment is available to carry out the levelling quickly and reasonably cheaply.[15] It may seem to be stretching our definition a little if a slag heap is to be classed as an industrial monument, but these horror areas are true evidence of the Industrial Revolution, just as significant and revealing in their way as an early iron-framed building or an old windmill. They deserve to be mapped and photographed and documented before the bulldozer sweeps them out of existence.

In Fife, a five-year scheme, begun in 1962, has removed the giant carbuncles of slag heaps and derelict industrial buildings which previously marred the otherwise pleasant face of the country, and Lancashire has done much to clean up its 100,000 acres of man-made dereliction. Probably the most massive and thorough-going attempt to survey and rehabilitate a devastated area is the Lower Swansea Valley Project in South Wales. This area, roughly three miles long and a mile wide is a terrible memorial to the ruthlessness and single-mindedness of nineteenth century industrial enterprise. The plan to restore it has engaged the attention of economists, botanists, biologists, civil engineers, geographers, geologists and social scientists. Old smelting and arsenic works have been demolished, an extensive grassing and tree-planting programme has been carried out, and different parts of the area have been reserved for housing, botanical research and new industries. The wounds inflicted by the Industrial Revolution are healing.

The industrial history of Scotland has followed a pattern of its own. Until the late eighteenth century, the main industry was linen, which mixed well with agriculture and was essentially domestic in character. At the same time, a very substantial tobacco trade was built up with the American colonies, much of the tobacco being subsequently re-exported to Europe. The American Civil War, and the nationalist feeling which followed, completely destroyed Scotland's profitable interest in tobacco and a cotton industry was established very rapidly as a substitute. Between 1780 and 1830, cotton became Scotland's major industry, its development coinciding with the introduction of important inventions, the spinning jenny, the water-frame and the mule.

The new industry was extremely popular. Robert Owen was able to say that

---

[15] On this, see Kenneth Browne's excellent article, 'Dereliction', in the *Architectural Review*, November 1955, and the Civic Trust's publication, *Derelict Land* (1965).

raw cotton could be bought at five shillings a pound and sold for nearly £10 when it was ready for the muslin weaver.[16] But by the 1860s cotton in its turn was collapsing. Paisley held out for a good deal longer, but by 1880 the famous shawls had gone completely out of fashion and the highly skilled weavers, whose craftsmanship had an international reputation, found themselves out of work. Fortunately for Paisley, the sewing machine was coming into general use at this time and the growing demand for cotton thread allowed some of the mills to stay in existence.

Meanwhile, linen manufacture continued in Forfar, Fife and Perth, although with recurring ups and downs.[17] Early in the eighteenth century a determined attempt had been made to improve the quality of Scottish linen. In 1729, as part of the campaign, a number of skilled weavers and their families were brought over from France to teach Scots people how to make a better product. Houses were built for them in an Edinburgh suburb and the site of this village is still called Picardy Place.

Before chemical methods were introduced in the late eighteenth century, bleaching linen cloth took eight months. Chlorine was discovered as a bleaching agent in 1785 and Watt introduced it in Glasgow in 1786. Tennant used chloride of lime for the same purpose in 1798, also in Glasgow.

A new textile industry was established in Scotland in the 1850s, when jute came to the help of flax. Dundee became a jute city in place of a linen city, and an important linoleum industry was built up at another old linen centre, Kirkcaldy. But before this, from the 1830s onwards, the metal industries had been gaining ground rapidly over textiles and by 1880 they were Scotland's principal source of income and employment.

Iron-smelting has had a long history in Scotland. In 1753, a Lancashire firm, Richard Ford and Company, built the Bonawe Furnace at Taynuilt, in Argyllshire. The furnace, which still exists and is in a good state of preservation, burnt charcoal and used Lancashire ore. The company built an industrial village at Taynuilt – houses, a farm, a school and a public house. The works finally closed in 1866.

Another charcoal furnace was set up in Argyllshire rather later, about six miles from Inverary, at a place that is still called Furnace. It was built by another Lancashire company, the Duddon Company, and it, too, depended on English ores brought in by sea. It stayed in business until 1813 and a part of the furnace, dated 1775, still remains.

The real beginnings of the Scottish iron industry, however, are to be found in the setting up of the Carron Iron Works in 1759. This event can be said without exaggeration to have been a turning point in the economic and industrial history of Scotland. Carron was the first works to use ironstone from the extensive carboniferous formations of central Scotland and it was at Carron that the process of smelting iron with coal was first used north of the border.

[16] Henry Hamilton: *The Industrial Revolution in Scotland* 1932, p. 123.
[17] See Hamilton, op. cit., p. 153.

It is interesting to speculate why the discovery made by Abraham Darby at Coalbrookdale in 1709 for using coke instead of charcoal in the furnaces was so slow in being adopted. Fifty years later, when Carron was founded, most pig-iron was still being smelted with charcoal. The reason for this conservatism was probably that for most of the eighteenth century malleable iron was a more important part of the industry than cast iron. It was the demands of the Army and the Navy for cannons and cannon balls which changed the emphasis of production and Carron, in fact, was set up chiefly to turn out munitions for the war of 1756–63.[18]

The activities of the Carron company extended a long way beyond smelting. It owned slitting and rolling mills at Cramond, using, in this case, bar-iron from Russia, and it also maintained warehouses at various places in the district in order to supply the nailmakers, who were domestic workers, with their raw material, rod-iron, and to receive back the finished nails.

Scotland's change of emphasis from textiles to iron and steel, to shipbuilding and to heavy engineering, is a remarkable example of the adaptability and resilience of an economy compelled to deal urgently with the problem of serious unemployment. A rather different kind of enforced flexibility occurred in Ireland. During the eighteenth century, the Lagan Valley,[19] the area westwards from Belfast through Lisburn, developed the manufacture of fine linen with many small mills involved in the industry and the capital investment per manufacturing unit quite small. In the 1780s cotton, which was heavily capitalised and spun by machinery from the start, first drove linen out of Belfast and then began to extend its factory system to the linen industry itself. But even well inland, the new methods came in through cotton first. In 1790, for instance, James Wallace, a Yorkshireman, set up one of James Watt's Glasgow-built steam engines in his new four-storey cotton mill at Lisburn, in the centre of the former flax and linen area. It was the first steam engine to be seen anywhere in Ireland.[20] And fifty years later, Samuel Richardson bought the old Lisburn chemical works, Vitriol Island, and put up a mill with 2500 spindles.[21] But, surrounding the up-to-date cotton mills built by Wallace and Richardson, was an essentially rural area, characterised by small-scale agriculture and by handicraft industries associated with it.

The Industrial Revolution was carried through by opportunists, who brought in new methods, not for the pure joy of experimenting, but because they provided a basis for increased production and increased profits. The capitalist manufacturers of the eighteenth and nineteenth centuries, like the industrial managers of our own times, watched their markets and worked their employees and their finances to the practical limit. For more than 250 years, the demand for English-made goods increased so steadily that the man of only average efficiency and

[18] For a discussion of this, see Hamilton, op. cit., p. 154 and T. S. Ashton: *The Industrial Revolution*, p. 65.

[19] On the development of this area, see E. R. R. Green: *The Lagan Valley, 1800–1850*, 1959. This illuminating study is sub-titled, 'A Local History of the Industrial Revolution'.

[20] Green, op. cit., p. 98.

[21] Ibid, p. 115.

single-mindedness could hardly fail to make money. But, as we have seen, this did not necessarily mean that all capitalist enterprises were large ones, nor that it was always easy to attract labour. In the eighteenth century as now, the working unit, the income unit, was the family and no man was likely to change his home and his own job if the result was to be unemployment for his wife and children.

This accounts for the curiously mixed character of a good deal of early industrial development. As one of the foremost historians of the Industrial Revolution has said: 'When an employer sought to engage a man from another district he often failed because he was unable to offer work to other members of the family. To surmount this difficulty ironmasters, like those at Backbarrow, sometimes set up textile works near their furnaces so as to provide employment for the women and children. Conversely, when an employer, like Oldknow or Greg, wanted juvenile or female labour, he was sometimes obliged to extend his operations to agriculture, lime-burning, and so on, in order to find work for the men. The industrial unit was often not a single establishment, but something approaching a colonial settlement.'[22]

This is no longer true, but the need to provide a satisfactory balance of employment persists. The New Towns have had to give a great deal of thought to the problem of ensuring work for women as well as men, and the difference in the standard of living of towns like Birmingham, where the whole family can work, and Barnsley, which is a man's place, is very marked.

[22] T. S. Ashton: *The Industrial Revolution* 1948, p. 112. In the 1770s and 1780s, when Samuel Arkwright built his mills at Cromford, the men and older boys of the large surrounding villages were all engaged in lead-mining, which meant that he had an abundant supply of female and child labour.

5

What to Look For:
Coal and Metals

Coal

'For the industrial archaeologist,' A. R. Griffin has observed,[1] 'coal mining is normally an unrewarding study. Once a mine is closed, its shafts are covered or filled in, and usually its surface plant and buildings are removed. Mounds of debris and filled-in shafts are not, perhaps, the most exciting of archaeological remains but they present a detective-type challenge and, properly interpreted, they have a contribution to make to the story of one of Britain's oldest and most important industries.'

There is evidence that small quantities of coal were mined in Britain at the time of the Roman occupation, although in all probability easily won coal from surface workings had been used as domestic fuel in the immediate neighbourhood of outcrops for nearly a thousand years before the continuous record of coal-mining in this country begins in the thirteenth century. By 1400 coal working was being undertaken in almost all the main districts in which it is carried on today. In medieval times, however, the quantities involved were still very small and even as late as 1550 it has been estimated that the total annual output of all the British coalfields did not exceed 200,000 tons or 1.1% of their present annual production.

Over the next century and a half the uses of coal were considerably extended and by 1700 output was probably in the region of three million tons. Not quite half of this was mined in Northumberland and Durham, where the pits supplied not only the rapidly growing London market but also places as far away from New-castle as Exeter in the South-West, where easy access to the sea made water transport practicable. But, at the end of the seventeenth century, the main demand for coal still came from the domestic rather than the industrial consumer, so that the

[1] 'Bell-Pits and Soughs: Some East Midlands Examples', *Industrial Archaeology*, November 1969, p. 392.

Entrance to drift coal mine near Cinderford, Forest of Dean

Fife,[2] Cumberland and Somerset fields, with the towns of Edinburgh, Dublin and Bristol for their customers, were among those most intensively developed at this stage. During the eighteenth century industrial expansion, the building of canals, and the accelerated growth of population combined to increase the demand and encourage the development of the inland coal-fields, which had previously been sterilised, because it had been impossible to transport the coal in sufficient quantities. By 1800 output had almost certainly passed ten million tons.

In most areas, however, methods of working were still primitive by modern standards. Few collieries with records of continuous activity extending back to 1800 survive today and there are hardly any remains of this early enterprise still to be seen.

In the nineteenth century the coming of the railways and the huge demand first for iron and then for steel changed the scale and the techniques of British coal-mines. By 1850 production was already in excess of 50 million tons and with the growth of the export and bunker trades, an output of 200 million tons was reached before the end of the nineteenth century and an all-time peak of 287 million tons in 1913. The period since then has been one of considerable and sometimes acute difficulty. The industry has had to adapt itself to the problems created by wars and slumps in trade and, more recently, by the competition of oil and of nuclear energy, but the past sixty years has also been a period which has seen a revolution in the industry's technology, with the large-scale employment of coal-cutters, conveyors and mechanical loaders, and with the closing down of pits and seams where this kind of machinery could not be used efficiently.

Since the industry's beginnings, tens of thousands of pits must have been sunk in the widely scattered coal districts of the United Kingdom. No fewer than four thousand were located and mapped by the National Coal Board in a survey of the small North Staffordshire coalfields alone. But for a considerable proportion of these earlier workings 'pits' is hardly an accurate term. A large number of them were little more than scratchings and burrowings of the ground. For many centuries, coal was either quarried where the seam came close to the surface or approached by tunnels, technically known as 'drifts', driven into the hillsides. Where pits were sunk they were shallow and short-lived. It was not at all uncommon for one to be opened and closed within a matter of months. Little surface evidence of these early pits exists, although where there is an outcrop of coal in open country as, for example, in parts of Northumberland and Cumberland and in some Pennine areas, remains of bell-pits and early drift working may still be seen. More extensive evidence of early activity lies below ground beyond the reach of the archaeologist. When Newcastle-upon-Tyne Town Moor was

[2] In 'Culross Colliery: a Sixteenth Century Scottish Mine', *Industrial Archaeology*, November 1970, A. J. Bowman makes clear the importance of the coal industry during the sixteenth and seventeenth centuries in Fife, for domestic consumption and for the salt and iron industries. At Culross, he notes, a small mound can be seen at low tide. It contains the remains of three circular stone walls and traces of a jetty, all that is left of the sixteenth century Moat Pit, built by Sir George Bruce of Carnock and one of the wonders of its day.

prospected soon after the war with a view to modern open-cast working, the ground was found to be so honeycombed with primitive bell-pits that the project was abandoned.

From time to time, old underground workings are revealed and destroyed during open-cast mining operations. A group of bell-pits, probably dating from the sixteenth century, was uncovered in this way in the Tupton Seam at Heage, near Denby, Derbyshire, in the 1960s.[3] The pits varied from 5 ft. 10 in. to 16 ft. in diameter and they were from 5 ft. to 12 ft. apart and about 20 ft. deep. In the bell-pit method of working, a shaft was sunk down to the coal seam and coal was extracted from around the base of the shaft. When the sides appeared to be in danger of collapse, the pit was abandoned and another opened up nearby. The debris from the new pit was used to fill the old one. During open-cast working, the bell-pits can be easily seen, because the soil and rock with which they were filled is lighter in colour than the coal seam.

At the next stage of mining development, headings or galleries were driven out to the seam. Such workings, dating from the mid-eighteenth century, have been found in the Silkstone Seam at Denby, about 145 ft. below the Tupton seam. The method of extraction was very wasteful. Pillars 9 ft. wide were left and only about 25% of the coal was mined.

From the end of the eighteenth century it became possible to sink shafts much deeper. This not only allowed the pits to stay in use longer, but made it necessary to erect more permanent buildings and machinery on the surface. Districts already extensively worked by the old methods were among the earliest to 'go deep' and the Northumberland, Durham and Cumberland coalfields were the first in which depths of below 1000 ft. were reached. It is in these districts that we find the greatest number of collieries with continuous records of working going back 100 or even 150 years, although the existence of such pits as the Blücher at Madeley Colliery in North Staffordshire is a valuable reminder that there are equally long-lived collieries elsewhere. Where the exhaustion of a seam has ended the life of a colliery – as is the case with most pits sunk before about 1850 – time has usually dealt unkindly with surface remains. The machinery has been dismantled and removed and the buildings have been allowed to fall into ruin. The chances of something surviving are greater where individual pits have been closed, but where new shafts have been sunk to make it possible for the colliery to continue.

The most typical visible evidence of coal-working is, of course, the headstock at the top of the shaft and the winding gear associated with it. Winding machinery developed from hand and animal powered windlasses to simple beam engines and then to engines of increasing power and complexity driven by steam and electricity. A number of notable examples of early winding and haulage machinery

---

[3] For a full description and diagrams, see Griffin, op. cit., pp. 392–394. The existence of old bell-pits and shallow pillar-and-stall workings has been revealed by aerial photography in Nottinghamshire and Leicestershire. See F. A. Henson and R. S. Smith, 'Detecting Early Coal Workings from the Air', *Colliery Engineering*, June 1955, p. 256.

are to be found on the Durham coalfield. The Isabella Engine, still surviving at
Elemore Colliery, Hetton-le-Hole, was installed in 1836 and worked regularly
until 1956. Another beam engine of the same date, 1836, and in this case built at
Chester-le-Street, near Durham, is at Warden Law. It was used to haul coal
waggons on the line from Hetton Colliery to Sunderland dock. More primitive,
although actually later, winding gear is still to be seen at the fireclay pits of the
South Staffordshire coalfield and in other districts where workings are carried on
close to the surface.

Shafts and engines were required not only for winding coal and men, but also
for pumping and ventilation, and pits that have long fallen out of use for winding
have been kept in use for these secondary but important purposes. At the Glyn
Pits, near Pontypool, to take one example among many, old shafts and a winding
engine built before 1850 are still used for pumping. A pumping engine of the same
period, now disused, also survives at Glyn, and the Monmouthshire coalfield,
which was the first to be intensively developed in South Wales, has existing
examples of water-wheels and furnace ventilation.

In the Derbyshire-Nottinghamshire coalfield, many of the early nineteenth
century shafts were lined with bricks laid without mortar. This was partly for
reasons of cost and partly to make it easier to recover and re-use the bricks when

Tylorstown Colliery, South Wales, *c.* 1900. Demolished 1972

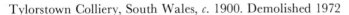

the coal in the pit was exhausted. Dry-brick shafts were dangerous. Coal was raised up to the surface in baskets, which swung freely on a rope and loosened the bricks. Men travelled up and down the shaft by passing their legs through short chains looped round the basket-hooks. Not infrequently, they were injured by hitting the side of the shaft, or by loose bricks falling on them.[4]

The surface equipment associated with coal-working includes machinery for screening and washing the coal – this was little used before the second half of the nineteenth century – pit-head baths, a nineteenth century amenity, and certain ancillary plant, such as coke ovens. These beehive ovens have survived, among other places, at the Victoria Pit in County Durham and at Waterhouses Colliery in Northumberland.

One of the most comprehensive archaeological surveys of a coalfield was carried out by Dorothy Vinter in Bristol during the 1940s and 1950s.[5] The last pit in this area, at the Coalpit Heath Colliery, closed only in 1949, but Mrs Vinter had great difficulties in finding surviving evidence of the once extensive coal workings in and around Bristol. New housing, new factories and new road developments had obliterated the former heaths, open spaces and waste-tips and swept away whole districts of eighteenth and nineteenth century houses. But, by walking round the district and combining exploration with research in manuscript and printed sources, she built up a detailed, lively picture of the rise and fall of the industry, showing an equal interest in techniques, profits, dangers, wages and living conditions. Much of what she learnt came from conversations with old miners. Parkfield Colliery, for instance, was plagued with thin seams and flooding. 'The pit,' she records, 'was very deep and the steam-boilers therefore became so hot that a retired boiler-man described to me how he had to stand in a bucket of cold water to be able to work at all.'

In 1970 a party from the Bristol Industrial Archaeological Society was guided round sites on the North Somerset Coalfield by A. H. Parsons, who had begun work in Bromley Colliery in 1917 at the age of fourteen. 'The occasion,' the Editor of *BIAS Journal* recalled, 'was a fascinating piece of industrial archaeology, enlivened by Mr. Parsons' commentary', and the old miner was afterwards persuaded to put some of his reminiscences down on paper, for publication in the *Journal*.[6]

He left home at 4.30 a.m. to cycle the five miles to work. 'We parked our cycles in a tin shed belonging to Mr. Slocombe, for which we paid 3d. per week, then went to draw our candles from the candle house. Sometimes you drew tallow,

---

[4] For this kind of accident, see *Children's Employment Commission (Mines)* 1842, 1st Report, Appendix, Part II, pp. 304–305.

[5] A report on her work, 'The Archaeology of the Bristol Coalfield', was published in Vol. 1, No. 1 of the *Journal of Industrial Archaeology* (1964). A more detailed, pit by pit account, is to be found in M. J. H. Southway's 'Kingswood Coal', published in the *BIAS (Bristol Industrial Archaeological Society) Journal*, 1971 and 1972. Mr. Southway acknowledges his debt to Mrs. Vinter, 'for stimulating my early interest'.

[6] 1970, pp. 26–27.

Monks Park Quarry: cutting out limestone blocks with converted 'Samson' coal-cutting machine

sometimes wax candles. The tallow ones were meant for working where there was plenty of air, the wax ones for where there was little air, as they would last longer. Our Cottage had boxes full of these candles because sometimes we brought home spare candles. With tallow ones we greased our boots and father his leggings.'

This kind of information usually dies with the men. It rarely finds its way into print, but it is an essential ingredient of history. Mr. Parsons was able to say exactly how the miners went about their work, how they had their baths, when they reached home, what food they had and what the dangers were. Every detail remained clear in his mind. There was, for example, a special way of moving a pit-pony up and down the shaft. 'To place the pony in the cage,' he remembered, 'they took the centre deck floor out, trussed the pony like a chicken ready for the oven, sat him on his behind, and down he went'. If industrial archaeologists fail to collect the memories of people like Mr. Parsons, who will? And such veterans are dying off very fast.

The bulk of mining activity takes place below ground. Underground equipment – lamps, picks, mechanical cutters and loaders – is necessarily worked hard and is replaced quickly once it becomes worn out or obsolete. The miner's tools of fifty and a hundred years ago have mostly disappeared, but it is very important to search for and preserve surviving examples of outdated equipment in order to document and illustrate the fundamental changes which have taken place in mining practice over the last half century. One can find examples of these old tools and machines in strange places. Two 'Samson' coal-cutters, built during the 1939–45 War and now totally obsolete, still perform a useful task cutting limestone in the mines of Corsham, in Wiltshire.

Iron

Iron is found in nature as an oxide, a brownish rock of varying degrees of purity. Before it can be turned to any commercial use, this natural iron oxide – ore as it is generally called – must be reduced to metal. There is more than one way of doing this, but all methods depend on the fact that if iron oxide is heated in contact with some other material which has a greater affinity for oxygen than iron has, the oxygen will leave the iron to form a compound with the other material, and more or less pure metallic iron will be left behind. In modern practice the iron ore is heated with burning coke, which not only provides the source of heat but also the reducing agent, carbon, of which coke mainly consists. Stated in its simplest terms, the oxygen in the ore unites with the carbon to form carbon monoxide, and the iron in the ore is reduced to metallic form.

After reduction from the ore the iron is known as cast or pig iron, and it can be used in that form for certain applications. But the greater proportion undergoes further metallurgical treatment in order to convert it into steel, either mild steel, which is really, in spite of its name, a commercially pure form of iron, or else into alloy steel, which, as the name suggests, is iron alloyed with one or more other elements to give it certain special properties such as strength or resistance to heat or corrosion.

As a rough guide, we can say that cast iron contains about 1/30 of its weight of carbon, and mild steel from 1/300 to 1/500. In between the cast iron and mild steel there is carbon steel. This can be hardened, which makes it suitable for certain tools. It contains about 1/100 of its weight of carbon. The addition of a very small amount of carbon to iron can make a lot of difference to its properties and the control of carbon content is, and always has been, an important feature of iron and steel making. Alloy steels contain percentages of other elements such as nickel, chromium or vanadium, and these steels are very new items in the long history of iron-making. In all cases certain other elements are present, often in very small quantities. They may have beneficial effects, or the percentage of them may be so small as to be of no practical significance. No chemically pure iron has ever been used commercially. It would be expensive and pointless to produce it.

Iron was known and used at least three thousand years ago. At first, and until about 1500, it was made from the ore, in what would now seem absurdly small quantities, by a process known as direct reduction, in primitive hearths and bloomeries. This process produced a form of wrought iron. In about 1500 the blast furnace was introduced into this country from the Continent, Sussex being the pioneering district.[7] This was a new technical process. It was quicker and more reliable and it produced larger quantities of iron with the aid of mechanical power – water power at first – than man's unaided muscles had been able to do previously. With the help of the blast furnace, all the iron was first produced in cast or pig form. A little was subsequently used for making castings, but for a long time most of it was converted from pig iron into wrought iron, so that the blacksmith could work it up into tools, weapons and other articles.

The blast furnace represented considerable progress, in that it enabled iron-making to develop beyond the domestic stage, but it created its own difficulties which, in time, became extremely serious. It used charcoal as a fuel and as a reducing agent, and by the seventeenth century the shortage of suitable timber for charcoal making was causing concern. Many inventors and capitalists tried to find the answer to the problem, but none of them succeeded until, in 1709 Abraham Darby, working at Coalbrookdale, in Shropshire, discovered how to use coke instead of charcoal. The historic eighteenth century furnaces at Coalbrookdale have been preserved. When one looks at them now, one's first reaction is likely to be, 'How small they are. How could they possibly have produced enough metal for all the work that the Darbys are known to have carried out?' Nothing could justify the preservation of industrial monuments better than these relics at Coalbrookdale. Without them, our sense of scale might well go seriously astray.

The Darbys experienced technical difficulties at first, but they were overcome and eventually coke-smelting became universal, helped by the improvement of the steam engine by James Watt and others, from 1769 onwards, and by the introduction of Henry Cort's puddling process for wrought iron production, in 1784. Cort carried out his experimental work at a little water-driven mill at Funtley, near Fareham, in Hampshire, an unlikely place for a process which required a great deal of fuel and scrap iron. Research at Funtley by R. C. Riley and M. D. Freeman [8] has shown the remarkable efforts made by Cort to increase the amount of water-power available to drive the rollers and hammers at the forge. With the nearly universal employment of coal for both the blast-furnaces and the reverberatory furnaces used in the puddling process, charcoal-smelting became a thing of the past and iron-making began to spread on a large scale from the traditional wood/ironstone/water-power centres, such as Sussex, to the newer coalfield centres, like Shropshire, the Black Country and South Wales. In the

[7] See Rhys Jenkins, 'The Rise and Fall of the Sussex Iron Industry', Parts 1 and 2, *Trans. Newcomen Soc.* Vol. 1 (1920–21).

[8] The results were published in *Industrial Archaeology*, February 1971. In 1974, the puddling process was being carried on at only one place in the world, Bolton, Lancashire, and ceased altogether at the end of that year.

opinion of Rhys Jenkins,[9] the decline of the Sussex iron industry was due not primarily to the scarcity of charcoal, but to a shortage of water-power for the bellows and hammers, to poor transport – the London market was more easily supplied from the Continent – and to the high cost of English labour.

With the help of several other technical developments, iron-making became a large and important industry, with two main products – pig-iron, which was used for castings and wrought iron, which could be rolled, forged and hammered into a multitude of forms. In 1856 Sir Henry Bessemer introduced a new method of making what was still called 'wrought' iron, but which was really quite a different form of the metal, now known under the name of mild steel. This soon revolutionised the trade. It was now possible to make steel in large quantities by several different methods, economically, and of consistent quality. Carbon steel had been made for centuries, in small quantities, by a process known as cementation, but the quality was unreliable and it was expensive.

Of the earliest, direct reduction, method, the only relics to be found are cinder or slag heaps and parts of hearths, usually buried. The excavation is an archaeologist's job, rather than a technical historian's. An excellent account of an excavation of such a site in County Durham is given in R. F. Tylecote's article, 'The Location of Byrkenott'.[10] A later site, at Melbourne, Derbyshire, which contains the remains of a small blast furnace, has been excavated privately by Mr. W. H. Bailey, of Sheffield. Clues to the existence of such sites are slag heaps – slag is a greyish, often glassy, stone – easily identified traces of charcoal just below the surface and earthworks of a type which are not clearly associated with other industrial activities. Most of these sites are documented, but Mr. Bailey's work provides a good example of one which was not known until he deduced its presence. This particular site has since been covered by the waters of a reservoir, and it would have been lost for good if it had not been discovered in time at least for a detailed record to be made.

From the eighteenth century onwards ironworks sites became increasingly well-known and, at the same time, much smaller in number. A few blast furnaces have survived at, for example, Coalbrookdale, in Shropshire; Morley Park, in Derbyshire; Apedale, in North Staffordshire; Brymbo and Acrefair, in North Wales, and Maryport, in Cumberland. An eighteenth century blast furnace is a massive brick or masonry structure, roughly square in plan, and easily confused with a lime kiln, unless the interior is examined carefully. Inside, the furnace is likely to be square or circular at the bottom, with the sides running up parallel for a short distance and then sloping outwards fairly sharply for a few feet more. Above this point, known as the 'boshes', the internal shape or 'stack' tapers in again, but less sharply, to the top. The interior may, and most likely will, show signs of vitrification from the heat of operations, though the firebrick lining may

[9] *Trans. Newcomen Soc.*, Vol. 1, 1920–21.

[10] *Journal of the Iron and Steel Institute*, Vol. 194, Part 4, 1960, p. 451 onwards.

have disappeared in part or completely, and in this case no fire marking will be seen, and the shape may be deceptive.

A few forges have also survived, either for the production of wrought iron, or for working it up. Abbeydale and Wortley Top Forge, both near Sheffield, are good examples. Both contain a certain amount of machinery, and have been well restored. So too has the very interesting Finch Brothers Foundry at Sticklepath in Devon, where the three water-driven tilt hammers, used to forge edge-tools, are all in working order, together with other machinery, such as the shears and the noble grindstone, at which a man had to lie down to his work, literally nose to the grindstone. Forges are usually housed in brick or stone buildings near a stream or an artificial channel from a dam to a water-wheel. Both the wheel race and the channel may have disappeared, but traces of them can sometimes be found. It is probable that most remains of blast furnaces and forges above ground are known already, but it is always worth investigating possibilities, because there may be parts of either buried somewhere. The East Sussex Industrial Archaeology Society, for example, discovered a tilt hammer completely buried by rubbish at East Grinstead, and which is now at the Weald and Downland Open-Air Museum.

Relics of the nineteenth century iron industry are not abundant, either because the old buildings and equipment have been demolished, to make way for new plant, or because of a curious and, to the historian, disastrous opinion that they were 'not old enough to be of interest'. A few nineteenth century plants survived until recently. The partly 1851, partly 1900, blast furnaces at Lilleshall, in Shropshire, were a good example of such a plant. They are now dismantled, but photographic and other records were made before this took place, and the two beam engines are now preserved at the Blists Hill site of the Ironbridge Gorge Museum Trust.

If there are indications that iron was made at any period on a site which is generally unknown or neglected, it is worthwhile investigating. A certain amount of preliminary work is always advisable before any surveying takes place. The site can be studied in relation to its ore and fuel sources, to water power, to transport and to markets, using both old and current maps and plans and any records which can be discovered. These records are not likely to be extensive. The Black Country, once the largest producer of iron in the country and among the largest in the world, is perhaps the classic example of the fecklessness of not preserving records and of not photographing in time. The area now has one very up-to-date furnace. Virtually nothing now remains to show that it once had two hundred blast furnaces and over two thousand puddling furnaces. A few photographs and records in private possessions are all that remain as descriptions of the old buildings. Modern houses and factories now cover the sites of such important industrial beginnings as John Wilkinson's pioneer furnace of 1757 at Bilston, although in this case its former existence is commemorated by a plaque, which appropriately is of cast iron. During the late 1960s redevelopment provided an opportunity for the Industrial Archaeology Group of Wolverhampton College of Technology to

Restored Cornish engine and engine house, near Camborne

carry out excavations on the site of Wilkinson's Bradley Ironworks at Bilston. The site was identified and plotted from an old engraving and a plan of 1836. Foundations of several buildings were revealed, including what was probably a boiler house. Metal found in slag heaps showed the iron produced here to have had a high phosphorus content, which would account for the reputation Wilkinson had for casting high-quality cylinders.

The archaeology of iron is the products of the foundries and forges, as well as anything that may survive of the foundries and forges themselves. Coalbrookdale's grates, cooking-pots, cast-iron fountains and bridges are as much evidence of its activities as the works that produced them.[11] If we disdain the product and concentrate on the factory or the foundry we can miss interesting and significant information. The Britannia Bridge[12] over the Menai Straits was badly damaged by fire in 1970. The tubes were made of wrought iron, which is a scarce commodity nowadays, and when the decision was taken to rebuild the spans of the bridge most of the iron was sold to Bolton, for reworking. A small part, however, went to Bristol, for repair work on Brunel's great steamship, the 'Great Britain', which is now being restored in the dock where she was built.

Lead, tin, copper and zinc

Lead, tin, copper and zinc ores are all vein minerals and traces of their mining will generally be found along the vein. Tin ores are hard and may occur as pebbles in stream gravels but the only evidence of shoading, the early method of washing for stream tin, is likely to be a chaos of disturbed gravels. Lead was worked from pre-Roman times, either by cutting trenches along the back of the vein or else by bell-pits – shallow shafts, each with its ring of debris, set close together along the vein rather like a string of beads. In the seventeenth and eighteenth centuries deeper shafts were sunk at greater intervals apart. The usual method of winding up the ore was by means of a horse gin, which was a drum, mounted on a vertical axis, that could be rotated by a horse walking round a circular track. Tracks of this type, with a central footstep bearing and an adjacent shaft, are common features of the older mining areas. The gins were used until the early nineteenth century.

In Cornwall and in parts of the Midlands the steam engine was used for pumping after about 1730 and the tall narrow engine house with its chimney is still a striking survival of many former mines. In most areas, water was an attractive source of power and with the improvements produced by eighteenth century engineers, water-wheels became very widely used for pumping, winding, breaking up the ore and blowing the furnaces. Few of these wheels still remain but the

[11] One learns a great deal about the nineteenth century iron industry from trade catalogues. See, for instance, N. W. Tildesley, 'The Early History of the Albion Works, Willenhall', *West Midlands Studies*, 1970–71, for the information about the Albion Works which can be obtained in this way.

[12] On the construction of the bridge, see Paul N. Wilson: 'The Britannia Tubular Bridge', *Industrial Archaeology*, August 1972.

wheel-pit, with its accurately cut masonry, provides useful evidence of the dimensions and type of wheel that once turned there and an estimate of the amount of water that was available, worked out from the traces of dams and water courses, can give a useful approximation to the power of the wheel. The layout of dams, water courses and wheels can be of great interest.

A recent example of a total investigation of a lead-mining area – its history, techniques, topography and people – is the work done by Martin Allbutt and Fred Brook on the South Shropshire mines.[13] Although lead was worked here in Roman times, the main development was in the nineteenth century and there are many visible remains of the activity of this period, engine houses, spoil heaps, abandoned shafts, drainage adits, dams, water-wheel pits and miners' houses, with their small plots of land attached.

Mr. Allbutt and Mr. Brook have worked through the papers of the old mining companies and trudged over the ground in search of surviving evidence of an industry which died just before the present century began. It is very clear from their report that, apart from giving extra life to their account of the rise and fall of the industry, the archaeology has increased their respect for the men who undertook this hard and dangerous work. Sites like this are perhaps best visited in the winter, when the harsh, arduous conditions under which our ancestors earned a living are more apparent.

The work of mining is essentially underground, so little remains to be seen, and the preservable material on the surface is almost all associated with the crushing and smelting of the ore. The entrance to a mine is by a shaft or a level, and occasionally the mouth of the level may be of good masonry, with a date or other significant feature. A survey of a mining field, however, should include not only the outstanding details, but every shaft and level, with their names, where these exist, and an estimate or record of their working dates. Much of the older mining evidence will only be seen in part where it has escaped being covered by the debris of later workings. Some copper ores are diffused in a rock mass, so that there are exceptional mines to be seen, like Parys copper mine, Anglesey, an open-cast mine over 300 ft. deep, or the cavernous workings of the Alderley Edge copper-bearing sandstone of Cheshire.

Until this century nearly all ore dressing depended on crushing and then washing with water. The mixed ore, spar and rock from the mine is called bouse and it was carried to stone hoppers or bouse teams, still a feature of most dressing floors. Bouse was drawn from the hopper and roughly 'dressed' – trimmed and broken by hand – on the floors. It then passed either into stamps, particularly in the case of tin ores, or to crushing rollers. The stamps were vertical timbers shod with a great cast iron foot and mounted in batteries of four or more, lifted and dropped in turn by nogs on a water-wheel shaft. The frame for the stamps and the crushing box at the foot often remain. Crushing rollers were introduced in 1804 and their foundations alongside a water-wheel pit are easily recognised.

[13] 'The South Shropshire Lead Mines', *Industrial Archaeology*, February 1973.

The crushed bouse was stirred in streams of water running through a series of troughs called buddles. The early buddles were built of timber and consequently they rarely survive but about 1825 a circular buddle made of fine masonry came into use. In this, the finely crushed bouse was distributed by a rotating arm and a concentrate of ore was obtained by the combined effects of gravity and the current of water. The buddle remains as a circular trough of well-cut masonry, with a central boss on which the distributors stood. These circular buddles generally date from about 1830 to 1870.

In the nineteenth century there was a tendency to concentrate ore dressing at larger floors where there was an adequate supply of water. The bouse was carried to these central floors from a large number of scattered mines. A few early tramroads remain between the mines and the dressing floors, usually only as tracks, but marked perhaps by cuttings and banks, and by paired stone sleepers. These are large square stones, usually with two small holes for the spikes which held an iron chair for the rail. The sleepers are set close together, because the rails were short and the gauge was very narrow.

The most prominent feature of many mining fields is the smelt mill. This can vary very widely in its arrangement. Zinc ore is technically difficult to smelt and for this reason it has usually been dealt with, not at the mines but at brass works in Bristol, Cheadle or one or two other towns, or exported to France or Belgium. Zinc working in this country does not go back much further than the mid-eighteenth century, and there are practically no traces of smelting sites at the mines, where zinc ores were generally by-products of lead ores.

Copper ores also present smelting problems and need far more fuel than either tin or lead. From the mid-eighteenth century onwards they were generally sent to a central point, such as Swansea or Tyneside, where Companies of smelters were established. The sixteenth century copper mining in the Lake District had smelters at Keswick but little trace of these activities remain.

The earliest traces of smelting are the widely scattered and very numerous bale or bole hills. These are now to be recognised mainly as patches of ancient slag and charcoal, a yard or two in diameter. The only structure likely to be found is a circular heath, with, at most, a very low surrounding wall. Bale hills are generally sited on a shoulder of a hill, where they could take the greatest advantage of the prevailing wind, but from the fifteenth century some were made near streams where a small water-wheel could operate a bellows. And in other places the bale was blown by a foot bellows. Their discovery is generally accidental. It is hardly possible to distinguish between bale hills for lead and bale hills for iron smelting merely by inspecting them. An analysis of the slag is always necessary.

In the seventeenth and eighteenth centuries the ore hearth was introduced as the common type of furnace for lead smelting. The smelt mill to house one or more of these hearths was often some distance away from the mine and on the banks of a reliable stream which provided sufficient water to drive the bellows wheels. The mill also had to be well placed for the transport of fuel and of the finished product. The ore hearth was capable of smelting 5 or 6 cwt. of ore at a time and it could be tended by one man, so it was part of the normal equipment of even the most modest mills, which were built near or even among small mines. A number of small mines or even a small company could afford an ore hearth and they would manage to find sufficient ore to keep it in fairly constant work.

The ore hearth has something of the appearance of a blacksmith's hearth. The actual hearth was about 2 ft. square and a little over 1 ft. deep, set in a masonry structure with a bellows place behind and a chimney above the hearth. The recovery of lead was never complete at a first smelting, so there was usually a second furnace, a slag hearth, very like an ore hearth, though a little more closed in, in which some of the lead left in the ore hearth slag could be recovered by further smelting. If the lead ore, as was commonly the case, contained some proportion of silver sulphide, then the smelted lead would contain silver which would spoil some of its quality. Many smelt mills would then require a refining hearth, which was again only a modification of the ore hearth. The basic plan of a fully equipped smelt mill may therefore remain as the foundation of three small furnaces, a bellows place, a water-wheel pit and water courses, and a fuel shed, which would be quite large if peat was a principal fuel.

The blowing house of the tin smelter, which was in use from the fourteenth century, had a square hearth built of massive granite blocks and served by bellows. The hearth was not covered and it was without a chimney. Few of them remain intact, but the ruins of a blowing house can be recognised by remains of the hearth, and often by the ingot moulds, which were cut into granite blocks and, after the smelter was abandoned, left about as no longer of any use.

In 1704 a larger furnace, the reverberatory furnace, was developed in Flintshire and after 1721 it spread into Derbyshire and the North of England for lead smelting on a large scale and into Wales for copper smelting. Such big concerns as the London Lead Company and substantial royalty owners, like the Duke of Devonshire and the Greenwich Hospital, built large mills with two or more reverberatory furnaces, but with slag hearths and refining hearths as well. The reverberatory furnace was a large oblong structure about 15 ft. long, 12 ft. wide and 6 or 8 ft. high, with the fire grate at one end and the chimney at the other. The high chimney used with the reverberatory furnace replaced the bellows in most cases.

The fumes produced in smelting lead contain volatilised lead and are very poisonous, and about 1772 Bishop Watson suggested that a long flue placed between the furnace and the chimney might condense some of the dangerous vapour. Most large smelters adopted this method by the beginning of the nineteenth century. The flue was built on the ground, with a remote chimney on a nearby hill shoulder and it is one of the most prominent of the still surviving features of the smelter. The flue was generally a trench in the ground, lined out with masonry and covered by a masonry arch at ground level. It ran up rising ground to a chimney and in this way the flue and the chimney together could have an effective height of 200 or 300 ft. This would produce an enormous draught in the furnaces, possibly enough to dispense entirely with bellows or to reduce their size considerably. To prevent too keen a draught and to increase length the flues were usually zig-zag up a hillside, so that they sometimes reached a length of two or three miles, with a corresponding increase in the condensing capacity.

Sometimes there were elaborate water systems, with a dam, and sluices, for turning a stream of water into the flues to wash out the condensed lead into settling ponds for recovery. In the course of time, various kinds of condenser were invented by which the flue length was reduced or the condensation improved and concentrated at one place. The basic principle of these condensers was a square house through which the fumes were made to take a devious course, either through water or among slats or brushwood which had water running over them. The clue to the existence of any form of condenser house will be a flue inlet and outlet, with some sort of water supply.

Apart from individual structures, the whole layout of a mine can be of interest and importance. Ideally, the survey should include the inter-relations of the mine entry, the winding arrangements, the dams, water courses and water-wheels, the dressing floor, the smelt mill, the local transport system by pony or sled track, or road or tram way, and the final link with a main road or canal. Each mine should be fully recorded with details of the royalty owner, the lessee, the equipment, the name and nature of the vein of ore, the approximate dates when the mine was worked, an estimate of its productivity, and the whereabouts of existing plans.

This, however, is a counsel of perfection and most investigators of mining sites have to content themselves with rather less. Metal-mining has, even so, been one of the most popular subjects among industrial archaeologists during the past twenty years. Its appeal is understandable, since so much of it has been located in exceptionally pleasant parts of Britain – the Peak District of Derbyshire, West Cornwall, North Wales, Loch Tay – where research can very easily be combined with holidaymaking. The tourist organisations are gradually coming to understand this and to publish brochures and guide books which are aimed at arousing the interest of the general public in the probably unsuspected industrial history of holiday areas. This is part of a welcome and overdue extension of the meaning of the terms, 'holiday' and 'holiday area'. In other countries, Austria, Germany and Czechoslovakia especially, the potential tourist attractions of mines have been well understood for many years, and considerable trouble has been taken to make mines safe to visit and to explain their history and technology to those who come to see them.

The changing attitude is well illustrated by *Lead Mining in the Peak District*, compiled by members of the Peak District Mines Historical Society and sponsored by the Peak Park Planning Board. 'Lead mining,' says this booklet, 'formed the backbone of the wealth of the Peak District for over 1500 years. The limestone uplands and valleys, and parts of the marginal shale and gritstone country are littered with derelict shafts, grass-covered spoil heaps and ruined buildings, forming conspicuous and characteristic features of many parts of the area.' *Lead Mining in the Peak District* is arranged in the form of a series of itineraries, designed to introduce visitors to the mining history and archaeology of different parts of the area – an admirable idea, which might well be copied in other parts of Britain.[14]

[14] The old mining areas have been used a good deal for study courses organised by universities and local education authorities. They offer opportunities to those whose interests lie in geology, speleology and natural history, as well as in industrial archaeology. The Somerset Education Committee's Field Study Centre at Charterhouse-on-Mendip, in the centre of the old lead-mining district, is admirably situated for broadly-based fieldwork. For some of the results achieved, see Frank Hawtin, 'Industrial Archaeology at Charterhouse-on-Mendip', *Industrial Archaeology*, May 1970.

6

What to Look For: Power

Animal power

The earliest use of animal power was for haulage, and this itself was a refinement of the primitive human situation in which men, and, even more commonly, women, did their hauling for themselves. The invention of the wheel represented a great increase of efficiency as far as traction was concerned. The use of animal power for driving stationary machinery should perhaps be regarded as a refinement of this, since rotary movement is almost invariably involved, produced either by a vertical action – the treadmill – or by a horizontal action – the circular path.

The treadmill falls rather outside the present field, because its use was mostly confined to the pre-industrial age, for such purposes as operating deep wells, as at Carisbrooke Castle in the Isle of Wight – the donkey-operated treadmill here dates from 1587 – and for turning spits.

The horizontal circular path, on the other hand, was employed for a variety of early industrial purposes. Three methods were available:

(a) *Direct operation* The equipment was directly attached to the horse. This is the method usually found in crushing mills, such as cider presses. Other uses included grinding woad, grinding bark for tanning, preparing clay in pug mills, and crushing sandstone and lead ore.

(b) *Rope-winding* The horse turned a horizontally placed drum on to which a rope was wound. An important example was haulage up mine shafts and up quarry faces. These machines were usually called 'gins' or 'whims' or 'whins'. Probably the only surviving example of a colliery gin is preserved at the West Yorkshire Folk Museum at Halifax, but there are many illustrations of this type of apparatus in contemporary literature, at collieries, tin mines, lead mines, and quarries.

In the Halifax area 'gin-pits' used to be common. They were characterised by a stone wall which surrounded the shaft and by a nearby 'race' or circular horse-track. The plan of this wall is roughly square or rectangular, with a semi-circular projection on one side, to incorporate the 'race'. Such walled enclosures have not been recorded elsewhere.

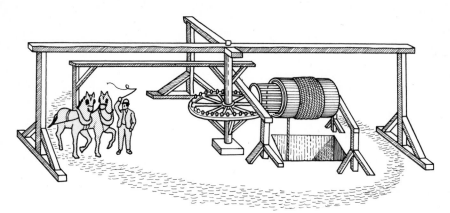

Horse gin, *c.*1650. The first improvement on the hand-winch for winding

(c) *Gear-turning* A circular machine, not unlike a roundabout at a fair, was turned by anything up to six animals. During the past 150 years these animals were usually horses, although occasionally oxen continued to be used. Attached to the roundabout was a large circular rack gear which meshed with other gearing to drive pumps, agricultural machinery, woollen spinning machinery and so on. Very few examples of the actual machinery remain. An eighteenth century horse-powered butter churn is exhibited at the Science Museum, London, and a late eighteenth or early nineteenth century three-horse wheel threshing machine are to be seen at the West Yorkshire Folk Museum, Halifax. A six-horse wheel intended to drive a threshing machine, a water-pump and a circular saw is still to be seen on its original site at Sawley Hall, Ripon. It was probably built in about 1830.

The threshing machine was invented by Meikle in 1788. It was frequently driven by a horse-wheel or gin-race, generally housed in a single-storey square or hexagonal building adjoining the barn where the threshing machine was. Although both the thresher and the wheel have almost invariably disappeared, the wheel-house, or round house, or pound generally remains, characterised by its shape, its size – about 25 to 30 ft. square – and its bearing beams. The main beam, which supported the centre pivot of the wheel, was usually placed parallel to the adjacent barn and from it a pair of beams about three feet apart ran to the barn wall. Between these, a short cross-beam supported the outer end of the tumbling shaft or main driving shaft to the thresher. Wheel houses are very common in County Durham, in the North and East Ridings and in some South Western counties, notably Dorset, Devon and Cornwall.

Determined searchers, such as Kenneth Major, who know what they are looking for, have discovered the remains of more horse and donkey wheels than one might think possible. Mr. Major's gazetteer of wheels used only for raising water occupies twenty-five pages of the May 1972 issue of *Industrial Archaeology*. These wheels are at country mansions, farms, waterworks and breweries, and the later horse-wheels, as Mr. Major notes, used carefully designed gearing and were highly efficient pieces of machinery.

Water power

The usefulness of water power depends directly upon the geographical characteristics of the area supplying it, in a way that is not true of animals, wind or steam. There must be an adequate fall and flow of water, if it is to be exploited. On the Norfolk Broads, for instance, there is plenty of water but no fall, while the mountain streams in Scotland have plenty of fall but no reliable flow. The industries dependent on water grew up where the conditions were best, and the method of developing the power was always the same. A weir was built across the stream, and a headrace was carried round the side of the hill until a suitable vertical fall could be obtained. This was the point where the mill and the waterwheel were built. As the water was discharged from the wheel, it was carried back to the river. The greater the fall, the greater the power which could be obtained from a given flow of water, but also the greater the capital cost of the development.

Water power was first used in Great Britain by the Romans, during the fourth or possibly late third century. There are three accepted Roman water-mill sites in England, all on Hadrian's Wall, but it is probably safe to assume that they were only erected because of a shortage of local labour to undertake the heavy, monotonous work of grinding corn by hand.

The Saxons used water-mills extensively, and more than five thousand are recorded in those parts of England which were covered by the Domesday Survey. From then onwards we have many records of manorial mills, all of which were corn mills, until 1185, when we learn for the first time that a water-mill was being used for fulling.

But the idea that water power could replace the work of men or animals for a wide range of purposes seems to have developed only slowly, both in Britain and on the Continent, until the Renaissance provided a favourable intellectual climate for the application of the discovery. By the end of the sixteenth century water was being used for pumping, hauling and ore-crushing in the mines of Cornwall and the Lake District, it was almost as essential to the Wealden iron industry as an adequate supply of charcoal, and it was soon being used for rolling copper and iron, for grinding gunpowder, and for many other purposes.

As industrial demands grew during the seventeenth and early eighteenth centuries, the provision of adequate power supplies from rivers and streams became an increasingly difficult problem. Today the power available to the early industries appears ludicrously small. Extensive capital resources, at a period when industrial financing was still in its infancy, might be devoted to weirs, water races, sluices and water-wheels in order to supply a factory with less power than could be obtained from a modern two horse-power electric motor, power which might fail completely in a dry summer or frosty winter. Remains of the earliest installations are consequently rare in districts which have had a continuous industrial history. Many small factories originally dependent upon water power have been transformed into huge modern works, often with the little stream which brought them into being discreetly led in a culvert below the shop floor, rather as if it were a slightly disreputable ancestor.

This pressure on supply resulted in a number of improvements in the design and construction of water-wheels during the eighteenth and nineteenth centuries. Both undershot and overshot wheels were in use before 1750. These were built almost entirely of wood and probably ranged in capacity from one half to twenty horse-power, using falls of from 3 to 20 ft. In 1752–53 John Smeaton, the famous eighteenth century engineer, carried out the first accurate experiments with models, and established the fact that overshot wheels – where the water falls on top of the wheel – were more efficient than undershot wheels – where the water hits the bottom of the wheel. He designed wheels more powerful and greater in diameter than any before, and found that the weakest points were the shaft and gearing. He introduced cast iron wheel shafts and gears about 1769, and advocated the use of wrought iron in place of wood for the buckets of overshot wheels.

At the end of the eighteenth and early in the nineteenth century the engineers, John Rennie, T. C. Hewes and William Fairbairn made great advances in water-wheel design. They built entirely of wrought or cast iron, overcame the difficulty of transmitting power through the shaft by building a gear wheel (engaging a small cog) on the rim of the water wheel, and achieved powers up to 240 b.h.p. from a single wheel.

The largest water-wheel in the United Kingdom is the Lady Isabella Wheel at Laxey, in the Isle of Man.[1] Commissioned in 1854 to drain the local metal mines, it is 72 ft. 6 ins. in diameter and developed 200 h.p. It has since been restored. The last of the giants was built at Rishworth Mills, near Halifax. The wheel was 57 ft. in diameter and developed 240 h.p. It was completed in 1864. Newcomen and Watt steam engines were used as returning engines to pump back the tail water of a water-wheel in dry times. Conversely, water-wheels seem sometimes to have been installed to make use of the surplus water pumped from mines by steam engines. Such hybrid devices were transitional. They heralded the

[1] The largest water-wheel on the English mainland is on a remote site near Blisland, in Cornwall. 50 ft. in diameter, it used to work iron flat-rods for a mile and a half to pump water from a china-clay pit. It has been restored by the Cornish Waterwheel Preservation Society.

disappearance of the water-wheel in favour of the much improved steam engine of the later period.

The chances of discovering water-wheels of special interest are comparatively slight. Indeed, in the majority of cases the wheel itself will have disappeared. In many cases where later developments have not obliterated the evidence, the weirs, the embankments of the mill race, the sluices and even the housings for the wheel and its consequent machinery are still conspicuous objects.

A number of local industrial archaeological societies have made careful surveys of the sites of watermills in their area, or along a particular stretch of river. In the summer of 1966, for instance, a group in Staffordshire surveyed the watermills on the Sow and its tributaries north of Stafford. Of the 16 sites visited, 13 still showed remains of one kind or another and of the 13 three were still in operating condition, a remarkably high proportion by today's standards.

The reports prepared by the group[2] varied from:

'SJ 860285 Chebsey Mill (Yates' map 1775)
All that can now be seen is the site of the mill pool. The stream has been re-coursed where it passes via a new bridge under the road.'
to 'SJ 792298 Walk Mill (Yates' map 1775) H. Howell, miller.
One breast mill 18 ft. outside diameter, 5 ft. 4 ins. wide, of cast and wrought iron. Recently repaired and in good condition but used only to work the sack hoist. There are 64 buckets, rim depth 12 ins. The upright shaft is of oak with iron bands at the ends, 20 ft. long. The drive is by crown and spur wheels. The bearings for main shaft and upright shaft are of brass; there is a spare set of brass bearings in the wheel house. The spur wheel and wallower are of cast iron and of more recent date than the rest of the gearing, having been cast to fit the upright shaft as a replacement for wooden gears. The other gears are of cast iron with wooden teeth which break if anything jams.
There are two pairs of French burr stones, originally four, none now in use. There are two sets of rollers, a Break Roller above and the Main Roller below; two sets of edge-runner stones; a Kibbler or Plate Mill for cutting grain; a cake breaker; a friction sack and a mixer.
Most of the building is probably of late 18th–early 19th century date. An adjoining building of similar materials and style has its date 1830 over the door, but Mr. Howell says this lintel is probably a later addition.'

This team had the great advantage of being able, at three of the mills, to talk to a working miller, a vanishing breed whose rarity is nowadays exceeded only by the millwright. One millwright, J. Harold Armfield[3] has fortunately set down

---

[2] Published in the *Journal of the Staffordshire Industrial Archaeology Society*, Spring 1970.

[3] The family firm was Armfields of Ringwood, Hampshire. Its history has been outlined by D. A. E. Cross, in 'Armfields of Ringwood', *Industrial Archaeology*, May 1967. The firm's turbine manufacturing business is described by M. D. Freeman, 'Armfield Turbines in Hampshire', in *Industrial Archaeology*, November 1971.

Restored overshot water-wheel, now at Castle Museum, York

on paper[4] exactly how his country business carried out this very skilled work. The cogs for the pit were always of English oak, which was bought in the plank and stacked to season. 'It was considered,' Mr. Armfield remembers, 'that the wood would season $\frac{1}{8}$ in. deep from each surface per year, so that $2\frac{1}{2}$ in. planks for 3 in. pitch wheels would require eleven years to season.' Cutting and fitting the cogs had to be done with great precision and since the life of the wooden cogs was 10–15 years, re-cogging was, for Mr. Armfield and his men, a normal operation. They served the local flour and paper-mills, knew the peculiar characteristics of each one's machinery and needed every minute of their seven years' apprenticeship. As Mr. Armfield rightly says, 'millwrighting was the most versatile of the engineering crafts'.

The first half of the nineteenth century saw the development, especially in France, of the turbine, in which blades or vanes attached to a shaft are rotated by the pressure of water directed on them. Water-wheels suffered from a number of basic defects. They rotated slowly, so that complicated gearing was necessary, if they were to run industrial machinery. It was difficult, too, to regulate them in order to maintain a constant running speed. Turbines were much smaller than water-wheels for an equivalent power output, and because they ran at high speeds, required little gearing. They could cope with a wide range of heads of water and generate much more power than the most efficient water-wheels. The first practical water-turbine was introduced by Benoît Fourneyron in 1827. From about 1840, when James Whitelaw produced his 'Scotch Mill', and more rapidly after 1850 when the much superior 'Fourneyron' outward flow and Thomson 'Vortex' inward flow turbines were manufactured in Northern Ireland and England, turbines began rapidly to replace water-wheels.

It was comparatively easy to take out a water-wheel and replace it by a turbine in the same pit, using the same head and tail races. Of the two thousand to three thousand water turbines installed in the United Kingdom between 1840 and 1900, probably half were water-wheel replacements. A notable example is the turbine at the Dinorwic quarry workshops, which took the place of the huge water-wheel still in position in its pit.

So far as can be discovered, only one example of a Whitelaw turbine still exists, and this is exhibited at the Science Museum. The discovery of all or even parts of one of Whitelaw's larger wheels would be a matter of considerable interest.

Wind power

In England, windmills were, for the most part, to be found east of a line from Newcastle-upon-Tyne to Portsmouth, in Anglesey, the Fylde, the Wirral and the Somerset plain. In some areas there have been windmills from the twelfth century until the present time. They were built chiefly in corn growing areas

---

[4] 'The Craft of Mill-Gearing', *Industrial Archaeology*, August 1972.

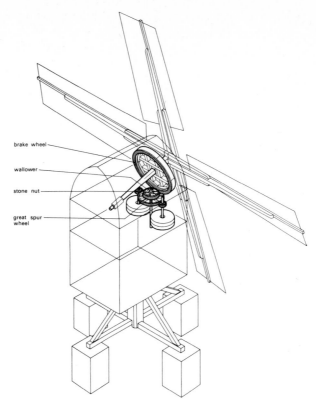

brake wheel
wallower
stone nut
great spur
wheel

Layout of gear wheels in a post mill

where the small volume and low fall of rivers or ponds made water power un-reliable. The earliest remains at present known are of the fifteenth century stone tower, now called 'The Beacon' at Burton Dassett, in Warwickshire, but the oldest remaining mills which are still complete date from the seventeenth century.

There are two main types of windmill. In both cases, the original design was probably imported directly from France. The post mill is built of timber and consists of a box-like body which contains the machinery and carries the sails. The body is mounted on a suitably braced upright post on which it can be turned so that the sails can face squarely into the wind. The post and its supporting sub-structure are frequently enclosed by a round-house, which serves to protect them and also to act as a store. The tower mill has a fixed tower containing the machinery and only the roof or cap carrying the sails is turned into the wind. It runs on a track on the top of the tower.

The tower is tapering and usually of brick, though other local materials were also used. Towers built of timber are called smock mills. Post mills and the caps of tower mills were originally turned into the wind by a long tail-pole reaching

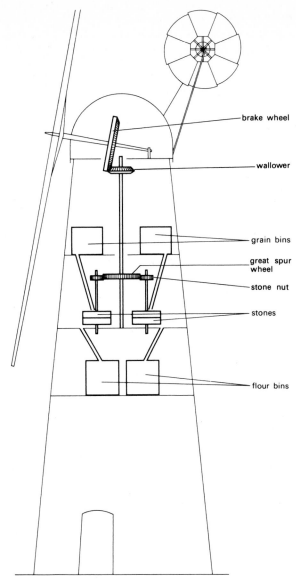

brake wheel

wallower

grain bins

great spur wheel

stone nut

stones

flour bins

Layout of a tower mill showing gear and grain mechanisms

to the ground. Later this was carried out automatically by fitting a fan-tail on a horizontal spindle.

The earliest type of sail is known as the common sail. It has a timber back or whip carrying a wooden framework over which sail-cloths can be set or furled. Later hinged shutters, like slats of a Venetian blind, were set in the sail frame and controlled either by springs or by a system of levers and chains and weights.

These are known as spring sails and patent sails. The sails were fixed to an axle or windshaft, which protruded from the top of the mill. Inside the mill the windshaft carried the geared brake wheel which drove the machinery in the body of the mill and on which acted the brake used to stop the sails turning. The sails themselves were fixed to the windshaft in two ways. In the South and East of England two long, heavy timbers, called stocks or middlings, were fitted into the front of the windshaft right through the poll-end, which consisted of two sockets at right angles to each other. In the Midlands and North a cast-iron cross was fitted to the front of the windshaft and the sails were fixed to its arms.

Early windmills were generally, if not invariably, used for grinding corn. It was not until the seventeenth century that the principle was adapted to raising water for drainage purposes. Smock mills were employed to drive wooden paddle wheels, known as scoop-wheels, which lifted water from a drain in a fen or marsh to a main drain or river on a higher level. The lift was equal to about one-fifth of the diameter of the wheel. Two main areas were involved, the Fens, and, somewhat later, the Broads.

Subsequently, the application of wind-power was considerably extended. Mills driving plunger pumps were installed to serve salterns or to pump water for domestic or industrial purposes. About a century ago their successor, the American multi-vaned wind-pump, made it appearance. Sawing timber, pressing oil from seeds, rasping logwood, grinding bark, cement clinker, chalk, flint, ochre, tobacco and white lead have all been carried out by wind-power. In all these developments Dutch designers played a leading part. It was not until the second half of the eighteenth century that the use of cast iron in place of wood put the English millwrights ahead of their continental counterparts, a lead which they kept until 1918.

A considerable number of windmills have been restored and preserved during the past twenty-five years. One of the best examples of the period when windmill technology was at its peak is at Ballycopeland, in County Down. It was carefully restored by the Northern Ireland Government in 1958. Built in the 1780s, it is a typical tower mill of the late eighteenth century. It has a wooden, boat-shaped revolving cap, fitted with an automatic fantail and four enormous patent sails. The hopper, stone, drive and ground floors are all maintained and equipped as they would have been in the mill's working days. Another mill of about the same period is at Upminster, Essex. This weather-boarded smock mill, dating from 1800, was restored by Havering Council. It is the largest complete mill of its type in the eastern counties, with four pairs of stones and a windshaft and sails brought in 1899 from a post mill at Maldon.

There are four tower mills in Sussex which still have their original sails, at Medmerry, Halmaker, Patcham and Polegate. Polegate, which was built in 1817 and continued in operation until the 1940s, is the only one to have its machinery in working order. Pitstone Green post mill at Ivinghoe, Buckinghamshire, has been extensively rebuilt and restored, but includes some timbers dating from 1627. In Lancashire, Marsh Mill (1794) at Thornton Clevelys has been restored by the local council and another on-site council restoration is a London mill, Brixton Mill (1860), in Blenheim Gardens.

The coming of electricity created fresh opportunities for windmills, In Denmark, at the beginning of the present century, La Cour was experimenting with the generation of electricity by wind power. Today the Dutch are successfully experimenting with using surplus wind power for the same purpose.

A mill is usually one of a group of buildings. Mill houses and granaries were usually sited end on to the mills. Those associated with post mills tended to be low, and even when tower mills became common the height of nearby buildings was usually kept down. Early post mills were small and were often erected on an artificial mound to give them more height and therefore more wind. A mill on a mound will generally be a replacement and often there will have been several previous mills on the site. It is not always easy to distinguish mill mounds from those of other origin, and in some cases the matter cannot be decided without excavation. From the thirteenth century onwards there were sunk post mills in England, the whole sub-structure of the mill being buried in the ground to give it greater stability. Remains have been dug in Lancashire, Yorkshire, Hertfordshire, Hampshire and elsewhere. In the case of Sandon Mount, Hertfordshire, an old burial mound had been used. Some of the others had been mistaken for burial mounds. At Lamport, in Northamptonshire, a mill mound was found to contain four walls of dressed stone meeting at a central point; they were the supports of the cross-trees of a normal post mill. This is the only case of its kind on record, but others may well await an excavator.

In some cases, mills have been converted into houses, so that obtaining satisfactory record of the original interior may well demand considerable power of deduction. An advertisement in the personal column of *The Times* was inserted by a lady who wished to sell: 'Windmill. Unique residence, artistically converted. Brick structure. Situated in picturesque Essex village. Three bedrooms, circular lounge, bathroom, kitchen, dining recess, garage.' This turned out to be Debden Mill. Further investigation revealed a handsomely illustrated article about the conversion in one of the more expensive women's magazines. The industrial archaeologist must, of necessity, be catholic in his reading.

One of the most ambitious mill conversions to have been undertaken in Britain is of a watermill, not a windmill. It is at Stamford Bridge, near York, where the former corn mill is now The Corn Mill public house and restaurant. The mill was built on rock and the wheel chamber, which can be seen from the Mill Wheel Bar, with the undershot wheel restored to full working order, is partly carved out of solid rock. The machinery has been preserved and is all on view to visitors. A staircase from the Mill Wheel Bar leads past the grinding machinery to the Flume Bar on the ground floor, where visitors can look down through the glass floor to the water-wheel and to the flume or water-channel leading to the wheel. On the same floor is the Mill Race Restaurant and above the Granary Grill. Most forms of preservation involve a certain measure of compromise and what has been achieved at Stamford Bridge will be acceptable to all but extreme purists.

Steam power

The history of steam engines covers more than 250 years, of which the first hundred are hardly represented at all by archaeology. The oldest surviving example is the Elsecar Pumping Engine, near Rotherham in Yorkshire. It dates from 1787, worked until 1930 and is preserved by the National Coal Board, a symbol of the fact that coal-mining created the steam engine.

By 1700 the development of mining in England was seriously handicapped by flooding of the pits. The available sources of power, such as horse-gins, water-wheels and windmills, for driving baling appliances and pumps, were inadequate for raising large quantities of water. The first practical engine was the atmospheric pumping engine, using steam, invented by Thomas Newcomen (1663–1729), an ironmonger of Dartmouth, in Devon, who made expeditions to Cornwall in order to sell tools to the tin-miners and had noticed the difficulties they experienced. After ten years' experimental work, Newcomen built his first engine in 1712, at a coalmine near Dudley Castle, in Staffordshire, and his second at Griff Colliery, near Coventry, soon afterwards.

In these engines steam was generated in the boiler at very low pressure. When the steam valve was opened, steam flowed up the pipe into the vertical cylinder. The piston-rod, carrying the piston, and the pump-rod were attached by chains to the opposite ends of a strong wooden beam, which rocked on trunnion-bearings at its centre. As the pump-rod in the mineshaft was the heavier of the two rods, it descended and pulled up the piston to the top of the cylinder. The steam valve was then closed, the injection-water valve opened and a jet of cold water condensed the steam below the piston, creating a partial vacuum in the enclosed space in the cylinder. Atmospheric pressure on the top of the piston forced it down – hence the name 'atmospheric engine' – and this was the working stroke. The descending piston pulled up the pump-rod, which, in its turn, raised water out of the mine. When the piston approached the bottom of the cylinder, the injection-water valve was closed and the steam valve opened. The pressure was thus equalised below and above the piston, which was raised by the greater weight of the pump-rod. The mixture of condensed steam and water drained from the cylinder into a tank which supplied the boiler. As the valves were worked automatically by the engine itself, the cycle was repeated continuously.

The Newcomen engine was improved by John Smeaton (1724–1792). Pumping engines of this type, although uneconomical by later standards, even in their improved forms, continued in use into the nineteenth century in collieries where the coal was very cheap.

The next important advance was achieved by James Watt (1736–1819). In 1765 he conceived the idea of condensing the steam in a separate metallic vessel, called the 'condenser'. In its practical form, the condenser, cooled in a tank of cold water, was connected by a pipe to the engine-cylinder, which was kept hot by the boiler-steam. This led to a great saving of steam and coal, as the cylinder metal was not re-heated during each cycle. Watt patented his separate condenser

Beam engine from silk-throwsters in Taunton, *c.*1850, now in Somerset County Museum, Taunton

for use with atmospheric engines in 1769. Matthew Boulton, the Birmingham industrialist, (1728–1809), invited Watt to join him at his Soho Manufactory in 1775. The condenser patent was extended until 1800, and during their twenty-five years' partnership, they built about five hundred beam engines, with a total power of approximately 7500 horse-power. About two hundred were recipro-cating engines and three hundred rotative. Only three of the engines built during the Boulton and Watt period have survived.

Watt's early engines from 1776 onwards were single-acting beam engines like Newcomen's, mostly for pumping water out of tin-mines in Cornwall and from coal-mines elsewhere. But the cylinder was closed at the top, with a stuffing-box for the piston-rod, and the piston was forced down by the difference between the low-pressure steam above it and vacuum beneath it, due to the separate jet condenser below it. During the working stroke, the steam and exhaust valves were open; as the piston approached the bottom of the cylinder, they were closed and the equilibrium valve opened. The piston now had equal steam pressure above and below it and was pulled up again by the extra weight of the pump-rod.

By 1781 Boulton realised that the demand for steam power was increasing rapidly and urged Watt to produce an engine to give rotary motion for driving machinery. Watt accordingly modified his pumping engine by replacing the pump-rod with a connecting rod with sun and planet gear. The driving shaft and its fly-wheel were rotated and drove the mill-shafting through more gear wheels. In 1782 Watt made the engine double-acting by duplicating the valves and introducing boiler steam alternately above and below the piston, thus doubling the power for the same size of cylinder. By cutting off the supply of steam during each working stroke up and down and using its expansive force to drive the piston, steam consumption was reduced. Watt abolished the chains after inventing his parallel-motion so that the piston-rod could pull and push the beam. His earliest rotative engines were for driving a tilt hammer at John Wilkinson's Bradley Ironworks in 1783, and the Albion Flour-mill, Blackfriars, in 1784. After Watt's retirement in 1800, and as his patents expired, other engineers, some of whom were trained at Soho, were free to make engines of new types. Richard Trevithick (1771–1833), a Cornish mining engineer, took the lead in raising steam pressures from 2 to 50 lb. per sq. in. by discarding Watt's wagon-type boiler, with an external fire and substituting a cylindrical boiler, called the Cornish boiler, with one internal flue for the furnace. Trevithick pioneered the advance in steam engine construction in two directions. He developed the small high-pressure boiler with the vertical engine cylinder inside, but with no condenser. As a unit, this engine could be easily moved about for driving agricultural machinery and pumps and did not need an engine house. And in 1812 he applied high pressure steam to single-acting condensing Watt pumping engines, and used the expan-sion of the steam more effectively. Trevithick's Cornish pumping engine with high-pressure steam and early cut-off was superior to the Watt engine in both power and economy.

Cornish engines survived longest for the supply of water to towns but were superseded after 1850 by high pressure compound rotative engines with fly-wheels, built by Simpson of Westminster and others. The lives of some Watt engines were prolonged and their power increased by McNaught, who fitted a high pressure cylinder at the opposite end of the beam to the low-pressure

WHAT TO LOOK FOR: POWER

cylinder, and installed Lancashire boilers with two internal flues, patented by Fairbairn in 1844.

About 1825 the horizontal steam engine with its cylinder, slide-bars and crankshaft bearings mounted on a horizontal cast-iron bed-plate began to displace the beam engine. This type was made by several firms during the next seventy-five years, with increased power for driving machinery. In the 1880s, electric power stations had horizontal engines driving generators by long leather belts, a method that was not invariably safe. By increasing the speed of the engine and coupling it direct to a generator, avoiding the necessity for a belt drive, space was saved and danger eliminated. Vertical condensing engines were being built by many firms during the last quarter of the nineteenth century. The largest sizes developed several thousand horse-power. But after 1900 large steam-engines were being replaced by steam turbines, which were more powerful and more economical. Railway locomotives apart, the development of the steam engine proper came to an end sixty years ago, except for special duties.

The old steam engines have mostly vanished, but the old engine houses are a very fruitful field of study for the industrial archaeologist. The earliest of them were made either of local stone, or of brick. They were tall, impressive buildings. For Newcomen's boiler under the cylinder, the chimney was built as part of one wall. Watt issued detailed instructions for erecting his pumping engines and engine houses. The 'lever-wall' had to be the strongest, to support the 'great working beam', and the stones must be 'long and large'. Wagon-type, Cornish and Lancashire boilers were contained in a low building attached to the side of the engine house with a separate chimney. The beam of a Watt rotative engine, however, was inside the house and the bearings were supported on strong vertical and horizontal timbers attached to the floor and walls respectively; the engine and its house formed a unit. Steam engines built in the nineteenth century were independent of the walls and were installed in the mill or factory building.

The distribution of early engines naturally followed the relevant industrial development. There were Newcomen type atmospheric engines in the mining district of Cornwall, Staffordshire, Derbyshire, Durham and Northumberland. Of the 496 Watt engines built between 1775 and 1800, there were 57 in Cornwall, 84 in Lancashire, 37 in Shropshire, 28 in Staffordshire, 27 in Yorkshire, 19 in Durham, 17 in Northumberland, and in some other counties of the United Kingdom. By 1835 there were 1369 steam engines of various types in Lancashire and the West Riding of Yorkshire. During the nineteenth century, steam power spread to all industrial areas and to most water-supply companies.

Very few Newcomen type atmospheric pumping engines are preserved. In addition to the Elsecar engine, there is another, of 1791, in the Science Museum, which also exhibits the original Watt engines of 1777, 1788 and 1797. The Cornish Engines Preservation Society, formed in 1935, owns five beam-engines and is preserving on the original site the Levant mine winding engine (1840) and Cornish pumping engines at South Crofty (1854) and East Pool (1892). A single-acting Cornish rotative engine (1851) is in Holman's Museum, at

Camborne. The Metropolitan Water Board has four large Cornish engines (1820–1871) and a Harvey-Bull engine (1859) at Kew Bridge Pumping Station, London. There are several historic steam engines at the Science Museum, in London, in the Museum of Science and Industry in Birmingham, and at the Royal Scottish Museum, Edinburgh.

Last surviving row of weavers' cottages, Trowbridge, Wiltshire, *c*.1790

7

Manufacturing

The range of manufacturing in Britain, as in most other industrialised countries, has been and is so wide that it would be absurd to try to select examples from every industry or branch of industry to illustrate the characteristics and usefulness of its own particular archaeology. What is more reasonable and more helpful is to concentrate on a few of the more important industrial groups and to draw certain general conclusions from this restricted amount of material.

For the present purpose, we have chosen textiles; pottery and glass; brewing and distilling; and in Chapter 8, building materials.

Textiles

The textile industries of this country present one of the most interesting and important fields of research for the industrial archaeologist. It is a field, moreover, in which architects and to a lesser extent town planners have the closest interest. Economic historians have shown a great, perhaps a disproportionate, interest in the textile industries so that adequate background material is generally available. The localisation of British textile industries in relatively compact regions makes them particularly suitable for intensive field-study. Even within these regions the need of water for power and for finishing cloth meant a concentration of sites in river valleys and these valleys make excellent subjects for more or less self-contained surveys on a manageable scale. During the past ten years especially there have been a number of detailed studies of particular textile areas, bringing together the evidence of the surviving buildings, the historical material derived from books and documents and the information gathered by talking to former workers. P. S. Richards, for instance, has done this with regard to the Holywell textile mill in Flintshire,[1] and J. R. Hume has carried out research into the old-established Glasgow carpet industry.[2]

[1] 'The Holywell Textile Mills, Flintshire', *Industrial Archaeology*, February 1969.
[2] In *Industrial Archaeology*, August 1971.

Historically, a broad distinction can be made in the textile industries between organisation on a domestic basis and under a factory system. This division cannot be made at any particular date or even within any short period of years. Mechanisation generally came first in the finishing processes. It was then dramatically extended to spinning in the last quarter of the eighteenth century, and it was applied to weaving last of all. In the Irish linen industry, for example, machinery operated by water power was fairly extensively applied to the bleaching of cloth by the end of the first quarter of the eighteenth century, but power-spinning was delayed for another hundred years, and hand-loom weaving persisted into the twentieth century.

Two seventeenth century weavers' cottages at Golcar, in the Colne Valley of Yorkshire have recently been restored and converted into a museum of folk-life and industrial history.[3] This steep valley, containing the towns of Golcar, Linthwaite, Marsden and Slaithwaite, has been traditionally a centre of the manufacture of woollen, as distinct from worsted cloth. There are now a number of large mills in the valley, but previously the cloth was made domestically, and here, as in the neighbouring valleys, there are dozens of weavers' cottages facing south and west into the sun. The top floors have large windows, to allow the maximum amount of light to fall on the looms. Until about 1800, the weaving room was also the bedroom, but from then until the middle of the century, when weaving was finally absorbed into the mills, most of the new cottages were three-storeyed, with the workshop on the top floor completely cut off from the living accommodation below. This was a reflection of the development of workshops which represented a transitional stage to the factory, when a manufacturing weaver would employ people from outside his own family to work in his mini-factory.

Handloom-weavers' cottages in mid-Lancashire have been investigated by Robert F. Taylor.[4] 'Many workers,' he has noted, 'kept their bulky machinery in a room in an ordinary cottage, or in a temporary shed which never survived to the present day, but some weavers were fortunate enough to have a room specially provided for their work.' These purpose-built cottages he has divided into three main groups, according to the position of the weaving-room.

(a) 'below the living accommodation in a cellar. This is generally the only type found in towns, but is not confined to them. The type is economical in space, which would have recommended it to the urban builder.'

(b) 'on the first floor, in a room often used as a bedroom as well. This is a Rossendale type, and frequently such cottages are built against the hillside so that the upper storey can be reached by a door opening directly on to the hill at the back. This makes it easy to carry beams and machinery in and out of the weaving room.'

[3] Hugh Bodey: 'A Colne Valley Weaver's Cottage', *Industrial Archaeology*, August 1971.

[4] 'A Type of Handloom-Weaving Cottage in mid-Lancashire', *Industrial Archaeology*, November 1966.

Early nineteenth century woollen mill at Bradford-on-Avon, Wiltshire. Since the disappearance of the woollen industry from Bradford in the 1830s, this solidly constructed mill has been used for a variety of industrial purposes, but its future is not bright.

(c) 'on the ground floor, alongside the domestic accommodation. This is essentially a rural cottage, rarely found even in villages. Its distribution appears confined to the western edge of the Lancashire cotton-weaving area, stretching from the Ribble valley near Blackburn, to the Mersey, but the type does not appear to intrude into the steep valleys of Rossendale. It marks the western limits of the early cotton industry.'

Studying the construction and the layout of these cottages, Mr. Taylor noticed a significant fact, not previously remarked on by historians. In Mellor, where hand-loom weaving remained an important industry as late as 1870, and where the standard of building was exceptionally high, all but the latest cottages are outside the village and out on the moor. They are widely scattered along the lanes, and many have land attached, an indication that they belonged originally to families who drew their income from both farming and weaving, and who, for this reason, were able to continue as weavers long after this occupation provided an inadequate income on its own.

So far as the industrial archaeologist is concerned it might be as well to concentrate on studying the textile industries in instances where they can be shown to have progressed beyond the production of yarn and cloth for mere family or local use. The only industrial buildings of the earlier type of textile manufacture are likely to be small fulling mills.

Once a considerable surplus of cloth to local needs was being produced and capitalist organisation had begun to spread, a number of characteristic industrial developments took place. The growing wealth of cloth merchants enabled them to build on a scale which often equalled that of the landed gentry. These great houses, such as those of the Longs and the Halls at Bradford-on-Avon, are certainly the concern of the industrial archaeologist. So, too, are the industrial plant for finishing cloth or preparing yarn and the warehouses which are frequently associated with the houses. Bleach-works and fulling mills are the only truly industrial buildings of those textile trades where neither the spinning nor the weaving processes were mechanised, but to concentrate on them alone would be too narrow an interpretation of industrial archaeology. Field study can be usefully concerned with population distribution, the association of agriculture and manufacture, the organisation of yarn distribution and cloth manufacture, and with the finishing processes. It is worth remembering that field and other place names can often be a valuable lead in locating sites.

The development of the factory system is a field in which the industrial archaeologist can make a unique contribution. In the past this has been treated entirely as a matter of industrial and social organisation. Such subjects as the location of factories, the use of water and steam power, the structural problems involved in such large buildings, and the provision of housing for industrial workers have only recently attracted much attention.

A number of eighteenth and nineteenth century textile manufacturers erected housing for their workers and a study of the examples which remain shows what was considered appropriate for a working man and his family at the time.

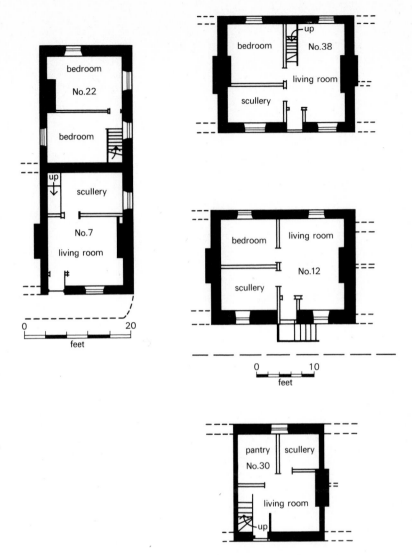

Housing at Cronkbourne Village, Kirk Braddan, Isle of Man (from *Industrial Archaeology*, August 1969)

Cronkbourne Village, near Douglas in the Isle of Man[5] was built in the late 1840s by the Moore family for the workers in their sail-cloth mill. The forty-two houses are of local slate and were modernised in the 1960s by the Braddon Parish Commissioners. The mill itself no longer operates as such. It is now a laundry. Some of the houses have one storey, some two. The single-storeyed houses were divided

[5] The village has been described by Larch S. Garrad in *Industrial Archaeology*, August 1969.

Mills and tenements at New Lanark. An early nineteenth century painting

New Lanark: aerial view (1952)

from back to front into a living-room running the full depth of the building and a scullery with a bedroom behind. The two-storeyed houses were either two rooms up and two down or three down and two up. A school and a reading-room were also provided by the company and Cronkbourne was the first community in the Isle of Man to have electric street lights.

By 1861 about 150 people were employed in the mill and the majority of them lived in Cronkbourne village. The census returns show that many of the workers were Irish, recruited from linen mills, and that a number of children aged between 12 and 14 were employed.

The earliest such settlement of note was at Cromford in Derbyshire, where Sir Samuel Arkwright[6] began building houses for his workers in the 1770s. The best example is North Street. The houses here are of three storeys, the top storey being one continuous room running the whole length of the street. This room was used by his employees in the evenings, for making stockings. In addition to the houses, Arkwright built a school, a chapel and the Greyhound Inn, which still stands, with its frontage practically unchanged. Cromford Village, which has altered very little during the two centuries since it was built, is now protected as a conservation area. The original mill (1771), the Upper Mill, can still be seen; the village cornmill and the manager's house have been converted into an Arkwright museum. Arkwright's own mansion, close to the mills and overlooking the Derwent, is now a conference centre.

One of the most famous of the 'model' industrial housing schemes in Britain, at New Lanark, dates mostly from 1790–1815. In 1800, when Robert Owen became managing partner of the mills, 2000 people were employed there. Owen took over the housing constructed by David Dale, the original proprietor, added Nursery Buildings, a four-storeyed tenement to house pauper apprentices, together with a group of community buildings, the three-storeyed Institution for the Formation of Character, a school and a village store. There have been great problems in preserving these buildings, and the mills which gave rise to them, but modernisation of the tenements has been carried out and, with financial assistance from the Government and initiative from the New Lanark Society, the future of this historic settlement now seems assured.[7]

All factory buildings should be studied from the point of view of structure, power, any surviving machinery, and of associated housing for the workers. The use of iron-framing was developed in textile factory buildings in this country to reduce fire hazard, and it was only incidentally that the structural advantages were discovered. The earliest known examples are at Milford in Derbyshire and at Shrewsbury. A much more extensive survey is needed to decide the period at which iron-framing was generally introduced and the rate at which it became known and widely used.

[6] See John N. Merrill, 'Arkwright of Cromford', *Industrial Archaeology*, August 1973.

[7] See J. R. Hume, 'The Industrial Archaeology of New Lanark', in *Robert Owen, Prince of Cotton Spinners*, 1971.

In the first stages of industrialisation, corn mills and fulling mills were frequently converted into factories. A careful note should be taken of this wherever the evidence is available and it is also useful to look for signs of parts of older buildings incorporated into the present structure. The persistence of local methods in the handling of masonry and woodwork should also be observed. Water-wheels must be measured and described and the source of the water supply noted. Wheels often bear the label of the foundry that made them. Unfortunately, old steam engines and other machinery have considerable value as scrap, especially in war-time, and since in any case they are much easier to dismantle and remove than water-wheels, they will usually prove rare and important finds.

Everything possible must be done to work up a history of each individual factory. If the original records of the business are not available, a good deal of valuable information can be discovered in parliamentary publications, such as the Reports of the factory inspectors, as well as in local histories and topographical works.

Many of the early cotton mills possessed apprentice houses, and these need to be carefully described. Later mill villages should be treated as a group, not ignoring the houses of the mill owner or managers, the school house, or the churches. Every effort should be made to discover what these buildings cost and how they compared with the housing available for other types of workers in the district.

The woollen cloth industry of the Stroud valleys: an example of a local survey

The Stroud area of Gloucestershire is well-known nowadays for the diversity of its industries. The factories are spread out along the River Frome and its tributaries, and most of them occupy the sites and often the buildings of earlier cloth mills. Much of the history of cloth-making in the area has been lost, but a great many details can be filled in by means of a careful examination and comparison of the surviving buildings.

The textile industry developed slowly in the hands of a few wealthy families. Richard Whittington, Lord Mayor of London, appears to have been one of the local mill owners, and he may well have played a considerable part in the later development of the cloth industry.

The siting of these mills in the Frome valleys was governed by a number of factors, the most important being the availability of Cotswold wool, the constant flow of water, and the suitability of the natural salts in solution in the local springs for cleaning and dyeing. Dyeing was carried out both in the wool and after fulling, according to the dyes used. The area did not limit itself to one colour alone, though it did specialise. Stroudwater scarlets and Uley blues were very famous.

As a means of power the water operated the fulling stocks and gig mills only. Space was not given to looms until a later date. The function of the mills was only to treat the raw materials in ways which were not possible in the houses around. They were not primarily a means of saving labour.

A. T. Playne gives a good account[8] of the processes involved. After sorting, the raw wool was scoured by boiling in stale urine, dyed, sorted to remove foreign bodies, then carded and spun in the cottages. The yarn was then sent out again to local weavers, after which it was returned for a lengthy fulling process before being placed on the gig where the nap was raised by a revolving drum of teasels. The final stages were shearing, followed by repeated stretching, steaming and pressing.

Alterations in the eighteenth and nineteenth centuries have removed all the early machinery from the mills, though conjectural reconstructions may be possible in a few instances from the few surviving mortices and shaft openings.

The oldest industrial building in a complete state is not at a mill, but in the centre of the village of Leonard Stanley. It adjoins a mercer's house and dates from the latter half of the fifteenth century. It consists of a ground-floor weaving room, with two storage rooms above, which opened out from the principal bed chamber. By the late seventeenth century the use of attics in clothiers' houses as warehouses seems to have become general practice.

Improvements in the standards of dress and living in the eighteenth century brought prosperity to the industry, and many of the so-called 'gentlemen clothiers' stood out by their extravagant living or by their services to the community.

Lesser families joined in the quest for wealth and many more mills were put up in the closing years of the eighteenth and early nineteenth centuries. Most of these are shown on Bryant's Map of the County of Gloucester, 1824, which, together with other sources, gives us a total of over 150 mills dependent upon the waters of the River Frome and its tributaries. A number of these must have been corn or grist mills. Documentary evidence shows that several cloth mills contained millstones as well, so the existence today of old millstones on any site need not rule out the possibility of cloth-working. Unlike the earlier mills which catered for all the preparatory and finishing processes required, the new mills were often able to deal with one process only. Some of them were so small as to make it easy to mistake them for cottages. The water-wheel was in a semi-basement and the family lived at first floor level. The little shear mills were smaller still.

The clothier usually lived near his mill. When this was not the case, fine cloth was often carried some distance to be dried on racks in fields around the clothier's house where theft was less likely. Most of the outworkers, the spinners and weavers, lived in groups of small cottages, built between about 1750 and 1820, high above the mills on land taken from the edges of the commons. Evidence of industry in the slightly larger houses is often lacking, though many must have contained looms. One does contain tanks, probably for dyeing lists,[9] and two

---

[8] *Minchinhampton and Avening*, 1915, pp. 141–148.

[9] The side or edge of a piece of cloth. It was of a stouter material than the cloth itself, and often of a different shade.

others have devices which may have been used in the sizing of warp for the looms.

Many cloth mills stopped working during the depressions of the 1830s and 1870s and there was considerable emigration of skilled workers and their families to Australia, South Africa[10] and America. Many of the mills that closed went over to wood-working or to cloth derivatives, like silk, mill puff, flock and shoddy, and even paper. The millwrights became general engineers. Even today most of the industries of the Stroud valleys can be placed in these same three categories, cloth, wood and engineering. Piano-making, one of the most successful introductions, draws on all three types of craftsmanship.

With the notable exception of Stanley Mill (1813), with its splendid interior iron columns, brackets and beams, most of the mills in this area are of stone and wood, although iron window-frames are almost universal.

The mill ponds in the Stroud valleys are exceptionally interesting. The form of the mill pond is governed by local topography and by the economic and structural history of the mill it serves. The stream may flow through or by the side of the pond. Two ponds on either side of a road may serve one water-wheel, or the ponds may be side by side for two wheels. In one instance two ponds lie on different streams, and in another the principal pond lies below the mill, with a culvert back to the mill head. The alignment of the water-wheel is almost invariably at right angles to the line of the roof. There are very few exceptions to this and they all appear to be the result of later alterations. The water-wheels were usually of cast-iron and overshot. The large number of mills in the area made heavy demands on the very modest rivers and streams and on several sites there is evidence of efforts to increase the head of water and, in this way, the power available to the mill machinery. Beam-engines were used to augment the water-power, but none has survived.

Pottery

Pottery was made in North Staffordshire long before the industrial age. The thrower's wheel was in use in Roman times and a two-compartment circular bee-hive updraught kiln of the same period was recently discovered at Trent Vale, Stoke-on-Trent. The history of pottery manufacture is, however, discontinuous. A great deal of pottery was made at Sneyd Green, within the present Potteries area, in the early Middle Ages. The kilns used had five fire-mouths and were of the updraught type. They were, moreover, fired with coal instead of wood. There is increased evidence of pottery making in North Staffordshire in the sixteenth century, but the modern concentration of the industry dates from the end of the seventeenth century, following the short stay of the Dutchman, John Philip Elers, in the district. Redware decorated with slip was made in every part

[10] On one such family, see 'A Gloucester Mill in South Africa', *Industrial Archaeology*, August 1967. Samuel Bradshaw emigrated from Cam, Gloucestershire in 1820 and built a mill at Bathurst, Eastern Province.

Southampton Water, looking towards the former flying-boat station (1930s) on Calshot Spit. Remnants of old landing stages, used at one time to load pottery clay carried over a network of tramways from inland, can be seen in the foreground

of England where suitable clay was to be found, and, from the latter part of the sixteenth century, tin-enamelled pottery, or delftware, was made in London and later in Bristol, Liverpool and Glasgow. The chief forms of pottery made in Staffordshire were, until well into the nineteenth century, the redwares of the country potter, salt-glazed stone-ware which was also made at Fulham, Nottingham, Southampton and in Derbyshire, and cream-coloured earthenware, which was also produced on Tyneside, in Scotland and in Leeds. Various ornamental types of pottery were being made in Staffordshire from about 1700 onwards and its porcelain competed with that of Limehouse, Bow and Chelsea, in London, and with Lowestoft, Worcester and Longton Hall. Hard-paste porcelain was a speciality of Plymouth, Bristol and New Hall, Staffordshire, and bone-china was produced at Stoke-on-Trent from the end of the eighteenth century.

The potter's chief machine-tools were the thrower's wheel, which might be of either the kick or rope-driven type,[11] and the lathe, which had been introduced about 1695 by Elers. Some kind of 'fire-engine' had been working at the factories

[11] Wedgwood's wheel, dated 1785, is in Hanley Museum.

of Turner of Lane End and Spode of Stoke-on-Trent before 1781. A 10 h.p. Boulton & Watt engine was installed at Etruria in 1793, following earlier experiments with steam engines in 1782 and 1784. It was expected to grind flint, enamel colours, operate a saggar-crusher[12] and to temper or mix clay. Machines for making pottery or for producing decorative engraved transfers in quantity date from the second quarter of the nineteenth century. The former were not extensively used in the Pottery districts of Staffordshire and Yorkshire until later in the Victorian age. Full mechanisation awaited the economic pressures that followed World War II. The Potteries' symbol of the first Industrial Revolution, the bottle-shaped oven, fired intermittently with coal, has given place to continuous tunnel-ovens, fired with gas or electricity.

Early pottery factories were situated at or near to the intersection of roads or, after the construction of the Trent and Mersey Canal, on the canal banks or near to the wharves. Running water was frequently laid on to larger factories. It was used in the manufacturing processes and also to turn a water-wheel to grind materials The difficulty of disposing of shraff and shards partly accounts for the wasteful use of land in North Staffordshire and the tendency to construct factories on the brows of hills where the slope formed a natural tip or shordruck. The stratification of most shordrucks is not horizontal, but diagonal, with a tendency for each deposit to drag.

At first, the factory workshops were irregularly grouped round a courtyard behind the master-potter's house, with the ovens in the rear. Following the lead given by Wedgwood at Etruria, manufacturers began to build on more rational and practical lines. The typical late eighteenth century earthenware factory consisted of a symmetrical two-storeyed façade with oval arched entrance lodge, and a three-light Venetian window over it, surmounted by a triangular pediment which enclosed an oval cartouche bearing the name of the factory and the date when it was put up. The Venetian window over the principal entrance remained a feature of local factory building until late Victorian times. Bell-turrets frequently surmounted the roof above the pediment, as at Etruria and at Cobridge. Factory bells are preserved at Ashworths (originally Baddeleys), although they are no longer in their original position. The principal workshops were arranged in two or three parallel lines running at right angles to the façade, providing one or two cobble-paved courtyards for internal communication and sufficient space to reduce the hazards of fire. Until early in the nineteenth century the owner's or occupier's house stood close to the factory, as at The Foley, Fenton, or formed an extension of the façade such as Davenports Factory, Longport. Uncovered wooden external staircases were common. Roofs were of the tie-beam or king-post type. The adze-hewn roofs of the workshops at Ashworths are preserved.

The more important features of the early 'sun-kiln factories' used by country

[12]Saggars – 'saggar' is a corruption of 'safeguard' – were fire-clay boxes used to protect pottery from the naked flame of the kiln in which it was fired. They were made both circular and oval and are usually about 9 ins. deep.

Bottle kilns at Etruria (*c*.1769), now demolished. The drawing, by L. G. Brammer, shows men carrying saggars of pottery into the kiln

Painting (early 1930s) of a scene at Stoke-on-Trent, showing different types of pottery kiln

The same part of Stoke-on-Trent, 1960. All but one of the kilns have gone, and so has the smoke

redware potters until the nineteenth century, were the stone-lined pit, or 'sun-pan', sunk into the ground, in which the clay was weathered by the action of the sun, and the hob-mouthed oven. The sun-pan was divided into compartments in which the clay was matured, blunged with water to a creamy consistency and run-off into a tank for evaporation. Ipstones, in the Staffordshire Moorlands, provides an example. There, clay, outcropping coal, white sand from a local stream, lead-ore, and good building materials were all close at hand.

A typical small factory in Lane End at the beginning of the nineteenth century comprised, in the terms of the industry, 'a squeezing-house, throwing-house, dipping-house, saggar-house, with or without chambers over them, a large slipping-house, a green-house, a marl-house, a commodious warehouse bank, and biscuit and gloss hovels'. The older bottle-shaped ovens, with their hovels, were constructed by stepping back the bricks, whereas the rather more recent ones usually have the bricks shaped or battered. The older ovens, too, were rather more squat than their successors, with a wide neck and few mouldings. Old fittings and furnishings which might well remain *in situ* at old factories, and are worth looking for, include throwers' wheels, turners' lathes, jiggers and whirlers, benches, three-legged stools, cast-iron stoves and pipes, wooden stillages, ware-house penning, pegs, nogs and trows, mill tubs and dipping tubs, grinding stones, biscuit and gloss saggars (ovals, twifflers, banjos) and tubs, tierces and casks. Disused saggars can sometimes be found built into dry walls. One such wall can still be seen, much decayed, in Tunstall, between St. Aidan's Church and the town cemetery.

Glass

Until the later nineteenth century almost all glass was made by hand,[13] the not-able exception being the larger pieces of the thicker plate glass, which were too heavy to be blown and had to be cast on an iron table and subsequently ground and polished. Outside this particular branch of the industry there was hardly any machinery in use at all and the archaeological evidence most likely to be encountered will consist chiefly of the melting furnaces in which the sand and other raw materials were heated to a working consistency, auxiliary furnaces, in which the glass was re-heated from time to time as it was being worked, and annealing kilns, in which the manufactured glass was cooled. Nearby may be found remains of warehouses and other ancillary buildings, remnants of large fire-clay pots, and, of course, large quantities of broken glass.

Before the seventeenth century, glass-making furnaces were fired with wood

[13] The techniques and organisation of an early nineteenth century glassworks have been well described by John C. Logan in his article, 'The Operations of a Glassworks in the Industrial Revolution', *Industrial Archaeology*, May 1972. Mr. Logan is concerned with the Dumbarton Glass Works Company, which operated from 1777 until 1850. Between 1814 and 1826 it produced 92 per cent of all the crown glass made in Scotland and the equivalent of 35 per cent of all English production.

and the industry was located chiefly in the south of England.[14] The development of the reverberatory furnace at the beginning of the seventeenth century made coal-firing possible and, after the royal decree of 1615 forbidding the use of wood, the centre of the industry moved to the Tyne. A few furnaces were also built elsewhere to supply the remoter parts of the kingdom.[15] Furnaces were at first housed in buildings of a normal rectangular type, but it later became customary to construct the outer building of the same shape as the furnace itself and the resulting cone-shaped glass-houses became the industry's characteristic contribution to the landscape. The earliest comprehensive list of their whereabouts is John Houghton's of 1696.[16] Francis Buckley collected eighteenth century newspaper references in a series of articles,[17] each dealing with a particular area. A later list, referring to the year 1832, will be found in the Thirteenth Report of the Commissioners of Excise Inquiry.[18]

During the eighteenth and nineteenth centuries, flat glass was made by one of three methods, to produce, according to the process, crown glass, plate glass or sheet glass.

Crown glass was produced by spinning glass into a disc. The workman first blew a globe of glass and then attached a pontil, or solid iron rod, to the side of the globe opposite to the blowing iron. The blowing iron was removed and then, by means of the pontil, the glass was spun rapidly at a re-heating furnace, opening out into a disc, which was cut up into pieces after it had been carefully cooled. The circular pattern at the centre of the disc can still be seen in old window panes.

The casting of thick plates of glass was carried out on a small scale in London from time to time from 1690 onwards. Large-scale production was embarked upon at Ravenhead, near St. Helens, in Lancashire, in 1776. Very little polished plate glass was produced until 1788, when a Boulton & Watt engine was installed to drive the grinding and polishing machines. Sand, first coarse and then fine, was used as an abrasive, followed by rouge as a polisher.

Ravenhead was followed, during the first half of the nineteenth century, by five other plate glass factories – two in the St. Helens area, one on the Tyne, one on the Thames and one in the Birmingham area.

An improved hand cylinder process of making glass, known as the sheet glass process, was introduced into England by Lucas Chance in 1832. A crude form of cylinder glass known as broad glass was generally used in England before it was almost completely driven out, in the eighteenth century, by crown glass. In the

[14] See S. E. Winbolt's *Wealden Glass* and his contributions in the *Journal of the Society of Glass Technology*, Vols. 16, 17 and 18.

[15] The main features of the coal-fired furnace are outlined in T. C. Barker's *Pilkington Brothers and the Glass Industry*, 1960, p. 34.

[16] *A Collection of Letters for the Improvement of Husbandry and Trade* (ed. Houghton, No. 198, 15th May 1696). The main details are summarised in *An Historical Geography of England before 1800* (ed. Darby), p. 420.

[17] In the *Journal of the Society of Glass Technology*, Vol. 13 and 14.

[18] 1835, p. xxi and Appendix 7.

Eighteenth century casting-hall at Ravenhead glassworks, St. Helens. This photograph shows the interior of the building as it was in the 1880s. Only two bays now survive in their original condition

manufacture of broad glass the cylinder was slit, while still hot, by a cold iron and clumsily opened out on an iron plate at the mouth of the furnace. At least one attempt was made to introduce sheet glass manufacture in England in the later eighteenth century but, because of the method of levying the glass excise duty, crown glass reigned supreme until well into the nineteenth century.

Between 20 and 40 lb. of glass was gathered on a blow-iron and blown to form a globe, and by 'blocking', formed into a shape which, when swung from side to side in a trench about 10 ft. deep, and further blown, became a cylinder about 5 ft. in length. The ends of the cylinder were then removed and it was allowed to cool, before being split along its length with a diamond. It was then re-heated in a flattening kiln and opened out into a flat sheet. The sheet was then annealed in another kiln. Larger panes of glass could be cut from rectangular sheets than from the circular discs of crown glass and there was not, of course, a 'bull's eye' in the centre. Because there was less wastage and because of the larger panes which could be produced, sheet glass gradually drove crown from the market. It was already in the ascendant by 1850 and almost universal by 1870.

In the mid-nineteenth century growing competition sharply reduced the number of window-class concerns and by the 1860s 75 per cent of the British output of this type of glass came from the three firms operating at St. Helens, Smethwick and Sunderland. The brick cone which used to belong to one of the casualties is still to be seen at Old Swan, near Liverpool, and pot arches, furnace foundations, an office building and glass-makers' cottages of another at Nailsea, near Bristol. Not far from Nailsea, at Stanton Wick, are the surviving traces of a much older concern. Some cones used for the manufacture of tableware still survive at Stourbridge. The introduction of new techniques during and since the later nineteenth century has resulted in the destruction of the obsolete plant at St. Helens and Smethwick. The Sunderland works, which were closed in 1894, were soon demolished and the site built over.

The materials used for glass-making are commonplace, and in consequence glass-making is a widespread industry, although the largest centre of production

Sunderland glass goblet (1825), showing Wearmouth Bridge and Sunderland Exchange

has remained in Lancashire. The buildings needed for the manufacture of cast plate glass were among the largest industrial premises of their day but, apart from the premises at Ravenhead, none of the early examples has survived as glass-works, although the buildings often stand and are now used for other purposes.

Large heaps or lodges of sand, deposited after grinding, may still be seen in their vicinity. The Ravenhead works, which contained the original casting hall, and other features of its early days, is now owned by Pilkington Brothers Limited, the sole producers of plate and window glass in Great Britain. The Museum of Glass, which forms part of the Company's premises at St. Helen's, is probably the finest industrial museum and historical research centre in Britain.

Brewing

By the close of the eighteenth century, most of the small market towns, and all the larger towns, had their Common Brewhouses – some already over a century old. There were about 1000 Common Brewers scattered over the country in 1750, and 2500 in the 1870s. Many of them owned more than one brewhouse. More-over, continuity in the main extractive processes of brewing, though not in the final preparation, packaging or distribution of the product, continuity of local markets, type of product, site of enterprise and of family ownership or control have all led to the original premises surviving in a considerable number of cases, even though they may subsequently have been incorporated in a larger building. All this makes old breweries and brewers' houses, so often built in association with the brewhouse, an interesting field for the industrial archaeologist.

The slaughter of breweries has been ruthless. In Hertford,[19] for instance, there were eight breweries in 1841, two in 1961 and one only in 1966. This was the trend all over the country. As the railway network improved, it became easier for the big brewers in London and Burton to distribute their beer over a larger area and to put the local breweries out of business. The local firms survived only when they had enough capital to buy public-houses and so develop a tied-house system. The struggle for a bigger share of the market led to an increase in the scale of production by the brewers who survived. Each amalgamation led to the closure of breweries and maltings, or their conversion to mere depots or bottling plants.

The basic structure of the brew-house was determined by the technical pro-cesses involved. Malt – germinated barley – was first coarsely ground, 'mashed' in hot water, the extract run off, boiled with hops and fermented with yeast. Having once raised malt and water to the highest level in the structure it was convenient and economical to allow gravity to transfer the liquids as much as possible between processes. For this reason, the malt mill and boiler, mash-tun, fermenting rooms and the 'racking stages' for barrelling were, as far as space allowed, on successively lower levels. This commonly gives the brewery a height

[19] On this, see E. J. Connell, 'Hertford Breweries', *Industrial Archaeology*, February 1967.

greater than that of the usual run of buildings in a market town. Often today, height, in a fairly narrow building, can be the first clue to an old brewhouse, even where it is now being used for another purpose. Tetbury brewery, for instance, is now a laundry.

The characteristic ground plan of an early brewery was a set of buildings grouped round a yard. The façade of the actual brewhouse often lay along the street. There was an entrance into the yard, often with the building continuing over it, between the brewhouse and the brewer's house or the counting house, which in this way had separate access to the street while being an organic part of the building. Round the yard at the back were the cooperage, stables, storehouses for large vats, in the case of porter breweries, casks, and often maltings

Breweries at Alton, Hampshire, taken from the tower at Watney's (formerly Crowley's) Brewery. Established in 1763, most of the buildings belong to the late nineteenth or early twentieth centuries. The maltings may date back to 1780. Opposite Watney's, and drawing on the same supply of excellent water, is Courage's (partly 1860). The new Harp Lager brewery is at the top right

in the case of country breweries, but scarcely ever with London firms. A major
part of the site would probably be in use for storage. Sometimes the stables have
survived without much alteration, as workshops, and usually the central group
of buildings has had a bottling store added to it. It does not take a very experienced eye to sort out the complex. The oldest parts of the structure are usually
the brewery offices and the central parts of the actual brewhouse.

Breweries have followed the changing architectural fashion of their different
periods, in the same way as other types of building. The functional tradition
remained at its least self-conscious in stores and warehouses, but in the brewhouse buildings themselves functional efficiency was everywhere under the
impress of aesthetic tradition. There are regular Georgian façades – Simpson's
at Baldock, and Payne's at St. Neots, for instance – with a pattern of fenestration
following the elegant town house which, indeed, part of it often was, for the brewer
was rich enough to live in the style appropriate to the wealthiest resident of the
town. With some Georgian breweries, symmetrical proportions are balanced
round a pediment, in country house style, as at Elwood's North Brink Brewery,
at Wisbech, and Cobb's at Margate. The steady rise in the number of commercial breweries means that stylistic development, through Victorian Byzantine
and Italianate, can be well plotted from new foundations, quite apart from the
reconstruction and enlargement of older buildings.[20]

Distilling

It seems likely that the distilling of potable spirits was first discovered about 1100
A.D. at the University of Salerno. Distillation is a simple process, the basis of
which consists of heating a substance, which may be anything from wine to
potash, in a retort so that the liquid is driven off as a vapour and led into a cooling
chamber, when it reliquifies in the form desired. By careful management, the
flavour can be taken off at one temperature, and stored separately, and the bulk
of the liquid at another. Commercial production began on a modest scale in
Northern Italy and spread across Europe in the wake of the Black Death, when
spirits were prescribed as the appropriate medicine. At first they were distilled
from wine only, but at the end of the fourteenth or beginning of the fifteenth
century it was discovered that spirits could be distilled from cereals or from beer.
Gradually the production of brandy and other spirits became the specialised
function of the distiller, instead of, as formerly, a sideline of the apothecary.

By the end of the sixteenth century, distilling was an important industry in
Holland. The earliest Dutch recipe for 'aqua juniperi', or Hollands Gin, distilled
from grain and flavoured with juniper berries, appears in a handbook published
in Amsterdam in 1622. The flow of exports to Britain stimulated English distillers
to copy the Dutch product.

[20] For illustrations of particularly handsome early breweries, see *The Functional Tradition*, by
J. M. Richards, 1958.

In 1638 the Company of Distillers was incorporated in London. By the beginning of the eighteenth century, the industry was divided between the malt distillers, who made the basic spirit from grain, and the rectifiers, who prepared the final product by re-distillation and flavouring.

There are several surviving examples of early stills and distillery buildings. Three Mills Distillery, at Stratford, in Essex, now owned by J. and W. Nicholson, dates from 1730.[21] No distilling has taken place here since the war and the original beam engines have been removed. But a beam engine of 1835 at Nicholson's distillery in St John Street, Finsbury was described some time ago in *The New Model Engineer*.[22] According to Pevsner, the older part of this distillery dates from 1828.

Gordon's and Booth's distilleries in Finsbury are modern, but they contain elegant copper stills preserved from an earlier period. There is a still at Booth's which is described as dating from about 1740, and a flavour still dated 1828. Gordon's has a hand-riveted still said to date from about 1800.

The distilling of pot-still whisky from malted barley became a small-scale industry in Scotland in the second half of the eighteenth century. The rise of the industry dates from an Act of 1823 which allowed distilling in return for a licence of ten pounds for each still containing over 40 gallons. Smaller stills were made illegal. This Act killed home-distilling.

The early stages of malt whisky production – malting, mashing and fermentation – are roughly identical with the brewing process. The fermented wash undergoes two distillations, first in a wash still, which must be filled, emptied and filled again and finally in a spirit still. In 1827 Jean-Jacques St. Marc patented a fire-heated continuous still, which he set up at Nicholson's gin distillery at Clerkenwell. In the same year a Scotch whisky distiller, Robert Stein, invented a steam-heated continuous still, one of which was erected at Cameron Bridge Distillery, Fife, in 1832, and another at Port Dundas Distillery, Glasgow, in 1833. An improved version, by Aeneas Coffee, then of the Dock Distillery, Dublin, was patented in 1831. The 'Coffee Still' was adopted generally.[23] It permitted whisky to be made more economically and in much greater quantities than by the traditional method. It was, and is, used for making grain whisky. Malt whisky is still made by the pot-still method.

Between 1860 and 1865 the blending of pot-still malt and patent still grain whiskies was pioneered by the firm of Andrew Usher of Edinburgh. A growing market for blended Scotch whisky was developed from the 1880s onwards. The '80s and '90s saw the building of probably the majority of existing whisky distilleries.

---

[21] See Pevsner: *The Buildings of England: Essex*, p. 343.

[22] 10th November, 1955.

[23] See Ross Wilson, 'The Evolution of the Continuous Still', in *Wine and Spirit Trade Record*, October–November, 1962.

A few maltings or warehouses built earlier than 1880 exist here and there, but the industry's production has increased enormously since then and the great majority of the distilleries in operation today are modern in both their buildings and their equipment. Examples of plant dating from before 1880 are rare museum pieces.

Paradoxically, however, a modern distillery may be its own museum, since the new equipment is frequently almost identical in design to what it replaces. At the Talisker distillery, for instance, in the Isle of Skye, the new pot-stills installed during 1962 are exact replicas of the old stills, because it is believed that the shape of the still can influence the character of the whisky.

8

Building Materials

The archaeology of building materials is to be found both in the places where they were made or processed and in the places where they were used. Every building is a museum of building materials.

Cement

The cementing materials which were used in building during the eighteenth and nineteenth centuries fall broadly into three types: gypsum plaster, various forms of lime and a group of artificial cements.

Gypsum plastering was first introduced into England from France in the thirteenth century. It was mainly used to give a smooth, hard finish to walls and ceilings but, by the mid-eighteenth century, builders both on the Continent and in England were including it as an ingredient in fire-resistant floors, the reinforcing materials being either wrought iron or reeds. Examples of this type of floor have been discovered in the Nottingham area, but others must exist elsewhere and are worth looking for, especially when buildings are being demolished.

The main centres of gypsum production in England are in Nottingham, near Newark, at Fauld, in Staffordshire, Chellaston, in Derbyshire, in Cumberland and Westmorland, and at Robertsbridge, in Sussex. The method of processing the raw gypsum depends on the type of plaster to be produced but, basically, the technique is first to grind it and then to calcine, or roast, it in open 'kettles'. Originally – and this is still the practice in the Middle East – lumps of gypsum were stacked into a primitive, beehive-shaped kiln and burnt. It is unlikely that any of these early kilns are still standing, even in a ruined state, but it might be worth searching for their foundations.

Lime, as a builder understands the term, consists of pure lime, which has little

137

strength and which can only harden as a result of gradual carbonation, and so-called hydraulic lime, which sets under wet conditions and is made either pure by burning limestone containing clay or else by adding natural or artificial pozzolanic materials, such as pumice or burnt clay, to pure lime.

The remains of early lime-kilns are to be found in many areas where chalk or limestone are readily available. The kilns usually had the shape of an inverted cone with a grating at the bottom and a draw-hole beneath. They were often built into a hillside, so that access for filling the kiln with fuel and raw material could be had from the upper slope.

There are a number of such kilns, mostly dating from the late eighteenth century along the North Devon coast from Glenthorne to Hartland. Particularly well-preserved specimens can be seen at Haddon's Mouth, Lee Bay and Woodley Bay, and on the promenade at Lynmouth a group of old kilns has been converted, very pleasantly, into a shelter for holidaymakers. Another series of Devon kilns, in a ruinous condition, is along the Tamar, between Gunnislake and Plymouth. On the island of Lindisfarne, in Northumberland, there is a battery of lime-kilns in a good state of preservation, with a track linking the kilns to the quarry on one side and a jetty on the other. The site of the new Black Country open-air museum at Dudley, Worcestershire, includes a group of large early nineteenth century kilns, built here to take advantage of the canal running close by.

Earl of Dudley's limekilns, Dudley, Worcestershire. The pool lapping the walls is sewage overflow from the treatment plant nearby. This no longer occurs

One especially interesting limeworks, near Merstham, Surrey, has been recently revealed by a team of archaeologists working under the direction of Eric S. Wood. The site is close to the southern end of Merstham railway tunnel and the limeworks was set up by the contractors who built it, Jolliffe and Banks. Two circles were excavated and provided evidence that they had been used for mixing mortar to line the tunnel.

The kilns were either intermittent or continuous in operation. In the former case, the fuel, consisting of wood faggots and coal, was placed on the grate and the lump chalk or limestone piled in above. The kiln was allowed to burn itself out. In continuous operation, the fuel and raw material was placed in the kiln in layers; as the lower ones burned away and the calcined lime fell through the grating to be collected in the draw-hole, so the kiln was replenished with more layers of fuel and raw materials filled in at the top.

By the mid-nineteenth century there were three available types of material derived from chalk or limestone which could be used for making mortar or concrete which would set under water or in a damp atmosphere. The first group comprised various hydraulic limes and natural cements, made by calcining stone that contained a suitable mixture of lime, alumina and silica. These included Parker's 'Roman' cement, patented by James Parker in 1796 and supposedly made of nodules of septaria, collected on the beach and from deposits along river estuaries at, for example, Harwich, the Solent and the Isle of Sheppey.

The second group was the artificial, proprietary cements, made by mixing limestone or chalk either with clay or shale in the right proportions – which were discovered and controlled empirically, not scientifically – and then burning the mixture at a temperature of between 1100 and 1300°C. What was originally known as Portland cement probably belongs to this group. It was invented in 1824 by Joseph Aspdin and was given the name because a wall rendered with it was optimistically reckoned to resemble Portland stone.

By the 1850s the true Portland cements formed a third group on their own. They were artificial cements in which the materials were mixed and then burnt at 1400–1500°C, a point where the mix began to fuse. The resulting clinker is then ground fine to produce the cement. This is the sense in which the name 'Portland Cement' is understood today.

The first large-scale cement works were set up by Joseph Aspdin's son, William, at Northfleet, in Kent, in 1843. This was followed by a second works, in the North of England, at Gateshead, in 1843. Cement works were situated close to natural sources of chalk or limestone and mud or clay. This explains the concentration of works in the Thames Basin, where ample chalk is available in the North Downs of Kent, with London clay and the mud deposits of the Thames and Medway near at hand. The cement industry established itself in Kent during the eighteenth century and this area has continued to be of great importance ever since. In addition to the advantage of having supplies of chalk and clay near at hand, the North Kent cement works were well placed for shipping in coal by sea and for sending away the cement to London in river barges.

The early type of kiln used for burning Portland cement clinker was basically the same as that used for lime production. As a higher temperature was necessary, the open end was of considerably reduced diameter to conserve heat, and to induce a greater draught through the kiln.

Once cement was available, and could be transported to the site in sufficient quantity and of a consistently high quality, it became practicable to use it for civil engineering purposes. Lime-concrete had been used for bridge foundations, and occasionally for the foundations of large buildings, from the mid-eighteenth century, but the first major contract on which Portland cement was used was for the main drainage of London, between 1858 and 1875.

A useful and interesting secondary task for the industrial archaeologist is to collect and have analysed samples of plaster, mortar and concrete from structures whose date is known and in this way to survey the gradual spread of new techniques across the country and from large to more humble buildings.

During the 1870s a tunnel-type kiln began to replace the old kilns, which were built in the shape of a truncated cone. A wet mix was used and the slurry was pumped up to the top chamber of the kiln, to be dried by the hot air rising up from the roasting of the previous batch on the floor below.

A rotary kiln was patented by Crampton in 1877, but it was unsatisfactory. The basic principle was obviously sound, however, and in 1900, since the demand for cement was rising so fast that some form of continuous production was essential, the newly formed Associated Portland Cement Manufacturers' Association bought the rights to an improved American version of Crampton's kiln and built new plants of this type on their Thames-side site.

Improvements in the supply and the quality of cement made important developments in the use of reinforced concrete possible. For some reason that is not altogether easy to explain, although it may have something to do with the current building regulations, the majority of these experiments in the late nineteenth century were carried out in France and Germany, not in England, although British patents for reinforced concrete beams go back to 1877. By 1900 the technique was securely established in this country and much of this early work is worth looking for and studying, in order to observe its frequently excellent quality. Some of it, in fact, put into position when civil engineers were still nervous about its structural qualities, had exceedingly careful supervision and has often lasted considerably better than examples of reinforced concrete made in the 1920s, a somewhat slap-happy period when there was a regrettable amount of unfortunate building in this material.

The cement industry has so far not proved very attractive to industrial archaeologists. One needs more local studies of the kind carried out by Charles Dodsworth in Oxfordshire.[1] The Oxford cement industry, now extinct, was established in 1905 at Kirtlington and was later extended to Shipton-on-Cherwell. As Mr. Dodsworth has shown, it developed naturally from already existing limestone

---

[1] 'The Early Years of the Oxford Cement Industry', *Industrial Archaeology*, August 1972.

STOTHERT & PITT, Limited, Engineers, Bath, England.   29

HAND BRICK CRUSHING MACHINE.

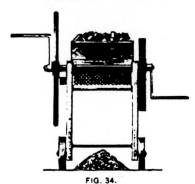

FIG. 34.

FOR crushing and breaking up old bricks, stones, &c., for Concrete making in moderate quantities, this machine will be found of great service and economical in results. The rolls can be adjusted so as to break up the materials coarse or fine, and being mounted on wheels can be easily removed from place to place.

Price........................ £18.

For gauging the material to different sizes and separating the sand, a screen can be fitted underneath the rolls, and another set of rolls for crushing the whole to powder can be supplied if required at a small additional cost.

Packing for Shipment 3 per cent. extra.

CONCRETE MIXER.

FIG. 35.

THESE Mixers are constructed chiefly of wrought iron, and are mounted on wheels, and may be used for mixing concrete, mortar, cement, &c. They are similar in design to the Hand Mixer, Fig. 33, and are made in two sizes, viz., No. 1 to be worked by steam power, No. 2 by hand or steam as may be required.

The door shown at end can be adjusted to check delivery, and at the same time it regulates the mixture of the different materials, and it is advisable the Mixer should be fitted with it. The additional cost of door and fly-wheel are given.

Size Number	1	2
Contents in cubic feet	30	15
Price	£18 0 0	£17 0 0
Price if fitted with Door at discharge end	1 10 0	1 0 0
Price if fitted with Fly-wheel	1 10 0	1 10 0
Approximate Weight	15 cwt.	10 cwt.

Packing for Shipment 3 per cent. extra.

London Office:—CORNES, CALVERT & Co., 30, Walbrook E.C.

Early hand-operated concrete mixers, from Stothert & Pitt's catalogue, *c.*1880

Brickwork at Layer Marney, Essex, *c.*1485

works. The quantity of cement produced each year was very small by comparison with modern standards, a maximum of 20,000 tons a year, and it is interesting to notice that it was considered worthwhile to operate such a works as late as the 1920s, when the industry as a whole was organised on a basis of large-scale production. The reason for this seems to have been that the quality was high and had a good reputation with tramway, railway and sewerage authorities.

Mr. Dodsworth's mixture of fieldwork, documentary research and discussions with old workers has produced a complete picture of the company's activities between 1905 and 1928, when operations finally came to an end. One of the most charming archaeological items is a small concrete farm building (1907) near the Kirtlington works. This has the company's trade mark, a cow standing over water, similar to the one used by Morris Motors for so many years.

Bricks

For nearly seventy years, the making and using of bricks and tiles in Britain was bedevilled by the brick tax, introduced in 1784 and not finally repealed until 1850. One effect of this iniquitous tax was that the building of the canals, the early railways and many mills and factories was made unnecessarily expensive. There was also an incentive to use stone wherever possible.

The railways were great customers of the brickmakers. In 1821, before railway building began, the number of bricks on which duty was paid was 915 million. Ten years later the total had risen to 1,153 million, and in 1840 to 1,725 million. An ordinary road bridge over a railway required 300,000 bricks and the lining of a tunnel about 14 million a mile.

Throughout the eighteenth and nineteenth centuries bricks were fired in clamps, and in up-draught kilns, similar in principle to those of ancient times. Nowadays, there are also down-draught kilns, in which not only bricks but roofing tiles, flooring tiles, pipes and other products are made. The burning of bricks in clamps was often carried out near to the building under construction. A foundation consisting of a layer or two of burnt bricks was formed as a level site to protect the clamp from damp rising from the ground. Channels were often arranged in this foundation in such a way as to provide fire-holes or flues running the length and breadth of the clamp. These flues held the fuel, while the 'green' bricks were stacked into the spaces between. Burnt bricks and mud were laid over the top of the stack to protect it from the weather and to reduce heat losses. The clamp was set on fire and allowed to burn itself out, a process which often lasted several weeks.

The second method of burning bricks was in up-draught kilns, in which higher and more uniform temperatures than in clamps were obtained. The bricks became vitrified, or practically so, and this made them more durable. The kilns consisted of two chambers, one above the other. The fuel was burned in the lower chamber and in the upper one, the oven, the products were stacked for firing. Remains of these early kilns exist all over the country, but, more frequently, the only surviving

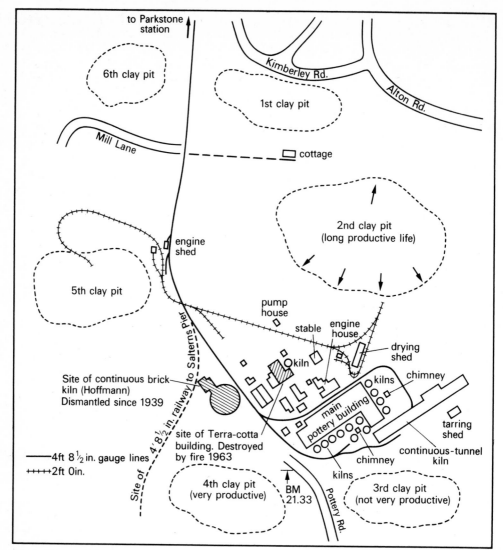

Site of South-Western Pottery, Poole (from *Industrial Archaeology*, May 1969)

evidence of early brickworks is provided by overgrown clay-pits. Names like Brickyard Plantation, Brick Kiln Plantation, Brickyard Spinney and Brick Kiln Covert are clues to vanished brickworks. So, too, are Brickyard Lane and Brick-yard Cottages. Many kinds of clayey materials were used for brick making, ranging from the almost pure and plastic clays, to marls and shales.

Brick moulding was generally done by hand, but compaction of the clay by rolling was introduced by William Bailey in 1741, and by pressure under a heavy weight by Francis Farquharson in 1798. The process known as wire cutting, in which a slab of clay was cut up into brick sizes by dragging a wire through it, was devised by William Irving in 1841. The first brick-extruding machine in Europe is reputed to have been made and used in Bridgwater in 1875. This type of machine continued in use with no significant modification until 1919. It was extremely simple; extrusion was carried out by means of a shaft which pushed the mass of clay between knives placed at right angles to each other.

Until the 1860s all kilns were what is known as intermittent, that is, they worked to a cycle of fill-fire-cool-empty. Intermittent kilns are still used to make the more expensive kinds of facing brick, but nowadays the great majority of building bricks are burnt in some form of continuous kiln. Such kilns have

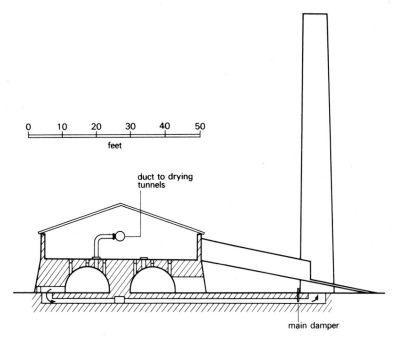

Continuous-burning kiln at Crook Hill brickworks, Weymouth

existed since 1856. They consist essentially of a series of connected chambers arranged in a circular or rectangular pattern, which allows the fire to be led gradually and progressively round the whole circuit. Burnt bricks are taken out of and 'green' bricks placed in the chambers which, at that point in the cycle, are furthest away from the fire. Kilns working on this principle use much less fuel than intermittent kilns, partly because the fuel – coal dust – is dropped in through feed-holes in the roof and burns actually among the bricks, and partly because much of the heat given up by the burnt bricks as they cool is re-circulated to dry and warm the 'green' bricks and to heat the air passing to the fires.

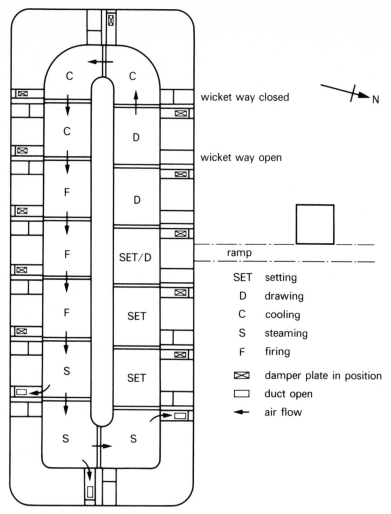

wicket way closed

N

wicket way open

ramp

SET	setting
D	drawing
C	cooling
S	steaming
F	firing
⊠	damper plate in position
▭	duct open
←	air flow

Continuous-burning kiln at Crook Hill brickworks (from *Industrial Archaeology*, May 1972)

Brick making has been carried out wherever suitable clay deposits exist. There are many derelict sites, a high proportion of them very inadequately recorded. The significant features are usually the scars in the surrounding land where the clay was dug, the shallow pits in which the clay was soaked and allowed to settle and perhaps a pug-mill for kneading the clay. It is often possible to note, too, the remains of the open sheds where the moulding benches were situated, a flat area where the green bricks were placed for preliminary drying, and the kilns in which the bricks were fired.

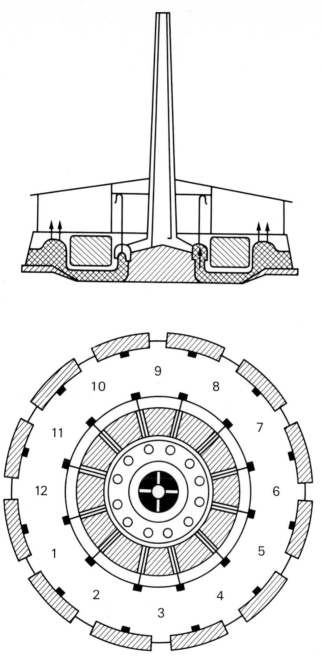

The Hoffman kiln, which revolutionised brick-making in the nineteenth century (from *Industrial Archaeology*, August 1972)

A revolution in brickmaking occurred at the end of the nineteenth century, when the manufacture of bricks from the Lower Oxford Clay was begun at Fletton, near Peterborough. It was found that the shale-like Fletton clay could be pressed into a brick which could be fired immediately, without any previous drying. An equally important advantage was that this clay contained about 10 per cent of carbonaceous material, which produces sufficient heat during firing to reduce the amount of coal required to something like a third of what has to be used with other clays.

Three companies making Flettons produce more than half the bricks used in Britain. The London Brick Company is the largest brickmaker in the world. It was the inability to compete with Flettons which caused so many local brickyards to close between 1920 and 1960.

Stewartby village, which adjoins the great Stewartby works in Bedfordshire, owes its existence entirely to the brick industry. It was named after the Chairman of what later became the London Brick Company, Sir P. Malcolm Stewart, and a former Chairman, Sir Hailey Stewart. The first houses were built in 1926 and there are now about 1000 people living in this model village.

A number of careful surveys of local brickworks, tileworks and potteries have been made during the past ten years. B. P. Lenman and E. E. Gauldie have investigated the remains and history of the Pitfour Brickworks, in Perthshire,[2] which were established in the 1830s by a local landowner, Sir John Stewart Richardson, and continued in operation until 1914. Pitfour was remarkably successful, mainly, no doubt, because there was no other brickfield in the whole of Angus and Perthshire. The latest machinery was always installed and the works had a continuous kiln only a few years after the original patent was taken out. The remains of this kiln are still clearly visible. A tramway was built to transport bricks down to the River Tay and some large contracts were secured, including that for supplying the bricks for the piers of the Tay Bridge.

Donald Young, a mechanical engineer working in the nuclear power industry, has devoted his energies to the Weymouth area, which had a brickmaking industry from the late eighteenth century until 1969,[3] and to Sandleheath, Hampshire,[4] where the brickworks operated over a similar period. In Weymouth, where there were massive deposits of Oxford clay, the two works were fully mechanised by 1926. One, the Putton Lane works, concentrated on bricks and tiles and the other, at Crook Hill, produced drainpipes, pottery and stoneware as well.

At Crook Hill, as in Bedfordshire, the clay contains combustible material, which reduces the amount of coal required, and, in the past, powdered dry clay has been used as fuel. A particular layer of clay was selected for this purpose. It was known as 'fiery' or 'coal strike' clay, because it was used during the 1926

[2] 'Pitfour Brickworks, Glencarse, Perth', *Industrial Archaeology*, November 1969.

[3] 'Brickmaking at Weymouth, Dorset', *Industrial Archaeology*, May 1972.

[4] 'Brickmaking at Sandleheath, Hampshire', *Industrial Archaeology*, November 1970.

Old King's Dyke Brick Works, Whittlesey, Peterborough

miners' strike. During the Second World War, the kiln once ran for three months without either coal or the clay substitute. The bricks literally burned themselves.

At Sandleheath, near Fordingbridge, Mr. Young obtained much of his information from the last owner and operator of the brickworks, S. R. Read, whose family had been brickmakers in the area for at least 180 years. A tile in Mr. Read's possession, taken from the Greyhound Inn, Ringwood, in 1912, carried the inscription, 'Wm. Redd Maker June 10th 1793', written in a copperplate hand in the soft clay.

A moulder at Sandleheath was expected to make 100 bricks an hour, or 5000 in a $5\frac{1}{2}$ day working week of 55 hours, reckoning that some time would be lost owing to bad weather. This included preparing the clay and stacking the bricks for drying. The kilns produced about 84 per cent top quality facing bricks, 8 per cent underburnt and 8 per cent overburnt. It took 8 cwt. of coal to burn 1000 bricks. The market for the bricks was mostly within twenty miles of the works, with Bournemouth as the most important area.[5]

Roofing tiles

The flat clay tile has remained practically the same size for five hundred years, about $10\frac{1}{2}$ by $6\frac{1}{2}$ by $\frac{1}{2}$ in.

The curved pantile was introduced into England in the seventeenth century and became a common type in the Eastern and Northern counties, where many were imported from Holland and Belgium. The manufacture of this type of tile was well established in East Anglia before the end of the eighteenth century. They were mostly red in colour and unglazed, but some were occasionally given a black vitreous finish. The moulding of the tiles was usually done by hand, using wooden pallets, although machine pressing was gradually introduced during the nineteenth century, and firing was carried out in kilns very similar to those used for firing bricks. The tile trade was conservative and on the whole probably under-capitalised, so that the units of production tended to remain relatively small throughout the nineteenth century and well into the twentieth, and both buildings and equipment were constantly repaired along the old lines, so that it is very difficult to know whether one is looking at something originally constructed in 1900 or 1850.

With the steady concentration of both the brick and the clay tile making industries into fewer and fewer units, there are a great many abandoned and derelict small works all over the country. The equipment is not very attractive to a museum hard pressed for space, as most are, and few of the works have been surveyed and photographed before they closed down. There is a strong case for preserving at least one on its original site, as a museum for the industry. Something in the Bridgwater area, an important centre of roofing-tile production until 1939, might well be practicable, although tile-making came to an end here in the 1960s and the remains of the old works are decaying and being cleared away very rapidly.

Stone and slate

The British Isles contains a wide range of stones suitable for building purposes – granites, slates, marbles, sandstones and limestones, with many different colours and qualities within each category.

[5] Other recent studies of the brick and tile and pottery industries include B. Nicholls, 'The Tamar Firebrick and Clay Company', *Industrial Archaeology*, August 1972; A. J. Cooksey, 'Jennings South Western Pottery, Parkstone', *Industrial Archaeology*, May 1969; and Kim C. Leslie's long article on the Ashburnham Estate Brickworks, published in *Sussex Industrial History*, Winter 1970–71, which is a most useful study of a works, until its closure in the 1960s, illustrating the art of brickmaking as it was before the nineteenth century revolution in techniques. Mr. Leslie has also provided a model of how to weld the reminiscences of old workers into the writing of industrial history.

Entrance to gallery of eighteenth century stone quarry, Combe Down, Bath

Some of the finest building granite has come from Dartmoor. Quarrying here began to develop on a larger scale during the 1780s, with the construction of the roads across the moor, and, later, with the coming of the railways. By 1820 large quantities were being exported, especially to London. The best-known of the quarries, at Haytor, provided the stone for London Bridge, now re-erected in the Arizona Desert, as a tourist attraction.

A good deal of Cornish granite was used locally on civil engineering work during the nineteenth century. The railway viaducts at Ivybridge and Cornwood were built of granite from Western Beacon, on the south of the moor, and the material for the dam at Burraton came from a quarry very close at hand. The only Dartmoor quarries still in production are those at Merrivale and Bridford, but there are impressive remains of deserted workings at many places, including Haytor and Swell Tor.

During the early years of the nineteenth century, a new industry, known as sett-making, grew up on Dartmoor. The stone was dressed into small paving-blocks, or setts, by men working under rough shelters on the slopes of Staple Tor and, a little later, at Merrivale Quarry. The trade was ultimately killed by the introduction of tarmac roads. Granite kerbs, another Dartmoor speciality, continued for much longer, however.

The Lake District has been another important centre of the granite industry. The present quarries at Shap were opened in the early 1860s. They supplied the masonry for the Cockermouth, Keswick and Penrith Railway (1864) and for the

Ruston & Hornsby steam navvy removing overburden at Portland quarries, *c.*1910

Thirlmere waterworks project (1894). Efficient polishing gear was installed at Shap quarries during the 1890s, and this created a large demand for the reddish local granite which was much used by the Victorians as a facing material for prestigious buildings. Examples of it can be seen on the Albert Memorial in Kensington Gardens.

Granite has been quarried on a large scale in Aberdeenshire for over 200 years, the principal quarries being at Kemnay, Peterhead, Cluny, Moneymusk and Rubislaw. Aberdeenshire granite went south to provide the material for many important public works – London Bridge, the Bell Rock Lighthouse, and the West India Docks were a few of them. Kerb stones were also in great demand in London and other English cities. They were supplied in lengths ranging from 5 to 6 ft. and in a standard width and depth of 1 ft. by 9 in.

The production of slates and stone tiles has always been as much of a craft as an industry. It has never been more than marginally mechanised, apart from transport and the stripping of overburden, and consequently it is hardly possible to think of it in industrial terms, although the quarrying and preparation provided a livelihood for a considerable number of people until quite recently.

The quarries themselves are museums of the industry and it is instructive to visit them and to find out as much as possible about their history and techniques and about their importance in the locality. They are well scattered over the country.

Entrance to Monks Park underground quarry, near Corsham, Wiltshire

Monks Park Quarry: haulage system and pillars of stone left to support roof

Monks Park Quarry: hand-sawing blocks at face

The fissile limestone tiles were derived from the inferior oolite beds at Colly-weston and Duston in Northamptonshire, and Bradford Abbas in Dorset; from the great oolite beds at Stonesfield, near Woodstock, in Oxfordshire and from the Forest Marble in Wiltshire, Gloucestershire and Oxfordshire. Other fissile tiles came from the Slatt beds at Purbeck, and some of a similar character from the calcareous sandy Horsham Stone in Sussex. Although some carboniferous limestone is fissile and was often used for tiles, gate-posts, kerbs and gravestones, it has much wider uses, as a flux in blast-furnaces, for example, to produce steel, for lime and cement making, and for road-stone. Some, like that near Oswestry, was used for making troughs and mangers, while some, like Fosterley Marble in the North of England, could be polished and used for mural decoration.

The main sources of supply of slates have been North and South Wales, the North of England and Scotland, and Cornwall. The North Wales deposits of slate run from the neighbourhood of Bangor, in a south-easterly direction towards Machynlleth, and include the Bangor and Caernarvon veins, Festiniog or Portmadoc veins, and the Corris or Aberdovey veins. In South Wales slates were obtained from the Prescelly beds, mainly in the Gilfach quarry. In the North of England the sources were Broughton Moor, Buttermere, Tilberthwaite in West-morland; and the Burlington quarries at Kirby-in-Furness in North Lancashire. The Delabole quarry in Cornwall, probably the oldest in Great Britain, has been producing slates for over four hundred years. In recent years the market for its products has become increasingly difficult and there have been some reductions in the number of men employed there, although changing architectural fashion makes it seem possible that there will be a growing demand for Delabole slate for wall-cladding and, in the case of the smaller pieces and inferior grades, for the more durable and expensive kind of garden wall.

Both limestone and sandstones are found in great variety within the British Isles. Until the late eighteenth century, when canals brought about far-reaching changes in the inland transport of heavy, bulky freight, builders would normally use a local stone, unless an easy route by river or sea were available. The industrial towns of Lancashire, for example, were to a large extent built of the sandstones and gritstones which occur abundantly within the county. Stone from the quarries at Haslingden, Rawtenstall, Bacup and Whitworth made the factories, town halls and workers' houses, lined the railway cuttings and tunnels, and provided the masonry for the bridges and viaducts. What could only be discovered by ex-perience was how well or how badly a local stone, well tested and successful in villages and clean country air, would cope with the soot and sulphur of a heavily industrialised area. A stone had to be assumed satisfactory until it was proved otherwise, and, in any case, it was only with the coming of railways that there was anything like a free choice of stone, at least for expensive buildings, practically everywhere in Britain.

Portland stone stood up particularly well to a city atmosphere, but the demand for it always exceeded the supply. In 1812 eight hundred men and boys were employed in the Portland quarries. They produced about 25,000 tons of saleable stone a year, which meant that Portland stone was a scarce commodity. Bath stone was more plentiful. Extracted from mines as well as quarries, five million cubic feet a year were being sold by 1900. The vast mines at Box and Corsham remain as evidence of how important the industry once was. Only one of these mines, Monks Park, is now in operation. Using mechanical cutters, themselves museum-pieces, a dozen men now produce as much as a hundred did in 1939.

Iron and steel

The medieval builders were able to appreciate the value of wrought-iron fastenings as a means of strengthening the stonework in arches and roof-trusses and they made use of iron girdles round the base of their masonry domes. But it was expensive, and continued so until the eighteenth century, and as a reinforcing material it was unsatisfactory so long as it had to be used in conjunction with stone, which was porous and therefore allowed moisture to reach and rust the iron. The availability of Portland cement during the nineteenth century changed the position completely and provided architects and engineers at last with the opportunity to exploit the possibilities of a cheap and strong method of construction.

A parallel technological advance was in the production of cast iron, and, later, of wrought iron on a much larger scale. Cast iron had been used in England for cannons in the mid-sixteenth century and in the seventeenth a new outlet was found in the form of fire-backs, many of which were well-designed and beautifully made and have recently become collectors' pieces.

Cast iron was beginning to be applied to civil engineering purposes by the early eighteenth century. A good deal of it was employed in the new waterworks constructed at London Bridge in 1704. Smeaton made extensive use of it for gearing and other mill-machinery in the 1750s and by the end of the century it had become an increasingly popular structural material, particularly in large buildings, like mills, where disastrous fires were all too frequent and where something less vulnerable than wood, especially oil-soaked wood, was urgently needed.

The eighteenth and nineteenth century builders showed considerable ingenuity in the use of structural iron. Cast pillars, window-frames and door-frames were in use from the 1790s and there are a number of early surviving examples of iron beams protected by earthenware pots, to give them a high degree of fire resistance. The Bank of England's new vaults (1792) were supported by this type of beam and during the same decade William Strutt incorporated them in his new mills, at Belper and elsewhere.

It is important to remember, however, that the original reason for using iron, instead of timber, was to lessen the fire-risk, not to provide a stronger or cheaper structure.

Rolled beams of **T** and **L** section were available during the 1820s and light **I** sections were being made in France by the mid-forties. Heavy **I** beams, for which there was an evident demand, were too expensive to make from wrought iron, since the blooms weighed less than 200 cwt. each, and consequently to produce a heavy beam of the kind of length that was needed, it would have been necessary to weld several blooms together, a process that was much less economic than riveting plates and angles together to form the section required. Heavy rolled beams only became possible in the 1860s, with the introduction of relatively cheap mild steel, that could be cast in large ingots. By that time, the universal mill had been developed. This was invented about 1853 and had two sets of rollers, one vertical, the other horizontal, running at the same speed and in this way it was an easy matter to produce **I** beams with wide, flat surfaces. It was found practicable, however, to make this type of beam in mills which were fitted only with rollers on horizontal axes, by working the metal in a series of progressively diminishing grooves, so as to produce a section in which the inner edge of each half of the flanges is slightly curved and at an angle to the outer edge, instead of parallel to it, as with a modern beam.

When a nineteenth century building is being pulled down or rebuilt in some way, there is often an excellent opportunity to study the use made of iron in its construction, and it is useful to note the dimensions and sections of the beams, whether they are rolled or riveted, and, wherever possible, to obtain a sample of the metal for expert analysis. A similar survey of pillars, frames and reinforcing materials is also valuable.

It is only very recently that the early use made of iron in buildings has been recognised and studied. At one time, for instance, it was believed that the cast-iron façade was an American invention. Professor Hitchcock, however, has shown[6] that the first, and most notable of these buildings were put up during the 1850s, in Glasgow. One of them, now occupied by a firm of cabinet-makers and upholsterers, stands on the corner of Jamaica and Argyll Streets and the other, subsequently refronted and therefore disguised, is an outfitter's shop. It is very probable that further examples of this type of façade are still to be discovered, possibly underneath cladding or advertisements put on in recent years.

Completely steel-framed buildings were being erected in America from about 1890, mainly in order to make it possible to have very tall office blocks, on expensive sites. The technique soon crossed the Atlantic and in 1896 a fully steel-framed furniture warehouse was put up in West Hartlepool, probably the first example of its kind in Great Britain. The Ritz Hotel, in London, was built with a steel frame in 1904, but it was another five years before the real advantages of this form of construction could be used. Until 1909, the building regulations in London compelled architects who designed steel-framed buildings to pretend that the steel-frame was not there, since the walls had to be as thick and solid as if they were still carrying the load of the building.

For much too long, the history of iron and steel, as applied to the building industry, has been obsessed, understandably, perhaps, with the larger and more

---

[6] In an article in the *Architectural Review*, February 1954.

spectacular buildings. It is clearly important to realise the technological importance of the Crystal Palace (1851), with its pre-fabricated sections and its 3500
tons of cast iron, and of the Forth Bridge (1883–90), the first major structure in the
world to be built entirely of steel. What is now wanted is a great deal more
evidence of the extent to which iron and steel were used at an early date in the
kinds of buildings which it has hitherto been rather unfashionable to notice –
shops, warehouses, mills, office blocks. The accumulation of this evidence is an
important task for industrial archaeology.

Wood

Timber engineering, too, has been much neglected. The great solid beams to be
found in large medieval buildings were becoming increasingly difficult to get, and
therefore increasingly expensive, during the seventeenth and eighteenth centuries
and a good deal of experimental work was carried out, both in Great Britain and
even more on the Continent, to discover alternative ways of supporting roofs and
ceilings. The problem was mainly one of finding a cheap and reliable method of
fastening the separate parts of a wooden structure together. Hand-made nails were
extremely expensive and bolts even more so. By the 1830s, however, long, strong,
machine-made bolts were available at a fraction of the former price, and the
railway engineers took full advantage of this to design some most impressive
wooden roofs for their new railway stations.

The first of the great wooden roofs was at Crown Hill, Liverpool (1830).
It has a 35 ft. span. This was followed by the more ambitious Lime Street Station
(1836), with a span of 55 ft., Paddington (1837) with 30 ft., and Bristol (1840),
with 72 ft. The most notable achievement of this kind, however, was at King's
Cross (1852), which was given two barrel vaults, carried on semi-circular wooden
arches, each with a span of 105 ft., springing from cast-iron shoes resting on piers
in the brickwork. The shoes are still there, but the wooden arches eventually had
to be replaced by wrought iron, the first in 1869 and the second in 1887. The wood
itself stood up excellently to the corrosive elements in the engine-smoke, but the
iron fastenings went to pieces rapidly, against the dual attack of smoke and damp
from the wood. The wooden trusses at Bristol, however, are still in place.

Even more remarkable, perhaps, than the station roofs were the great wooden
viaducts used by Brunel to carry his railway line through Devon and Cornwall.
These have long been replaced by masonry arches, but the original piers remain
in many places, abandoned and slightly to one side of the present position of the
track.

The mechanisation of wood sawing in England dates from the middle of the
eighteenth century. The first power-driven saw-mill was probably designed and
erected by James Stanfield in Yorkshire in 1761. It had three reciprocating vertical
frame-saws driven by a water-wheel. A second machine, in this case driven by a
wind vane, was built by Stanfield for a London timber merchant named Charles
Dingley at Limehouse. In 1779 Samuel Miller of Southampton built a machine

Roof timbering in Machine Shop, Railway Workshops, Swindon, in 1964

with circular saws, also driven by a windmill. Some years later, in 1808, William Newberry of London invented the band-saw. In spite of these inventions most of the timber continued to be cut by hand, by pit sawyers, at least until the middle of the nineteenth century.

Samuel Bentham invented the first planing machine for wood in 1791; and later some other machines which were set up in the house of Jeremy Bentham, his brother, in 1794; and this became the first mechanised wood-working factory in England. In 1794 the Admiralty set up Bentham machines in their dockyards at Portsmouth and Plymouth, and by 1803 some of these machines were driven by steam engines.

9

What to Look For: Transport

Roads

So far as Great Britain was concerned, there was no scientific road-building at all from the time the Romans left until half-way through the nineteenth century. The only known methods of making the highways more or less passable were to scrape off the mud and to fill in the worst of the holes either with brushwood or with stones.

The position probably got worse during the seventeenth and eighteenth centuries, with the increase in wheeled traffic, and in many areas the roads became so bad that they were practically unusable for anything more ambitious than riding horses and packhorse trains.[1] Before the coming of the railways, the only dependable way to transport heavy loads was by water, the possible exception being the route between London, Bath and Bristol – the two largest cities in the country and the main pleasure resort – where an exceptionally determined and expensive effort was thought to be worthwhile.

The nineteenth century saw only a very gradual improvement. Capital, and public interest, was devoted to building railways, not roads, partly because it was commonly believed that, in time, roads would inevitably be replaced by railways except for purely local traffic. The contrast with the position today is ironical.

When the problem was eventually grappled with, half-way through the nineteenth century, a number of new factors had arisen which made radical improvements essential – the urgent need for faster travel between London and

---

[1] A useful article on packhorse roads is Harry W. Hodgson's 'Packhorse Roads in Todmorden', *Industrial Archaeology*, November 1969. Mr. Hodgson walked over many miles of these old moorland roads and found them almost as they must have been in the eighteenth century (the new nineteenth century roads were constructed along the valley, not on the uplands). The Todmorden packhorse roads were carefully paved with slabs of the local gritstone.

the provinces, and for a more reliable method of moving raw materials and manufactured goods, the creation of administrative bodies suitable for dealing with transport and the revival of interest in road building among engineers.

It is curious that British engineers were so backward in turning their attention to the opportunities presented by the building of highways suited to contemporary traffic. The first real attempts since Roman times to build roads on scientific principles were made in France, in the seventeenth century, with an investigation into the methods used by the Romans. The French monarchy's dream of military grandeur, with the accompanying urge to move troops and equipment rapidly from one part of the country to another gave considerable impetus to this branch of civil engineering, and also to bridge building, and gave the engineers what they acquired only much later in Great Britain, prestige, administrative backing and reasonably adequate funds. It was the French who were the first to realise that an adequate road system was impossible without a proper centre for training the men who would have to design and build the roads. Formal, systematic instruction for this purpose was established in France in the early part of the eighteenth century, at a time when England was contenting itself with a not very effective combination of make-do-and-mend and learning on the job.

It is easy, none the less, to underestimate what was achieved in improving British roads during the eighteenth century. The ever-present problem was to finance the necessary work. Until the second half of the seventeenth century the only available way of getting roads repaired was to use statutory labour. Each individual local authority, and over most of the country this meant the parish, had a duty laid on it by Parliament to provide men and materials for maintaining the roads in its own area. The task was greatly disliked, and widely avoided, both by the men who actually carried it out and by those who were supposed to administer it. In 1663, the first turnpike was set up, on the Great North Road, on the theory that the people who used the roads were the people who ought to pay for them. By the 1830s there were more than 3700 separate turnpike trusts, controlling some 20,000 miles of highway; and spending perhaps two million pounds on repairing the roads under their charge. The majority of the turnpikes had gone by the 1880s, after a series of Public Health Acts had set up local governing bodies capable of maintaining the roads themselves.

An unusually thorough local survey of turnpike roads was carried out in the Bristol area during 1967–71 by members of the Bristol Industrial Archaeological Society, under the supervision of S. Allan Rees. The results were published in two issues of the *BIAS Journal*,[2] the fieldworkers' survey forms and maps having been deposited with the Department of Technology at Bristol City Museum. Working over a large part of North Somerset and South Gloucestershire and extending eastwards as far as Chippenham, Mr. Rees and his fellow-researchers set down every piece of evidence of the turnpikes they could find; boundary stones and posts, milestones and mileposts, and tollhouses. The quantity and variety of their

[2] 1968 and 1972.

Bath Turnpike Trust milestone

discoveries was remarkable, and a great encouragement to those contemplating similar projects in other districts.

The difficulties experienced by the turnpike trusts were technical, quite as much as administrative and financial. The roads they were attempting to maintain were, for the most part, quite unsuited to the traffic they were expected to carry. Until the end of the eighteenth century, the enormously heavy and cumbersome vehicles, with their huge, broad wheels, were extremely destructive of the road surface, and it was only the development of much lighter and better sprung carriages, coaches and, to a lesser extent, wagons, that made it rewarding to think in terms of a smoother type of road.

The fundamental attack on bad roads is quite reasonably associated with two men, who were exactly contemporary. Thomas Telford (1757–1834) pinned his faith to a carefully laid and packed foundation of large stones, covered with a relatively thin layer of small stones which the traffic would gradually consolidate. It was a vast improvement on anything seen before, but it had two failings. The top layer of fine material was too easily worn away and thrown aside by heavy traffic, a defect of no consequence in the case of Telford's highways in the sparsely populated Highlands, but serious elsewhere. And the foundation was very expensive to build.

John McAdam (1756–1836) worked on a different principle. For him, drainage was everything. If the road bed and the road surface could be kept dry, they would survive both bad weather and hard wear, with a minimum of maintenance. His method used small stones and avoided the costly base of hand-placed large stones and it proved popular with the authorities, who were always worried about their budgets. By 1900, approximately 90 per cent of the main roads of England and Wales had been rebuilt according to McAdam's theories, a fact not unconnected with the growing use of rubber tyres. Solid rubber tyres were available for carts by 1850, and for bicycles by 1865, while pneumatic tyres were coming on to the market in the last decade of the century.

Both Telford's and McAdam's methods have been described, documented and argued about in great detail. What is missing from a study of their work is a series of carefully planned excavations on suitable sites to show what a Telford or a McAdam road of the early nineteenth century really looked like from top to bottom and, as a secondary purpose, to discover what time has done to it. It is hardly reasonable to disrupt main road traffic in order to carry out an exploratory dig of this kind, but such an investigation is not impossible where the route of an old road has been changed and where the former highway has reverted to something little more than a lane or a track.

What is normally much more practicable, however, is to consult with the highway authorities and to find out when the trenches are to be dug for some purpose along or, even better, across one of these roads of the Industrial Revolution, in the hope that an archaeologically useful section may result. The modern carriageway, in many cases, was laid directly on top of the old water-bound surface and a great deal of the work of the pioneers like Telford and McAdam must be more or less safely preserved beneath the unknowing wheels of modern cars and lorries.

The same degree of co-operation with the local surveyor's department can also provide opportunities for studying the design of early nineteenth century sewers, gas and water mains, which have often had a phenomenally long life in suitable soils and where the community needs have not required the complete replacement of the old system. These services were an indispensable part of industrial growth and they deserve more adequate attention than archaeologists have so far given them. So, for that matter, do the sanitary facilities provided in eighteenth and nineteenth century factories. This, so far, is an almost totally neglected field of study.

The toll-houses, which are the one remaining feature of the old turnpike system, have never been surveyed in any systematic or comprehensive way. The trusts varied a good deal in the amount of money they felt able to spend on the accommodation for their turnpike keepers, but a careful study of the interiors of these often very pleasant little houses would be well worth making, partly from the architectural point of view and partly to reconstruct the kind of domestic life that was considered appropriate to these universally disliked servants of the Industrial Revolution. The present writer lived for some years in an eighteenth century toll-house and never ceased to wonder how a typically large family of the eighteenth and nineteenth centuries would have managed in it.

The later developments in road making techniques seem to fall rather outside the field of industrial archaeology, although quite conceivably posterity will not agree with this view. But, in case any early asphalt surfaces should somehow have happened to survive, it may be worth mentioning that by 1900 three different types of asphalt were in use.

One was made of rock-asphalt, broken up by heating and then spread and rolled. Another was a mastic, with sand and a filler added to it. This mixture was poured in position and smoothed out with a trowel. And the third type consisted of a hot mixture of bitumen, sand, a filler and fairly large stones, rolled down to provide a firm, smooth running surface. The engineers who laid the early asphalt roads had an essential tool which was not available to Telford or McAdam – a steam roller.

Other surfacing materials call for a brief note. Tar-bound macadam was laid experimentally in Nottingham in 1832. This is the first known instance in Great Britain, although research might well yield earlier examples. One or two stretches of woodblock roads were put down in London in the 1830s, but, despite the great advantage of their silent-running qualities, they were very slow in catching on. Even so, considerable stretches of Victorian and Edwardian woodblock, and of old tramlines, too, must still lie buried under modern asphalt, as road-making operations often reveal. And a good deal of the stone paving and kerbing that survives is certainly more than a century old. There are some excellent examples in Bath, for instance, and in one or two of the Lancashire industrial towns.

The most elaborate survey so far undertaken of the archaeology of a section of British roads was that planned and carried out in 1969 by the University of Southampton's Industrial Archaeology Group. The whole of Hampshire was covered. 'Compilers,' said the Group's published report,[3] 'were asked to record visible evidence of past road use, in the form of coaching inns, with their attendant livery stables, plus smithies, horse-troughs, any unusual non-standard road signs, hand water pumps, and the early type of petrol pump. It was not intended to confine attention solely to the past, but to record the situation on Hampshire roads at the time of the survey; hence more recent road works, widening, straightening and re-alignment, as well as the construction of new roundabouts and new routes, have been included.' Twenty-four people took part and allocated routes were surveyed by groups of three in a car – driver, observer and recorder. The complete record, together with field-books, was deposited in the Southampton University Library.

[3] D. J. Viner: 'The Industrial Archaeology of Hampshire Roads: a Survey', *Proceedings of the Hampshire Field Club*, Vol. XXVI, 1969.

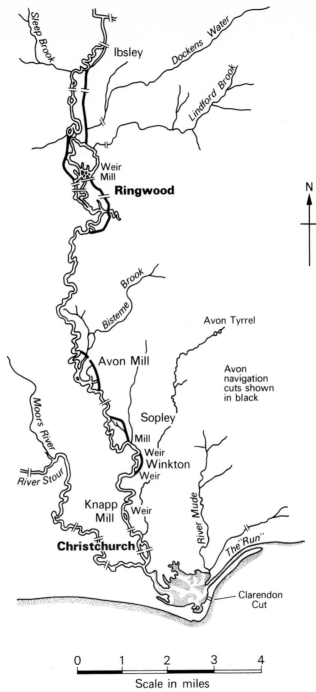

Canalisation of the Hampshire Avon (from *Industrial Archaeology*, May 1970)

Inland waterways

Navigable canals were being constructed in Britain from the sixteenth century onwards,[4] but the real development of the canal system of Great Britain can be dated from the Act for making navigable the Sankey Brook (St. Helen's Canal) in 1755. Before that date, rivers had been much used for transport, and on some of these artificial cuts had been made to shorten and straighten them, and locks built to make them more easily navigable.[5] From then until the middle of the nineteenth century, but mainly between 1765 and 1805, about 3000 miles of canals were added to the existing thousand miles of navigable rivers, and improvements were also made in the older form of water transport. After 1850, very little was done to extend or improve the system, although Britain's largest canal, the Manchester Ship Canal, was opened in 1894, unique among British canals in having been dug, not by spades and wheelbarrows, but by Ruston steam navvies.

British canals were of four main types: those to take ships of the coasting and foreign trades, with the necessary depth and size of locks and basins; those which usually communicated with river navigations, took river barges, and had locks about 14 ft. wide; narrow canals with locks about 7 ft. wide; and tub-boat canals, found mainly in the hilly parts of Shropshire and the West Country and taking boats some 20 ft. by 5 ft. that could be carried over inclined planes.

The main lines of canal, and their bigger branches, were usually built by public companies, occasionally by individuals, but many smaller branches, often to collieries or works, were constructed privately by their owners. The system of canals and navigable rivers, much of it still in existence, therefore reflects the industrial and agricultural trading needs of the period that ended about 1850, and it should be considered, together with the contemporary horse railways and tram-roads, the turnpike and parish roads, many of which acted as canal feeders, and with port development, as one part of a transport complex.

The features to look for along navigable, or formerly navigable rivers include:

Wharves Most riverside villages once had their own wharves where coal, road-stone, limestone, lime and other heavy and bulky goods were landed, and agricultural produce loaded for shipment away. There might be a small warehouse and a public-house nearby. Bigger places, such as Bewdley, had extensive warehouses and wharves where goods were trans-shipped to and from packhorses

---

[4] The Exeter ship canal, running from Exeter to Topsham and begun in 1564, was the first canal in England to use the pound-lock.

[5] The Salisbury Avon, for instance, was made navigable from Salisbury to Christchurch during the late seventeenth and early eighteenth centuries, following the River Avon Navigation Act of 1664. The Salisbury and South Wiltshire Industrial Archaeology Society has explored the river in order to identify the canalised stretches of the river and a report on their discoveries (Donald A. E. Cross: 'The Salisbury Avon Navigation', *Industrial Archaeology*, May 1970) has been published. A curious fact which emerged from this survey is that there is very little evidence of a towpath anywhere along the route.

One of the flight of locks on the Kennet & Avon Canal at Devizes, Wiltshire

and wagons. Certain towns, such as Gainsborough, were trans-shipment points from river to sea-going craft. They consequently needed a great deal of warehouse accommodation for goods waiting for ships and also houses for merchants, sailors and bargemen.

Locks These were usually built in connexion with mills. Riverside mills needed a head of water to drive their wheels and therefore had a weir across the river below the mill-stream intake to maintain it. In order to pass boats through, part of this weir was made moveable. Sluices were opened and water allowed to run past the weir till the level on each side had equalised. The boat then passed through the weir, the moveable part, called a flash-lock,[6] was restored, and the level of the water raised again. Alternatively, a single pair of gates, called a half-lock, or staunch, was built across a side-cut from the river, the water-level of the river being again equalised before a boat could pass. Mill sites will often show

---

[6] Flash-locks were so called because they helped boats over shallows or a weir by releasing a 'flash' or flush of water. They were extremely wasteful of water and often failed to work at all during a dry season. A survey of flash-lock remains was carried out in the 1960s by M. J. T. Lewis, W. N. Slatcher and P. N. Jarvis. They found and recorded ('Flashlocks on English Waterways', *Industrial Archaeology*, August 1969) 73 sites, nearly all in three areas, the Thames basin, some tributaries of the Severn, and the rivers on the edge of the Fens.

the position of the weir also, while that of old staunches can be located from the masonry or brick remains of the side walls. The most easily traceable examples are usually in East Anglia.

On some rivers the flash-locks and half-locks were replaced by pound-locks, each with two pairs of gates enclosing a chamber in which the boat rises or falls as the necessary sluices are worked, or pound-locks were built at new sites. The ruined masonry of many of these old locks can still be found upon such rivers as the Yorkshire Foss or Derwent, or the Western Rother or the Ouse in Sussex.

Artificial cuts Some of these shortened the course of the river, as on the Kennet or Itchen. Others by-passed a length of it, as on the Welland, near Stamford; and others again form a branch from it, as at Cassington, near Eynsham, on the Thames.

Towpaths Some river navigations had no horse towpaths, the hauling being done by men. Where a path was provided, it was sometimes controlled by one or more separate bodies, as on the Severn and the Wye. The old paths can often be traced, toll houses found and the points identified at which ferries were provided to carry the horses across when the path changed sides.

Boat-building yards Most of the boat-building yards have vanished almost without trace, but diligent enquiry will enable the sites of many of them to be identified on, for example, the Severn, the Wye and the Trent.

Limekilns

Limekilns were often built alongside navigable rivers and canals. The Rolle Canal,[7] along the valley of the River Torridge in North Devon, was built in the 1820s specifically to transport limestone and the coal to burn it inland from the coast. Limestone is not found in North Devon and, since burnt lime corrodes timber, it could not be carried in the wooden ships of the eighteenth and early nineteenth centuries. The practice was consequently to ship limestone and coal from South Wales to kilns on the coast. The farmers who were close to the sea found this was an efficient system, but for those inland the bad North Devon roads made carriage impossibly expensive. The eight miles of canal, from south of Landcross to east of Little Torrington were built to remedy this situation. The whole cost of between £40,000 and £45,000 was met by a local landowner, Lord John Rolle.

The Rolle Canal was only 13 ft. wide and 2 ft. 9 ins. deep. It was just wide enough for two tub-boats to pass. Each boat carried four tons of cargo and the boats were towed, in sets of six, by a horse. The route included an aqueduct and an inclined plane. The Canal closed in 1871 when the Bideford to Torrington railway was built. Part of the railway ran over the bed of the canal.

[7] On its history, see Barry D. Hughes, 'The Rolle Canal', *Industrial Archaeology*, February 1970.

The following details of canals are likely to be of particular archaeological interest:

Types of construction of the waterway

It is broadly true that the earlier the canal, the more it followed the contours, and the later, the more likely it was to use embankments and cuttings in the interest of a straighter line. We may compare the curving line of the Oxford Canal,[8] between Braunston and Banbury (early 1770s) with the Shropshire Union main line from Nantwich to Autherley, near Wolverhampton (early 1830s). A few of the contour canals were subsequently straightened, notably the northern part of the Oxford – Braunston to Hawkesbury – and the original line of the Birmingham Canal between that town and Wolverhampton.

Locks These pound-locks can be single, staircase – the top gates of one forming the bottom gates of the next – or double – side by side. They are often grouped in flights, such as those at Tardebigge, near Bromsgrove, which has thirty locks and Devizes, with twenty-nine. Various means of saving water can be noticed, such as side-ponds – small reservoirs into which water from an emptying lock could run, so that it could be used again – or sluices, with the same purpose, to interconnect double locks. A few locks are not of the usual rectangular-chambered shape, and some have gates of the vertically rising or guillotine type. A stop or regulating lock was built where one canal joined another, even if there were no change in level. This prevented loss of water by one company to the other, should a burst or leak cause a change of level. A single pair of gates is sometimes found. These are stop-gates, used for shutting off a section of canal, so that it can be drained for repairs. More often, planks are slipped into slots provided under bridges or at specially narrowed places.

Inclined planes, to carry boats up and down a railway laid between two sections of canal. About twenty were built in Great Britain. None are now working, but almost all can be traced.

Lifts, which raised boats vertically from one level to another. Only a few were built. One was still working at Anderton in Cheshire until a few years ago, and there are ruins of others in Somerset.

Tunnels About forty-two miles of canal tunnel were built, varying from those a few yards long to Standedge (5415 yards) under the Pennines, near Huddersfield.

---

[8] The archaeology of James Brindley's Oxford Canal (1790) is described by Ron Davenport in 'Warwickshire's Forgotten Canal to Oxford', *Industrial Archaeology*, May 1972. Its 'river-like appearance' is contrasted with William Cubitt's route, $13\frac{1}{2}$ miles shorter, with deep cuttings and tall embankments.

The usual method of construction was by vertical shafts, the material being lifted by horse-gins. The sites of shafts and of spoil-heaps can be found. The dimensions of canal tunnels varied from 35 ft. high by $26\frac{1}{2}$ ft. wide at Strood, Kent, to $9\frac{1}{4}$ ft. high by 6 ft. wide at Morwelldown, Devon. The earlier tunnels had no towpath through them, so horses were led over the top. The old horse-paths can still be found. The one over Harecastle tunnel, near Stoke-on-Trent, has become immortalised as Boathorse Road.

Aqueducts James Brindley built the first notable canal aqueduct over the Irwell, near Manchester. It was replaced later by the existing Barton swing aqueduct over the Manchester Ship Canal. The abutments of the original structure still remain. Most aqueducts are built of masonry with a puddled channel for the canals. Some of these impressive memorials of the engineers are at Lancaster (Rennie), Marple (Outram), between Bradford-on-Avon and Bath (Rennie), and the Kelvin aqueduct on the Forth and Clyde Canal (Whitworth). An important single-arched brick aqueduct is over the Rea near Tenbury on the derelict Leominster Canal. In the 1790s and later, some aqueducts with iron troughs were built, first at Longdon-on-Tern, in Shropshire, and also at Derby Bearley (Warwickshire), Wolverton, over the Great Ouse, and, most notable of all, at Pont Cysylte, near Ruabon.

Road or accommodation bridges These were fixed bridges, usually of stone or brick, and varying slightly in design on each canal. Some were specially elaborated to suit the taste of local potentates. They usually have a towpath running

Footing a barge through a tunnel on the Peak Forest Canal, *c.*1950

Canal-side maltings, Devizes, Wiltshire. Built *c.*1815, to take advantage of the cheap freight available on the Kennet and Avon Canal

underneath, and sometimes a guard strip or rollers is fitted to prevent towlines rubbing on the masonry edge of the arch. Occasionally, as on the Stratford Canal, iron bridges with a divided arch are to be found. The towline was passed through the slit in the arch. Many patterns of lifting and swing bridges are found, some of them most attractively designed.

Mileposts, usually of iron, sometimes of stone, the design varying with the canal.

Houses, now sometimes used for other purposes. These could be:

(a) for lock-keepers. These houses were placed near one or more locks. Each canal had its own special design for them, the single-storey barrel-roofed type of the Stratford Canal, for instance, or those of Dutch appearance on the Droitwich Canal.
(b) for lengthsmen – maintenance staff – as in the case of the round houses on the Thames and Severn Canal.
(c) toll-houses, sometimes with a look-out window, and usually placed at junctions or where a canal entered a basin, as at Stourport.
(d) for bridge-keepers. One thinks, for instance, of the little classical houses on the Gloucester and Berkeley Canal, where the men lived who helped to swing the bridge.

(e) for wharfingers. These are found on both village and town wharves. They are usually plain structures, but sometimes they are of special design, like the combined wharf and warehouses at Cricklade and Kempsford on the Thames and Severn, and harbour-masters' houses at basins or sea-locks.

(f) for boatmen. These are normally found in terraces near old canal basins or junctions.

Other buildings to be looked for are warehouses, old stables for the boat-houses, smithies, and canal-side public-houses. Not infrequently the public-house preserves the memory of a long vanished canal. In London, for example, there are at least two instances where public-houses give the clue to the former terminus of a canal which was replaced many years ago by a railway – the 'Grosvenor Basin' in Wilton Road, Victoria (demolished in 1960) and the remarkable and otherwise inexplicable collection of pubs in Warwick Road, Kensington, where the Kensington Canal formerly terminated.

Water supplies Each canal had one or more reservoirs, and usually rights to take water from local streams, and feeders from such supplies are therefore found. Another source of water was by pumping from a river, perhaps by water-wheel, as at Claverton on the Kennet and Avon near Bath, or by steam, as at Crofton on the same canal near Savernake. A number of the old pumping engines still exist.

Structures associated with boats Few traces remain of the early boat-weighing docks that were used to index boats, that is, to find out what weights they carried at various depths of loading. However, a number of dry-docks and boat-building basins still exist, as at Stone in Staffordshire.

Canal branches There are usually short branch canals running to works or collieries, or to a former wharf beside a road. Many sites can only be found with the help of early Ordnance plans or by consulting tithe or similar maps. A large number of early horse railway or tram-road feeders to canals were also built, and the remains of them can often be traced.

One difficulty involved in any investigation of the history and development of canals in the eastern counties, and particularly in the Fens, is that some of the artificial waterways there were constructed for drainage purposes and it needs a good deal of further investigation to be sure whether they were at any time regularly used for navigation by freight-carrying craft, whether, in fact, they were canals in the usual sense of the word.

Ports and harbours

'Most of the buildings of the old port of Boston,' wrote N. R. Wright ten years ago, 'are Georgian granaries and warehouses, which have altered very little in structure, although their use has changed. Few later buildings intrude among them, and until recently the character of the area had been preserved for over 150 years. The situation is now ending, however, as the buildings are being demolished for modern developments.'[9]

Mr. Wright could not have carried out his research, taken his photographs, or written his article today. Of the seven warehouses he described, only two now remain. The others have been the casualties of road-widening and car parks.

Since 1945 the same fate has overtaken early warehouses and other port installations in many other parts of Britain. Weymouth, for example, has lost a group of elegant Georgian warehouses and there have been regrettable losses of a similar kind at King's Lynn, Penzance and Bristol. Civil engineering works are fortunately more difficult to destroy than warehouses, custom houses and post offices. John Rennie's great breakwater at Plymouth (1811–1848), a mound of limestone blocks tipped on to the sea-bed and faced with carefully dressed and fitted stone, is in as good condition as when it was built, and so are William Jessop's West India Docks (1799–1802) in the Port of London and the same engineer's Floating Harbour (1803–8) in Bristol, although the southern entrance lock was subsequently reconstructed to designs prepared by Isambard Brunel.[10] The most remarkable item of archaeology in the Port of Bristol is undoubtedly the nineteenth century dock where Brunel's 'Great Britain' was built and where she is now being restored after being brought back from the Falkland Islands as a mere hulk. The continued existence of the dock is miraculous, or, as some critics of the British economy might feel entitled to say, evidence of the disastrous failure of our industry to modernise itself. The historian's dream is the economist's horror.

Telford's splendid warehouse complex (1832–43) at Ellesmere Port, Cheshire, was completely gutted by fire in 1970, but Jesse Hartley's Albert Dock in Liverpool (1845) has met with a better fate. This five-storey rectangle of fireproof warehouses, one of the nineteenth century's greatest achievements in industrial architecture, has now been converted to educational purposes. The buildings, by Telford and Philip Hardwick, at St. Katharine's Dock in London have had mixed fortunes. One warehouse has been converted, very successfully, into expensive flats, another has been badly damaged by fire before a similar conversion could be carried out, and other buildings around the dock have been pulled down to make room for the World Trade Centre and a hotel.

At Gainsborough,[11] an important river port and entrepot in the eighteenth and early nineteenth centuries for goods from the Midlands and the Baltic, archaeological survivals are more plentiful, largely because the building of the railway to Grimsby in the 1850s caused Gainsborough to decline as a port. The old warehouses, wharves, granaries and shipyard were left to moulder quietly

[9] 'Buildings of the Old Port of Boston, Lincolnshire', *Industrial Archaeology*, December 1965.

[10] On this and other modifications to the Harbour, see Angus Buchanan, 'The Cumberland Basin, Bristol', *Industrial Archaeology*, November 1969.

[11] See Ian Beckwith, 'Gainsborough: the Industrial Archaeology of a Lincolnshire Town', *Industrial Archaeology*, August 1971.

away, because there was no particular point in pulling them down. The story
has been repeated in many other ports around our coast.

Railways

The earliest known railway in Great Britain was at Wollaton, near Nottingham,
brought into use in 1604. It had wooden rails and no trace of them remains. From
that date there was a continuous growth of horse-worked wagonways associated
with the mining and smelting industries, particularly in Northumberland,
Durham and Shropshire. Railways as feeders to canals were introduced about
1773 – the earliest definite case concerns the Chester Canal, and the first public
line, the Surrey Iron Railway, started work in 1803. Up to 1830, when the
Liverpool and Manchester was opened, railways were little more than an
extension of the turnpike road system. They were free to all on payment of a toll,
and hauliers provided their own horses and wagons and in one or two cases,
locomotives.

The early tramroads – railways over which the trucks were hauled by horses –
have become a popular field of study for industrial archaeologists. The authoritative work on them, Bertram Baxter's *Stone Blocks and Iron Rails*, was published
in 1966. The result of many years enthusiastic research, it included a gazetteer
with basic details of every tramroad in England, Scotland and Wales. 'The
entries there,' another tramroad devotee, Philip Riden, has written, 'coupled
with the bibliography, provide a very useful starting-point for local work on the
industrial archaeology of an individual line or group of lines.' Mr. Riden's
special interest is Derbyshire, and he notes[12] that Bertram Baxter lists fifty tramroads within the county, mostly based on one of Derbyshire's seven canals. Of
these fifty, seven were connected with the Chesterfield Canal and another three
within its immediate vicinity. Philip Riden based his own very detailed paper on
these ten entries, an interesting example of the way in which a local fieldworker
can develop a part of a national survey in much greater detail.[13]

Railways, in the usual sense of the word, date from about 1830. With certain
exceptions, the rolling stock and motive power were provided by the railway
company. Because of the nature of their business, it was necessary to plan and
construct early railways as an adjunct to industry, and the remains of lines built
up to about 1820 are mainly in well defined areas – Northumberland, Durham,
the Forest of Dean, Monmouthshire and Cornwall – though isolated lines
appeared in the rural counties of Brecon, Hereford, Surrey and Warwick.

From their earliest days, each of the railways developed individual characteristics of its own. The engineers, and later, the architects, had freedom to work out

[12] 'Tramroads in North-East Derbyshire', *Industrial Archaeology*, November 1970.

[13] On this, see D. E. Bick, 'Tramplates of the Gloucester and Cheltenham Railway', *Industrial
Archaeology*, August 1966. This particular tramroad was opened in 1811 to take coal, roadstone and
other heavy freight from Gloucester to Cheltenham and to bring back agricultural produce and
stone from Leckhampton quarries.

Early broad gauge railway coach in use as cottage and chicken house at South Cerney, Gloucestershire

Front panel of the South Cerney coach being removed for storage at the Bristol City Museum

their own ideas. Much depended on the affluence of the company. The first railways thought not of artistic design, but only of utility, and certainly too, of durability. Some of the early railway buildings were clearly a perpetuation of the turnpike and canal tradition, and particularly of the toll houses which had become a familiar feature of the English landscape.

The course of early railways which remain undisturbed, have substantial remains, which are often in good condition, either because of their solid construction or because of careful maintenance by their present owners. The surviving structures are most likely to be over- or under-bridges, culverts, toll and dwelling houses, tunnels, cuttings and embankments. The 1826 Stratford and Moreton Railway, in Warwickshire, retains a pleasing brick toll house and a graceful four-arch river bridge at Stratford-upon-Avon, with an under-bridge, in a poor state of repair and a well-preserved private road over-bridge, just outside the town. A portion of the site of the railway is now a public footpath.

The Hay and Kington Railways (1816–20) provide excellent examples of both stone and cast-iron river bridges, at Afon Llynfi and Kington respectively, and of a stone culvert, near Eardisley. These little-known remains are on private land, but they are readily accessible. It should be remembered, however, that the sites of some early lines have been obliterated by subsequent railway construction or, after they were abandoned, became covered over by roads or housing estates. In such cases it was usual to demolish all the buildings and it is rare for anything tangible to remain.

Where a railway has been closed, its former tunnels frequently remain as marooned holes in the hill to remind the investigator of the disused line which they once served. They are likely to be found as often in town centres as in more remote areas. A good example exists at Clifton, near Manchester, and there is another right under the city of Edinburgh. The first railway tunnel in the world (1809), at Bullo Pill, in the Forest of Dean, still survives.

As railways developed, there was a great increase in the number and variety of structures necessary to handle increasing goods traffic and to provide for the carriage of passengers by locomotive-hauled trains. Adjacent inns were no longer suitable as passenger accommodation and stations were built. Bridges spanned wider waterways, tunnels were longer and of larger bore, level crossings had to be provided with gate-houses, signal boxes and various line-side buildings began to appear. All these in due course gave scope to the architect and designer, though it is to be regretted so many of these have disappeared without record.

Railways and railway relics have been the subject of many years devoted, not to say fanatical study by railway historians, and an immense number of photographs have been accumulated over the years. No branch of industrial archaeology has received as much attention as railways. A careful and unbiased examination of even the best books about railways reveals, however, that enthusiasts and authorities in this field are very selective in their interests. Much, possibly too much, has been written about locomotives, signalling, operating methods and the permanent way, and remarkably little about wages, refreshment

Backs of houses in the Railway Village, Swindon (1840s), before modernisation

Houses in the Railway Village during modernisation (1960s). Work on the houses at the left of the picture has been completed. At the back of the terrace on the right the old wash-houses and outdoor privies have been demolished, but the new outbuildings have not yet been started

Railway Village: restored fronts of houses

rooms, booking-offices and fares. Opportunities for carrying out research into these neglected railway matters become more difficult each year, as stations are demolished and modernised and railway veterans die off, but even a late start is better than none. One could put the weakness in existing railway history in another way, by saying that what is urgently needed is a small supply of experts whose interests are social as much as technical. The historically and socially minded engineer is unfortunately a rare animal in any branch of industrial archaeology, nearly as rare as the engineering-minded historian or sociologist.

Station buildings have received a great deal of attention, although those of architectural distinction – the small minority – have received over-much publicity. In Britain, as elsewhere, the little country station was the norm, until the wholesale butchery of stations which took place during the 1950s and 1960s. The survival of the larger stations and the disappearance of the smaller ones is an archaeological falsification of railway history and every effort should be made to restore the true picture, especially for the benefit of the increasing number of younger people who never knew the railways in their prime.

David Lloyd's important article, 'Railway Station Architecture',[14] contains a descriptive list of the sixty stations which, in the author's opinion, are most worthy of preservation. They are divided into 'large', 'medium-large', 'medium-small' and 'small', which is as sensible a way as any of going about the business. Mr. Lloyd, a collaborator of Sir Nikolaus Pevsner, has a poetic feeling for buildings which allows him to sense the individuality and charm of these old stations. His description of the station at Newmarket, for example, shows how it is possible to transcend mere technicalities.

'The mysterious gem of East Anglia,' he writes, 'is the old station at Newmarket, opened in 1848, at the end of a branch (from Great Chesterford) which lasted only two years, and was then superseded by a line from Cambridge (with another station). Used for goods until recently, it is now slowly decaying, but its beautiful façade, with pairs of Ionic columns jutting out boldly between round-arched window openings, and an entablature with little turrets following the rhythm of the columns, is still intact. Nobody knows who designed it – Wood, Barnes, Thompson? An air of mystery regarding their authorship hangs over all these distinguished East Anglian stations.'

Ancillary railway buildings, such as stationmasters' houses and railway hotels have shown remarkable stamina, often surviving long after the station they served has disappeared or ceased to function. Many station-houses are surprisingly early. A notable example is that at Micheldever in Hampshire, which dates from 1839 and has an elegant verandah supported by iron pillars.

The smaller railway items are usually those with the most charm. One can often find, for example, cast-iron seats of unusual design incorporating some special device, such as a knot, in the case of the North Staffordshire Railway, or a

---

[14] *Industrial Archaeology*, August 1967.

squirrel for the Furness Railway. Awning brackets and lamp-posts are often fine examples of ornamental cast-iron work. In Scotland a few lamp-posts, though far from their original sites, include the railway company's initials on the ladder crossbar.

There are also a few surviving examples of early locomotive sheds, mostly of the round-house type. The best known of these is in London, at Camden Town. After a number of years' service as a wine and spirit warehouse it is now a theatre.

Every railway adopted its own design of signal box. Many of these are well proportioned and pleasing to look at. Few are now over one hundred years old, but at remote stations the original boxes may still be found, usually out of use. The construction was generally all-wood, or wood on a brick substructure. A small number of all-stone boxes are found in the North of England. One or two at level crossings have bow windows.

Crests, armorial devices and monograms of both companies and influential land-owners are to be seen in many places, often in unusual positions. When Bangor station was rebuilt, the Chester and Holyhead Railway monograms from the previous building were incorporated in the new one. The Midland Railway's wyvern decorates that company's Avon bridge at Bath. This example is in metal and a carved replica in stone is over a tunnel entrance at Heeley, Sheffield. A Furness Railway armorial device, also in stone, is found on one of the few stone signal boxes, now disused, at Carnforth, in Lancashire.

Mile posts were made compulsory in 1845, but most railways had them long before that date. Both stone and cast-iron may be found on line sites now abandoned. Cast-iron examples from 1815 exist in the Forest of Dean, though they are not easily found.

Necessity for replacement has swept away virtually all the early railway machinery and equipment, though some have been preserved by the Railways Board and its predecessors. The outstanding survival is probably the famous Butterley beam engine (1825), still hauling wagons up Middleton Incline, near Cromford, Derbyshire, and the equipment in the repair shops, dating from about 1835. It is unlikely that any earlier plant is now in active use.

Two other kinds of physical evidence bearing on railways might be mentioned. The first is the considerable number of spoil banks, to be found all over the country, where the surplus soil from tunnel excavations was dumped. Spoilbank Wood, near Potters Bar, is one such case and some of the great quantity of earth and rock from the Kilsby Tunnel, near Rugby, was dumped away from the railway, creating a now forgotten change in the local scenery.

There is physical evidence, too, in various places of the boundary of the property line relating to long-abandoned railways being given over to other purposes. Two examples of this are at Oxford and Cambridge. At Cambridge the boundary of the course of the former link between Cambridge station and the Newmarket line is clearly visible on the map appended to the volume published by the Historical Monuments Commission, and at Oxford the course of the long-disused line to the old Great Western terminus, south of Folly Bridge, can be picked up from the still existing garden boundaries behind the houses in Hinksey Road.

The sites of long-abandoned early railways are often no longer shown on maps (the new 25-inch maps omit virtually all these old lines), though an occasional stretch of embankment or cutting, or a length clearly marked by surviving twin hedges, may sometimes be marked 'track of old railway'. This indication on an Ordnance Survey map may, however, be misleading, since there are really three types of abandoned railway:

(a) Lines which were used for railway traffic for a number of years, and which have ceased to be operated.
(b) A few lines which were fully constructed, but never opened to traffic. These include, for instance, a section on the Cambrian system, leading from Llanidloes in the direction of Llangurig, on which for many years there was a fully equipped signal post.
(c) Portions of line on which construction was begun, but never completed, leaving a series of discontinuous pieces of work, like the Ouse Valley Railway, which joins the London and Brighton line immediately south of the Balcombe viaduct and of which intermittent traces can be seen near Lindfield and again near Uckfield.

There is very little trustworthy literature on this subject. The sites of all the more important and nearly all the lesser lines are known to railway historians, even if they have not yet been examined or written up in detail. The help of the Railway and Canal Historical Society is freely available to anyone requiring information on a particular line or area. Some pre-knowledge of the railway's history is essential to a survey of its remains. Without this knowledge, important features may well be overlooked, even by the most experienced fieldworker.

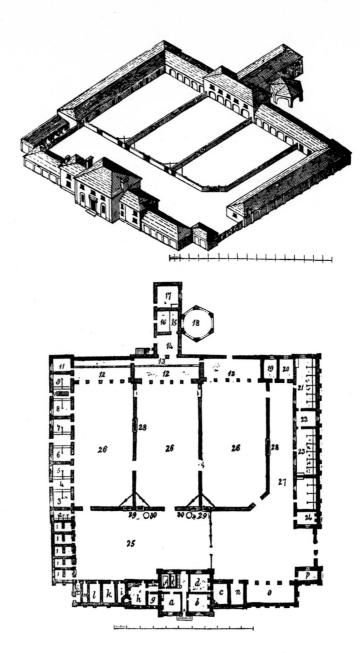

Mid-nineteenth century design for a large farmhouse and outbuildings. The six-sided building in the top right-hand corner was to shelter the horse-gear, for driving machinery in the barn behind

10

Farm Buildings and
Industrial Change

The rapid growth of population during the eighteenth and nineteenth centuries gave rise to an increased demand for food. Farming became primarily a commercial enterprise, an industry, in fact, and less a subsistence occupation. There was, as a result, considerable interest in the planning and rebuilding of farmsteads. New farming methods, new machinery, enclosures, the reclaiming of derelict land and an increasing tendency towards mixed farming made bigger and more conveniently designed farmsteads necessary. As a result, landlords and their more go-ahead tenants took a keen interest in designing buildings which would accommodate all the necessary farm stock and provide adequate room for the storage of crops and machinery, and enable the processing of crops such as threshing corn, making cider or butter, cutting chaff and breaking oil-cake to be done under cover.

A great deal of thought and ingenuity went into the design of these buildings and in the days of cheap and plentiful labour they served their purpose well. Until the 1860s, when it became possible to send milk by train, the liquid milk market was restricted to the areas surrounding the large towns and for this reason dairying, except in the traditional butter and cheese districts, like Cheshire and Somerset, was unimportant. Most of these farmstead, or farmeries as they were often called, were designed for a mixed system of arable and cattle fattening. Today these steadings, many of them monumental in conception, are too inflexible for modern farming systems and are either being radically altered or permitted to decay.

The majority of them were built between the end of the Napoleonic wars and the 1870s, when the competition from imported food brought a halt to expansion. Many of them were built of local materials, in the traditional styles – for example, stone in the Cotswolds and the north and wood in the east – but after the middle of the nineteenth century there was an increasing tendency, in all parts of the country, to use red brick, slate and cast iron. In cases where landlords provided new buildings for their whole estate, similar designs were employed throughout all the farmsteads and those can sometimes be spotted today from the marked similarity of design or from certain architectural features which the buildings and houses have in common. On the Ragley Estates in Warwickshire, for instance, the Marquis of Hertford appeared to favour mock iron cannons for the gateposts of the farm entrances. Landlords very often built large numbers of cottages at the same time to house farm workers. Not uncommonly, the same design was used for the majority of the cottages on the estate. A good example is Alscot Estate, in Warwickshire, especially in Alderminster village.

The system of buildings depended, of course, on the size of the farm. For the larger farms of, say, over three hundred acres, it was common to include provision in the centre of the buildings for a steam engine to drive all the barn machinery. There are a number of farms with the engine chimneys still surviving, though many of these stacks have been taken down. The engine room either contained a fixed steam engine or merely a place for a portable engine to stand when it was required, with its funnel under the chimney. In some places, although the engines have gone, the shafting which they drove still runs the length of the barn and occasionally some of the now redundant machinery – threshers, grain cleaners, chaff cutters, root slicers, cake breakers – is still in position. Government grants for the improvement and rehabilitation of old buildings have caused many of these installations to disappear without trace.

Another feature sometimes found in association with the barns was a small railway to bring the corn ricks in from the rick-yard to the barn. At harvest time the ricks were actually built on small bogies, so that a horse would pull them into the barn for threshing. No installations of this kind are still known to exist, although it is worth searching for evidence of them.

A good example of the heavy investment of capital which mid-nineteenth century landowners were prepared to make, in order to modernise their farm buildings, is at Childerley, near Cambridge. Here, on a thousand acre farm, two similar sets of buildings in brick and slate were put up in the 1850s. In each set there were three half-covered cattle yards for fattening with three long barns running end to end under one roof across the ends of the yards. The food for each yard was thus conveniently available close to it. The tall brick building with the weather vane housed the steam engine underneath and the mill on top. Shafting ran from the steam engine along the barns. The stables and implement sheds were at one end of the range. A number of cottages were built close to the buildings at the same time.

Uphampton Farm, at Shobdon, in Herefordshire, was the home farm of Lord Bateman. It was built in 1861, of the local blue stone and Welsh slate, and cost £4500. The machinery included a 12 h.p. steam engine, a combined threshing and corn dressing machine, fed by a railway which ran from the stackyard, a root pulper and cutter, a straw litter cutter, a chaff cutter, and cake, oat and bran crushers. The threshed grain was carried to storage bins by an Archimedean

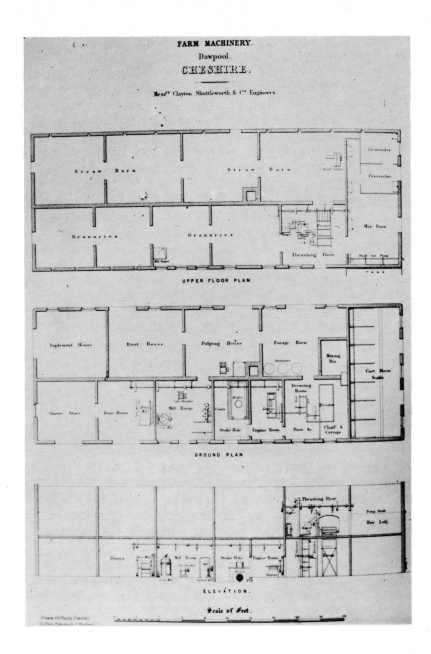

Layout of farm machinery installed (*c*.1870) by Clayton, Shuttleworth at Dawpool, Cheshire

screw and the straw was taken by elevators into storage barns. There was food steaming apparatus in the mixing house and also a cider press and apple mill from which cider was conveyed by $1\frac{1}{2}$ in. galvanised pipe to cellars.[1]

The most impressive agricultural enterprise of all, however, may well have been Buscot Park in Berkshire.[2] This 3500 acre estate was bought, in a very run-down condition, by Robert Campbell in 1859. He had recently returned from Australia, where he had made a fortune, and proceeded to transform his new property in the most adventurous way. A huge drainage programme was undertaken, an irrigation system installed and a six-mile light railway laid. The cuttings and other evidence of the railway are still visible and lengths of rail have been used for fencing. A telegraph provided instant communication between different points on the estate.

A large acreage was sown to sugar-beet – Campbell was one of the early pioneers of this crop – and a distillery and sugar factory were built to make use of the beet. Other industrial buildings included an oil-cake mill, a gas-works and a fertiliser factory.

Outstanding among all the buildings at Buscot was a magnificent, cast-on-site barn of mass concrete, in Buscot village, 162 ft. long, 60 ft. broad and 12 ft. 6 ins. to the eaves. Built in 1870, this pre-dates the other known concrete farm buildings by about thirty years.

A by-product of the vogue for reclaiming waste land was the large number of wind and steam pumps erected for drainage purposes. A number of these still remain in the Fen country and on the Norfolk Broads, though they have mostly been superseded by more modern engines. Many of the drainage channels cut to carry away the water from these large-scale reclamations are, of course, still in use. Underdrainage – the laying of clay pipes beneath the soil – which in the nineteenth century improved the quality of so much heavy land, though still functioning, is not visible on the surface and the only trace of it is the occasional decorated cast iron outfall along the banks of ditches.

It is interesting to speculate on what the appearance and equipment of British farms would be today if a series of agricultural depressions from the 1870s onwards, produced by the import of cheap foodstuffs from abroad, had not undermined the ability and the willingness of nineteenth century and early twentieth century landowners to clear away obsolete buildings and to mechanise agricultural operations wherever possible.

Since 1939, the opportunities presented by the war began an inflow of capital back into British farming which has done a good deal to turn a starved and backward industry into one more capable of surviving and prospering in the face of

---

[1] Nineteenth century textbooks abound with designs of such buildings. Good examples may be found in J. C. Loudon's *Encyclopaedia of Agriculture* (1831), J. C. Morton's *Cyclopaedia of Agriculture* (1855) and J. B. Denton's *Farm Homesteads of England* (1864).

[2] Described by John R. Gray, in 'An Industrial Farm Estate in Berkshire', *Industrial Archaeology*, May 1971. Another example of a narrow-gauge farm railway was on the Nocton Estate near Lincoln.

international competition. But this very process, with its amalgamation of small units and its demand for the type of buildings suited to a modern, highly mechanised agriculture, is inevitably sweeping away many of the remains of previous waves of improvement. This, coupled with the hunger of the war years for the scrap metal contained in old farm machinery, has removed much of the evidence of the revolution in agriculture which was a not unimportant part of the Industrial Revolution itself.

11

Recording, Publication and Documentation

Recording and publication

Communication of one's discoveries is implicit in any form of archaeology, but achieving this is not always easy. Much of the work carried out within the field of industrial archaeology within the past twenty years must still, for lack of inclination or opportunity, be lying hidden away and sterile in the form of unpublished, unwritten-up notes, or, somewhat less inaccessible, in the bulletins and newsletters of local societies. Nearly all societies have a publication of some kind. A frequently found pattern is to issue a journal once or twice a year and to supplement this by a newsletter, sent out perhaps quarterly. The journals, running to fifty pages and more, give members an opportunity to present the results of their work in a form which can be filed in libraries, reviewed and made available to other people with similar interests. The Sussex Society is exceptional in putting the production and distribution of its journal in the hands of a firm of commercial publishers, although one or two of the other societies are fortunate in being able to call on specialist help from particular members, which allows their publications to achieve professional standards.

A number of industrial archaeology groups are off-shoots of a larger society and rely on the parent society to provide the opportunities for publication. This happens in the case of, for example, Southampton University, which uses the *Proceedings* of the Hampshire Field Club, and Cornwall, where the area is covered by *Cornish Archaeology*. Where this is possible, the method has a good deal to recommend it, mainly because the larger the publication, the wider its circulation is likely to be. There are, however, great advantages in having a specialist publication, devoted entirely to industrial archaeology and industrial history. The editor of a county archaeological journal is almost certain to be under great pressure from the more traditional and more numerous type of archaeologist historian with articles to publish, and will not find it easy to allocate a great deal of space to the industrial archaeologist, especially when he considers, as he must, the probable interests of the majority of his readers and subscribers. Much the same consideration will apply to notes and to book reviews.

One very important point should be emphasised. A careful inspection of the details provided by societies, supported by discussions with a number of secretaries and treasurers, suggests very strongly that the average subscription is too low, sometimes much too low. Even with the maximum of unpaid labour, the preparation and distribution of good bulletins and journals is a costly business, made even more costly by rising postal charges. But it is a very necessary and useful activity, and members of industrial archaeology societies should become accustomed to the prospect of paying more in order to have the job done properly.

An encouraging number of industrial archaeological societies are now publishing above what may be described as the 'printing horizon', that is, the line which separates typeset or litho printed publications, staple or stitch bound, which are sent for review and deposited for copyright purposes, from the duplicated pamphlets of a more ephemeral nature. Apart from the obvious advantages of being able to reproduce good photographs, plans and drawings, results of research published in a properly printed journal are ensured permanence in libraries and archive offices and usually a much wider long-term availability than is the case with duplicated material. In addition, a well-designed and properly printed publication can often achieve wide sales through bookshops, museum publications desks and by mail, and thus recoup the additional costs involved.

The importance of good publishing cannot be over-emphasised as there is little point in printing the results of research work in a form which is not going to be available for other workers in the field in future years. Industrial archaeologists can learn a lot from the publications of 'traditional' archaeological societies in this respect, as their standards of preparation of visual material are often of the highest order. Despite today's high printing costs, there is no reason why individual archaeological societies should not achieve a much higher standard of academic and visual presentation and publication and thus establish, in a more authoritative way, the need for industrial archaeology as a study and the competence of the local recorder and researcher to make worthwhile statements on the sites and monuments in his area.

One form of recording, if not of publication, which is open to everyone is the National Record of Industrial Monuments. Since 1965 this has been in the care of the Centre for the Study of the History of Technology at the University of Bath, under its Director, Dr. R. A. Buchanan. About 10,000 record cards have so far been received and processed at the Centre. Three copies are made, one for the Council for British Archaeology, one for the National Monuments Record and one for the Centre staff. The third card is classified according to its county and industrial grouping.

Both the quality and the distribution of the NRIM record cards are very uneven. Some counties – Hertfordshire is a shining example – have contributed many hundreds of cards and others a bare half-dozen. But the existence of 10,000 cards is proof of a good deal of interest and activities, and a spur to further effort. As Dr. Buchanan himself has written: 'The value of the NRIM, in the last resort, will be in its comprehensiveness. As it approaches completion it will become a unique source of information for industrial remains in the country, and will be available for the compilation of local histories, industrial distribution maps and such like. Otherwise forgotten industrial processes and landmarks will be filed for posterity, and, as to the historian all information is good information, the Record will be a valuable archive. This is a longer-term objective than the short-term aim of selecting monuments for preservation, but it is no less valuable. To fulfil it, however, the NRIM will continue to depend utterly on the enthusiasm and co-operation of individuals and societies who are convinced of its value. It is much to be hoped that people who are at present sitting on piles of completed record cards in the hope of incubating books and other publications will let us borrow the cards for the extension of our Record. For while we would not deny that there is a great deal more to industrial archaeology than the completion of record cards, the construction of a really comprehensive and integrated National Record should retain a high priority in the endeavours of serious industrial archaeologists.'[1]

It may be, however, that interest is moving away from single buildings and towards groups of buildings. The concept of a total environment is growing stronger each year and it is becoming more and more realised that the district, rather than a single mill or canal wharf, is the meaningful unit, both for study and for preservation. This tendency has been noticeable for some time and it must to some extent operate against the one-site, one-card system on which the NRIM is founded.

In 1966, for instance, John Butt published his article, 'The Industrial Archaeology of Gatehouse of Fleet'.[2] Gatehouse, midway between Dumfries and Stranraer, is a tourist attraction, 'a rare and beautiful example of an arrested industrial village'. Its development began in the late eighteenth century and its industries – a soapworks, two tanneries, a cotton mill and a brass foundry – remained prosperous until the 1840s. But to understand one of the buildings, one has to develop a feeling for the whole town, its cottages, the solid homes of its manufacturers and merchants, the church, the river. And to record a whole town on record cards is difficult.

A. D. George has adopted a similar all-town approach in his survey of Carlisle.[3] He has noted and woven together Carlisle's railway archaeology, biscuit factory, brewery, canal and cotton mill (1836), which at the time it was built was the biggest in England. Ian Beckwith has approached Gainsborough in the

[1] In the *Industrial Archaeologists' Guide*, 1971–73.

[2] *Industrial Archaeology*, May 1966. The article owed a great deal to the work of an extra-mural class, under Dr. Butt's guidance.

[3] 'The Industrial Archaeology of Carlisle', *Industrial Archaeology*, August 1973.

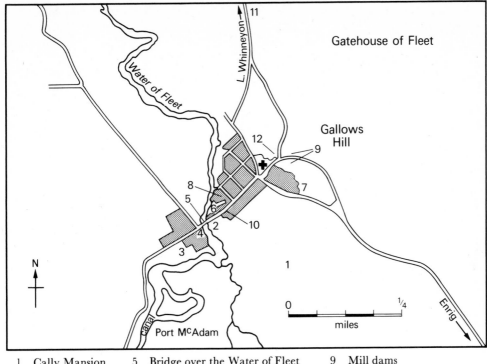

1	Cally Mansion	5	Bridge over the Water of Fleet	9	Mill dams
2	Tannery	6	Three cotton mills in the	10	Brewery
3	Tannery		Birtwhistle complex	11	Barlay Mill
4	Soapwork	7	Scott's cotton mill	12	Tollhouse
		8	Brass foundry		

Industrial buildings at Gatehouse-of-Fleet (from *Industrial Archaeology*, May 1966)

same way.[4] Having dealt with the port, which was effectively killed by the railway, he looks away from the river to the new industries which took its place as a source of employment. The major concern was William Marshall's agricultural engineering business, established in 1848. By 1904, 74 per cent of the population depended on Marshall's for a living.

And then there was Mr. Barnes, who began building bicycles in the 1880s. 'In 1885,' Mr. Beckwith tells us, 'Barnes's built a complete new range of buildings, now used by a firm of motor engineers. With their Italianate two-storey showroom faced with terracotta, with two large display windows, and crowned with a terracotta replica of a bicycle wheel, these buildings are of great interest

[4] 'Gainsborough: the Industrial Archaeology of a Lincolnshire Town', *Industrial Archaeology*, August 1971.

Late nineteenth century advertisement for gunpowder (from *Industrial Archaeology*, February 1968)

as a monument of the early days of the bicycle. To the north of the showroom are the old cycle workshops. The firm was expected to produce sixty bicycles a week.'

This, we might say, is dynamic recording, in which the archaeology comes alive and the town is appreciated as a single, changing unit.

Documentation

During the 150 years before 1800, the central government did not watch over local affairs with the care that it did later but, even so, much useful information can be found about particular industries both at the Public Record Office and at the Houses of Parliament, especially among eighteenth century Parliamentary papers. The records of certain branches of the national administration, such as the Patent Office, contain relevant material, but more important perhaps are the records of law suits, particularly of those heard in Chancery. In this court documents put in as exhibits were sometimes left behind by forgetful litigants and are now to be found among the class known as Chancery Masters' Exhibits.

In local government records, whether borough or parochial, rate books are an obvious source of information about premises, although, particularly in smaller villages these can be exasperating by their frequently unrevealing character. In counties where before 1832 the franchise depended on the forty shilling freehold, there are normally for the period 1780–1832 returns of land tax assessments, which, for all their pitfalls, can prove extremely useful. From 1792, plans of projected public works, canals, railways and the like, were deposited with the Clerk of the Peace as well as in the House of Lords. On these information is given not only about the proposed site itself but about properties immediately adjacent to it.

Probate records, which until the mid-eighteenth century frequently included inventories of the effects of the deceased, can from time to time offer interesting details of tools and equipment. As late as the mid-nineteenth century most testamentary business was conducted by the ecclesiastical courts, and the litigation which arose in these produces a surprising variety of useful facts.

It is perhaps in the records of property owners and of commercial and industrial firms that local topographical information is most easily obtained. The Crown and the Church were two of the greatest landowners in the country and their estate records therefore include some of the most complete and significant series surviving. It is also important to remember that a landowner may at one period have managed his industrial enterprises directly by bailiffs, as the Pagets and Willoughbies did in the sixteenth century, while at other times he was content to receive ground rents and royalties. It is always more satisfactory to have available the records of the day to day management of an enterprise; but in those cases, and they are the majority, where the landowner acted merely as a lessor of land and premises, the records of a large estate will have had a far better chance of survival than those of an ephemeral business enterprise. The deeds, maps, estate surveys, leases, manor court books, rent accounts and agents' correspondence of the local landowner may well be all that exists locally to document an industrial activity.

Nevertheless, the records of some of the firms themselves do survive, in the form of title and partnership deeds, account and order books, and correspondence. Among the larger firms the records of Boulton and Watt, of the Wedgwoods, and of some of the great London breweries can be cited as examples. A list of company papers which are now in Libraries and archives accessible to the public is maintained by the National Register of Archives, at its London headquarters (Quality House, Quality Court, Chancery Lane). The Business Archives Council (37–45 Tooley Street, London S.E.1) is active in promoting the proper care of business records and has a fine collection of histories and catalogues of industrial and commercial firms. Most of the professional and trade associations maintain fairly comprehensive archives. The British Iron and Steel Federation, the Cement and Concrete Association and the Institution of Mechanical and Civil Engineers, for instance, all have excellent and well-indexed collections of historical material. From time to time groups of books and deeds appear from the lofts and outhouses of long established, even long forgotten, industrial concerns, from the homes of descendants of partners, or from the premises of successors to the firm's solicitors.

In the case of the records of the central government or of property owned by the Crown, an enquiry at the Public Record Office in London will eventually – the Public Record Office is understaffed, ill-housed and underfinanced – produce an answer as to the present whereabouts of surviving documents. Similarly, ecclesiastical records will normally be at either the diocesan registrar's office or at a local record office designated by him. Most probate records have now been removed from probate registries and placed in the custody of local record offices. These Record Offices have now been established by most major local authorities, both county and borough councils, though there is considerable variation in the scope and arrangement of the collections. Frequently a Record Office will contain not only the archives of the council itself or of the Justices of the Peace, but also those of smaller existing or defunct local government authorities in the neighbourhood and quite possibly, in addition, those of the local archdeaconry or diocese as well as those of local families and commercial concerns. The records of other families however may well be at one of the national libraries or in the care of a local university or antiquarian society.

At least one nationalised industry, the National Coal Board, has a well-established policy of depositing archives in approved Record Offices. One such accumulation relating to Wemyss Colliery Company, is now in Register House, Edinburgh, and there are others in the Glamorgan County Record Office. Several more have also been deposited in the Lancashire and Durham Record Offices.[5]

[5] The Business Archives Council does excellent work in encouraging firms to look after their documents in a responsible and systematic way.

The Coal Board has followed this policy in order to give research students better facilities than can be provided at their own Divisional and Area Headquarters. The British Transport Commission archives, which includes both railway and canal material, is now housed, not altogether conveniently, in York.

The Department of the Environment includes a number of industrial monument in its lists of scheduled buildings. There are, for instance, special lists covering railway structure and Cornish engine-houses. Most local authorities have been provided by the Department with details of important buildings in their areas, but this information cannot be regarded as in any way complete, partly because new discoveries are constantly being made, and partly because a great deal of the work done by the Department investigators has never been made public, in the sense of being finalised in a statutory list. The Department is literally years behind with large tracts of the rural areas, as it was decided, in view of very limited staff, to concentrate on the urban areas, where the threat was supposed to be greatest. Consequently, it is sometimes necessary to rely on provisional lists, which are not always easy to get hold of, on the grounds that some of the buildings included in them may not eventually find their way on the final, statutory list.

For the London area a great deal of useful information is to be found in the volumes of the Survey of London, published by the Greater London Council and the London Survey Committee, and in the Inventories of London and the Home Counties, produced by the Royal Commission on Historical Monuments (England).

Local and county archaeological societies, sometimes have Records Sections, including libraries and publications of industrial interest. The Wiltshire Archaeological Society is a good case in point.

Early directories are indispensable works of reference. A detailed list of them is to be found in *The Guide to Directories (excluding London) published before 1856* (Royal Historical Society, 1950). The carefully printed eighteenth and nineteenth century maps and early editions of the Ordnance Survey are also very helpful. Lastly, it is advisable not to despise the work, whether printed or manuscript, of the earlier antiquaries and topographers. However inaccurate, credulous or garrulous they may appear to a more critical age, some of them did produce information which is accurate, useful, and otherwise completely unrecorded.

Photographic documentation

The outstanding national collection of photographs of buildings is that of the National Buildings Record, 23 Savile Row, London W.1., which has been accumulating material since 1941. The Record is, of course, concerned with all types of buildings, and photographs of industrial buildings make up only a small proportion of the many thousands which have been taken and filed.

The three Royal Commissions on Historical Monuments for England (23 Savile Row, London W.1.), Wales (17 Queen's Road, Aberystwyth, Dyfed) and Scotland (7 Coates Gardens, Edinburgh 12) respectively also have a considerable number of photographs which can be made available to serious students, but here, too, the emphasis has necessarily been on non-industrial buildings. The function of the Commissions, as laid down on their appointment in 1908, is to survey and publish in inventory form an account of every 'building, earthwork or stone construction' which they consider to be of historical importance and 'to specify those that seem most worthy of preservation'. It is only since the last war that they have been empowered to include buildings of later date than the beginning of the eighteenth century and, since the great majority of the monuments which are of interest to industrial archaeologists belong to the period between 1750 and 1850, this more liberal and enlightened attitude is very welcome. The Commissions are now free to make available their previously illicit photographs and to reveal publicly that they are personally aware of the existence of relics of the Industrial Revolution.

A number of public and private libraries and several County Record Offices – Essex and Worcester are good examples – have begun to build up reference collections of photographs of local life, scenes and buildings which can be of great value to the industrial archaeologist and local historian. Worcester now has more than 20,000 prints in its central collection; its photographic Survey Council depends largely on the organised work of amateurs. Old prints and negatives are

Nineteenth century roundhouse at Kidderminster, built to enclose a gas holder and now demolished. Reproduced from brochure to Open-Day at the Gasworks, 1922

also acquired whenever an opportunity occurs and a great deal of valuable historical material has been accumulated in this way.

The Manchester Public Libraries have had exceptionally long experience of this kind of work. Their collection, housed at the Central Library, goes back to the 1860s when the Library acquired a fine collection of photographs of local buildings, taken by a professional, Mr. W. Mudd. In 1888, the Reverend H. J. Palmer proposed that the recently formed Manchester Amateur Photographic Society should undertake a systematic, detailed study of the buildings of Manchester, and, in March, 1889, Mr. George Wheeler gave a talk to the Society, in which he said: 'In a few years hence the people who take our place will have but a vague notion of the general character of the streets and buildings as they are today, unless we or some other society come to their rescue'. He suggested that 'two prints be made of any subject, one of which should be presented to the Manchester Free Library'.

The original group made 232 prints in 10 years. After this very satisfactory beginning, a steady flow of prints continued and in 1937 an annual exhibition of Local History prints was started at the Central Reference Library. This lapsed during the war, but work began again in 1946, when the Survey was completely re-organised, direction being shifted from the Manchester Amateur Photographic Society to the Library itself.

The method now is for the Library, at the end of each year, to put forward 'a series of subjects that it considers to be of primary importance, or of sufficient historical interest'. The members of the Society pick their subjects from this list, the allocation and subsequent progress being supervised by a joint committee representing both the Society and the Library. The photographers are told to take useful, not pretty, pictures – 'Art is useless for this type of work' – and to realise that the object must be a photographic record of the Manchester area that students will be able to use with complete confidence in fifty years' time. They are told to get dating material into their shots wherever possible. Only good quality photographs of the required type are accepted. An annual exhibition is held and this, the Library believes, has been a great help in steadily raising the average standard of work.

Similar, but not so extensive, schemes are in existence in Eccles, Rochdale, Stockport, Birkenhead, Liverpool and Croydon. Croydon Library, like many others, has an arrangement with the local newspaper, whereby it is allowed to select any photographs from the files before they are destroyed.

The main shortcoming of most library and museum collections of photographs of local views and buildings is that they have grown up on a basis of the photographers' personal tastes and preferences. Consequently, they may well be rich in pictures of churches or street scenes, but poor in factories or slums. Only a deliberate policy which aims at the systematic filling of gaps can restore the balance. Meanwhile, anyone whose interest is in industrial buildings is very likely to find, when searching through a collection of local photographs, that what he needs is not there.

Workman sawing block of stone at Corsham, Wiltshire, *c*.1920

In some recently started collections, the photograph has been included on a comprehensive record card, which gives the necessary historical and technical details of the building or piece of machinery in question, as well as its picture. At a number of museums, such as Liverpool and Birmingham, a collection of films and still photographs is being built up, showing men and women working at traditional, but fast-disappearing crafts, such as file-making and rug-weaving. In some cases, these pictures supplement the information provided by the actual equipment of the same workshops which has been acquired by the Museum, so that an unusually full record of an old industry is available for students to consult.

Appendix One

Local Societies carrying out research, recording, publicity and political action within the field of industrial archaeology

Abertay Historical Society: IA Section
    Secretary: D. Bruce Walker, 149 Strathern Road, West Ferry, Dundee, DD5 1BR
Basingstoke IA Group (WEA)
    Chairman: P. P. Morris, 103 Maldive Road, Basingstoke, Hampshire
Bath & Camerton Archaeological Society
    Secretary: Peter J. Greening, 61 Pulteney Street, Bath, Avon
Batley Museum Society: IA Group
    Secretary: Mrs. G. Ashworth, 16 High Cote, Riddlesden, Keighley, Yorkshire
Berkshire Archaeological Society: IA Group
    Secretary: J. Kenneth Major, 2 Eldon Road, Reading, Berkshire, RG1 4DH
Birmingham & Warwickshire Archaeological Society: IA Research Group
    Secretary: Dr Jennifer Tann, Department of Industrial Administration, University of Aston in Birmingham, Maple House, 158 Corporation Street, Birmingham 4
Bradford Archaeology Group: IA Section
    Secretary: Stuart W. Feather, Bradford City Art Gallery and Museums, Moorside Mills, Moorside Road, Bradford, BD2 3HP
University of Bradford: IA Unit
    Secretary: Dr. John Diaper, The University, Richmond Road, Bradford, BD7 1DP
Bristol IA Society (BIAS)
    Secretary: Mrs. Joan Day, Hunter's Hill, Oakfield Road, Keynsham, nr. Bristol, Avon, BS18 1JQ
Brunel Society
    Secretary: Michael Williams, Bristol Polytechnic, Ashley Down, Bristol, Avon, BS7 9BU
Cambridge Society for IA
    Secretary: N. A. Smith, 4 Springfield Road, Cambridge, CB4 1AD

Map showing uneven distribution of industrial archaeological societies in Great Britain

Cheddleton Flint Mill Industrial Heritage Trust
>   Secretary: T. R. Copeland, Briton House, Tittensor, Stoke-on-Trent, ST12 9HH

Chester & District IA Society
>   Secretary: G. R. Coppack, Sunnycot, 1 Ash Grove, Little Sutton, Wirral, Cheshire, L66 1PP

Clackmannanshire Field Studies Society: IA Section
>   Secretary: Mrs. E. K. Kennedy, 26 Victoria Street, Alloa, Clackmannanshire

Cornwall Archaeological Society: IA Sub-Committee
>   Secretary: S. Beard, 6 Godolphin Way, Newquay, Cornwall

Council for British Archaeology, Group 2: IA Section
>   Secretary: Douglas B. Hague, Maesglas, Llanafan, Aberystwyth, Dyfed

Council for British Archaeology, Group 9: IA Sub-Committee
>   Secretary: J. Kenneth Major, 2 Eldon Road, Reading, Berkshire, RG1 4DH

Crofton Society
>   Secretary: Nicholas Reynolds, Vine House, 11 The Vineyard, Richmond, Surrey

Cumberland & Westmorland Antiquarian and Archaeological Society: IA Committee
>   Joint Secretaries: M. Davies-Shiel, Lilac Cottage, Lake Road, Bowness-on-Windermere, and Dr. J. D. Marshall, Department of History, University of Lancaster, Bailrigg, Lancaster.

Derbyshire Archaeological Society: IA Section
>   Sectional Secretary: L. J. Stead, 48a Sandbed Lane, Belper, Derby

Devon IA Survey
>   Secretary: Michael Dower, Dartington Amenity Research Trust, Central Office, Skinner's Bridge, Dartington, Totnes, Devon

The Devonshire Association: IA Section
>   Secretary: R. M. L. Cook, 18 Margaret Park, Hartley Vale, Plymouth, Devon, PL3 5RR

Dorset Natural History and Archaeological Society: IA Group
>   Secretary: D. Young, 20 Martel Close, Broadmayne, Dorchester, Dorset

Durham IA Group
>   Secretary: D. Wilcock, 26 Bede Terrace, Bowburn, Durham, DH6 5DT

Durham University Group for IA
>   Secretary: Christopher Hinde, Dunelm House, New Elvet, Durham, DH1 3RQ

The East Yorkshire Local History Society
>   Secretary: Group Capt. G. G. Robinson, RAF (Retd), Purey Cust Chambers, York, YO1 2EJ

Enfield Archaeological Society
>   Hon Secretary: G. R. Gillam, 23 Merton Road, Enfield, Middlesex

Exeter IA Group
>   Secretary: Mrs. B. Entwistle, 5 Elm Grove Road, Topsham, Exeter, Devon, EX3 0EQ

The Faversham Society
>   Hon. Secretary: Arthur Percival, 42 Newton Road, Faversham, Kent, ME13 8PU

Gloucestershire Society for IA
>   Secretary: Miss A. Chatwin, 6 & 7 Montpellier Street, Cheltenham, Glos., GL50 1SX

Greater London IA Society (GLIAS)
>   Secretary: Vere Glass, 69 St. Peter's Road, Croydon, Surrey, CR0 1HS

Historical Metallurgy Society
>   Hon. Secretary: K. C. Barraclough, 19 Park Avenue, Chapeltown, Sheffield, S30 4HW

Historical Model Railway Society
    Librarian: L. Mole, 43 Kent Drive, Hornchurch, Essex
Huddersfield IA Society
    Hon. Secretary: Robert Whitehead, 119 Coniston Avenue, Dalton, Huddersfield,
        Yorkshire
Industrial Steam Preservation Group
    Chairman: C. D. Topp, 146 Milner Chase, Hunslet Green, Leeds 10
Irish Society for IA
    Secretary: K. A. Mawhinney, 34 Lakelands Close, Blackrock, Co. Dublin
Ironbridge Gorge Museum Trust
    Hon. Secretary: E. Thomas, Southside, Church Hill, Ironbridge, Telford, Shrop-
        shire, TF8 7RE
Isle of Man Natural History & Antiquarian Society Field Section (IA Group)
    Secretary: L. Quilliam, c/o Manx Museum, Douglas, Isle of Man
Keynsham & Saltford Local History Society: Industrial Section
    Secretary: R. Milner, 15 Chelmer Grove, Keynsham, nr. Bristol, Avon
Kingston Polytechnic IA Society
    Staff Representative: Bryan Woodriff, Senior Lecturer, Kingston Polytechnic,
        Penrhyn Road, Kingston-upon-Thames, Surrey
Leicestershire Industrial History Society
    Secretary: R. N. Thomson, 'Three Gables', Queen Street, Markfield, Leicester
Lincolnshire History and Archaeology, Society for: IA Sub-Committee
    Secretary: Mrs. C. M. Wilson, Curator, Museum of Lincolnshire Life, Burton Road,
        Lincoln
Maidstone Area IA Group: Industrial Section
    Secretary: R. J. Spain, 'Trevarno', Roseacre Lane, Bearsted, Maidstone, Kent
Manchester Region IA Society
    Secretary: Dr. R. L. Hills, c/o Manchester Museum of Science and Technology, 97
    Grosvenor Street, Manchester, M1 7HF
Friends of Morwellham
    Hon. Secretary: G. Garlick, Warden, Morwellham, Cornwall
Norfolk IA Society
    Hon. Secretary: Mrs. J. Mackie, 2 Mill Corner, Hingham, Norwich, Norfolk,
        NOR 23X
Northamptonshire IA Group
    Secretary: G. H. Starmer, 17 Mayfield Road, Northampton, NN3 2RE
Northern Mill Engine Society
    Secretary: Trevor Lees, 2 Brocklebank Road, Rochdale, Lancashire
North East IA Society
    Secretary: D. Wilcock, 26 Bede Terrace, Bowburn, Durham, DH6 5DT
North-Western Society for IA and History
    Secretary: Mrs. P. Paget-Tomlinson, City of Liverpool Museum, William Brown
        Street , Liverpool, L3 8EN
Peak District Mines Historical Society
    Hon. Secretary: P. J. Naylor, 85 Peveril Road, Beeston, Nottingham.
Friends of the Pembrokeshire County Museum IA Group
    Hon. Secretary: R. A. Kennedy, c/o The Pembrokeshire County Museum, The
        Castle, Haverfordwest, Pembrokeshire

Poole (WEA) IA Group
    Secretary: Alfred J. A. Cooksey, 18 Parkstone Avenue, Parkstone, Poole, Dorset, BH14 9LR
Portsmouth Polytechnic: IA Society
    Secretary: Dr. R. C. Riley, Department of Geography, Portsmouth Polytechnic, Lion Terrace, Portsmouth, PO1 3HE
Railway & Canal Historical Society
    Secretary: J. R. Harding, 174 Station Road, Wylde Green, Sutton Coldfield, Warwickshire, B73 5LE
Redditch IA Society
    Secretary: C. A. Beardsmore, 127 Beaumont Road, Bournville, Birmingham, Warwickshire
Rickmansworth Historical Society
    Secretary: E. V. Parrott, 66 The Queens Drive, Rickmansworth, Hertfordshire
Rochdale Society for the Study of the History of Industry and Technology
    Secretary: D. Ternent, 298 Hatfield, Ashfield Valley, Rochdale, Lancashire
Rossendale Forest Railway Society
    Secretary: David L. Ormerod, 'The Hollies', Hud-Hey Road, Haslingden, Rossendale, Lancashire
Ryhope Engines Trust
    Secretary: S. A. Staddon, 3 Leominster Road, Sunderland, Co. Durham, SR2 9HG
Saddleworth Historical Society
    Secretary: Mrs. B. Booth, 'Ceann', Friezland Lane, Greenfield, near Oldham, Lancashire
Salisbury & South Wiltshire IA Society
    Secretary: Peter Goodhugh, 34 Countess Road, Amesbury, Salisbury, Wiltshire
Scottish Society for IA
    Secretary: D. M. Dickie, Teachers' Centre, Branshill Road, Alloa, Clackmannanshire
Scottish Vernacular Buildings Working Group
    Hon. Secretary: Geoffrey Stell, RCAHMS, 54 Melville Street, Edinburgh, EH3 7HF
Somerset IA Society
    Chairman: Frank Hawtin, Quaking House, Milverton, Taunton, Somerset, TA4 1NG
Southampton University IA Group
    Secretary: J. B. Horne, Heathermount, Moor Hill, West End, Southampton, Hampshire
South-East Wales IA Society
    Secretary: W. G. Hughes, 96 Wenallt Road, Rhiwbina, Cardiff, South Glamorgan
South-West Wales IA Society
    Newsletter Editor: P. R. Reynolds, 12 Beaconsfield Way, Sketty, Swansea, West Glamorgan
South Yorkshire Industrial Museum
    Secretary: John Goodchild, Curator, South Yorkshire Industrial Museum, Cusworth Hall, Doncaster, South Yorkshire
Staffordshire IA Society
    Secretary: F. Brook, 15 Widecombe Avenue, Weeping Cross, Stafford
Sunderland IA Group
    Secretary: George Edwards, 3 Broxbourne Terrace, Sunderland, Co. Durham

Surrey Archaeological Society
    Secretary: D. J. Turner, Castle Arch, Guildford, Surrey
Sussex IA Society
    Hon. Secretary: A. J. Haselfoot, Albion House, Cobourg Place, Hastings, Sussex, TN34 3HY
Teesside IA Group
    Hon. Secretary: D. M. Tomlin, 8 Loweswater Crescent, Stockton-on-Tees, Teesside, TS18 4PY
The Trevithick Society
    Hon. Secretary: A. P. F. Stephens, 23 Merrick Avenue, Truro, Cornwall
Tyne IA Group
    Secretary: R. M. Higgins, Waterhouse & Partners, Park View House, Front Street, Newcastle-upon-Tyne, NE7 7TZ
Watford & District Industrial History Society
    Secretary: R. Beattie, 23 St. Lawrence Way, Bricket Wood, Watford, Hertfordshire
Wiltshire Archaeological & Natural History Society (IA Committee)
    Secretary: D. A. E. Cross, Wyndhams, Shrewton, Salisbury, Wiltshire
Wolverhampton Polytechnic: Study Centre for Industrial Archaeology and Business History of the West Midlands
    Secretary: W. A. Smith, The Polytechnic, Wolverhampton, Staffordshire
Wolverhampton & District Archaeological Society
    Secretary: R. J. Ayers, 13 Vicarage Walk, Stony Stratford, Wolverton, Buckinghamshire
Yorkshire Archaeological Society: Industrial History Section
    Hon. Secretary: Mrs. N. M. Cooper, 307 Spen Lane, Leeds, LS16 5BD

National bodies

National Record of Industrial Monuments
    Director: Dr. R. A. Buchanan, School of Humanities and Social Sciences, University of Bath, Claverton Down, Bath, Avon, BA2 7AY
National Trust
    42 Queen Anne's Gate, London S.W.1
National Trust for Scotland
    5 Charlotte Square, Edinburgh
Newcomen Society for the Study of Engineering and Technology
    The Science Museum, London S.W.7
Standing Conference for Local History
    26 Bedford Square, London W.C.1
Victorian Society
    1 Priory Gardens, Bedford Park, London W4 1TT

Appendix Two

Films illustrating industrial and transport history

Food and drink
Stilton Cheese   1903–5 (BFI)
Manufacture of Stilton Cheese   1920 (BFI)
Processes at the Craigellachie Glenlivet Distillery   *c.*1925 (BFI)
Bottling White Horse Whisky   1925 (BFI)
Brewing at the Lion Brewery, Blackburn   *c.*1930 (BFI)
Visit to Peak Freans Biscuit Factory   1906 (BAC)
Village Bakery   1946 (EFVA)
Grinding Corn   undated (EFVA)

Mining, quarrying
Nine Centuries of Coal   1958 (NCB)
A Day in the Life of a Coalminer   1910 (BAC/BFI)
Black Diamonds (film of life in the Welsh coal mines, made by a working miner)   1932
    6 reels (BFI)
Coalface   Grierson: music by Britten   1935 (BFI)
Slate Quarry   (Lake District) 1947 (EFVA)
Tin Mining   1948 (EFVA)
China Clay   1949 (EFVA)
Slate Quarrying in North Wales   1935 (BFI)
Oil Industry (colour)   A historical survey   1963 (PFB)

Building materials, building
Cement   1949 (EFVA)
Building in Stone   1953 (LAMS)
Bricks and Brick Masonry   1963 (NFBI/Rank)
Bricks   1947 (EFVA)

Bricks for Houses   1947 (EFVA)
Brickmaking   1947 (EFVA)
Thatching   1965 (EFVA)

Power, metals, engineering
Diesel Story   1951 (PFB/SMBP)
Transfer of Power (history of the toothed wheel)   1939 (PFB)
Industrial Notebook I (generation and distribution of electricity until 1959)   1959
    (SMBP)
Industrial Notebook II (iron and steel from Ironbridge to continuous casting)   1950
    (SMBP)
History of the Oil Engine   1961 (SMBP)
Casting at Wilson's Forge (Bishop Auckland)   1947 (EFVA)
James Watt   1959 (BFI)
Welding steel bars by the alumino-thermic process   *c.*1910 (BFI)
Making steel by the Siemens process   1914 (BFI)
Manufacture of wrought iron chains   1939 (BFI)
Manufacture of puddled wrought iron   1939 (BFI)
The Village Blacksmith   *c.*1909 (BFI)
The Blacksmith   1935/51 (PFB)
New Bells for Old (bellcasting)   *c.*1918 (BFI)
Water Power   1937/1949 (EFVA/Rank)

Paper
In Black and White (history of paper)   1951 (Bowater)
Paper-making (Wiggins Teape)   1915 (BAC)
Paper-making (hand process)   1920 (BFI)
The manufacture of art paper   1921 (BFI)
The production of *The Times*   *c.*1927 (BFI)
How the *Daily Mail* is produced   1930 (BFI)

Pottery, glass
Glassmakers of England   1932 (BAC)
Glassblowing   *c.*1912 (BFI)
Bottle making up-to-date   *c.*1921 (BFI)
Glass-making   1921 (BFI)
The Glassblowers   1935/51 (PFB)
Bridging the Centuries (Doulton pottery)   undated (Rank)
Village Potter   1953 (EFVA)

Textiles, leather, footwear
Carpets through the Ages (colour)   undated (SSL)
Carpets in the Making (colour)   undated (SSL)
Manufacturing carpets at William Gray and Sons' factory, Ayr   1920 (BFI)
West of England (Stroud Mills) (colour)   1955 (CFL)
Woollen Mill   1936 (BFI)
Witney Blankets   1920 (BAC)
The Story of the Witneydown Blanket   1928 (BFI)

From Wool to Wearer (the factory of Peter Scott Limited, and the manufacture of
    'Pesco' garments)   1913   2 reels (BFI)
Lace-making   1930 (BFI)
Modern boot manufacturing   1920 (BFI)
Village Tannery   1953 (EFVA)

Other manufacturing
Boots Beeston Factory   1935 (BAC)
Devon Fishing Net Industry   *c.*1911 (BFI)
Matches (made in England)   1910 (BFI)
Women's Work in Wartime   1917 (BFI)
Women's Work on Munitions in War   1918 (BFI)
Empire's Money Maker: a visit to the Royal Mint   1910 (BFI)
Making Fireworks   1911 (BFI)
Manufacture of Top Hats   *c.*1923 (BFI)
Rope   *c.*1937 (BFI)
Soap-making   *c.*1935 (BFI)
Port Sunlight   *c.*1919   3 reels (BFI)
Port Sunlight (Lever Brothers)   1919 (BAC)
The Wheelwright   1935/51 (PFB)
The Tidemiller   1935/51 (PFB)
The Flintknappers   1935/51 (PFB)
The Cooper   1935/51 (PFB)
Coopering (colour)   1953 (EFVA)

Industry: general
Machines that Think (calculators)   *c.*1922 (BFI)
Industrial Britain (Grierson/Flaherty)   1931–32   2 reels (BFI)
Men who Work (Austin factory, Longbridge)   1935 (BFI)
Heavy Industries – Scotland   1936 (BFI)

Gas
Beckton Coke Works   1926 (BFI)
How London Coke is Made   1930 (BFI)
How Gas is Made   1935 (BFI)

Electricity, electronics, telephones
The Romance of Postal Telegraphy   1922 (BFI)
Power (grid; steel foundry; hydro-electricity; clay conductors; pylons)   *c.*1925 (BFI)
Power and Electricity (production and distribution)   *c.*1930 (BFI)

Railways
Electrifying the South Western   *c.*1915 (BFI)
Building a Locomotive at Crewe   1920 (BFI)
LNER Centenary Celebrations at Darlington   1925 (BFI)
Railway Ride over the Tay Bridge   1897 (BFI)
Building a LNWR Locomotive   1905 (BFI)
Trip on the Metro (Harrow to Aylesbury)   *c.*1910 (BFI)

The Making of a Modern Railway Carriage   1912 (BFI)
Giants of Steam (BBC film of steam pioneers)   1963 (BTF)
Elizabethan Express (London–Edinburgh steam run)   1954 (BTF)
Night Mail (GPO film unit classic)   1936 (CFL)
Right Down the Line (some historical details of railway signalling) (colour)   undated
    (CFL)
Under the River (the story of the Severn Tunnel and its Cornish pumping engines)   1959
    (BTF)
Isambard Kingdom Brunel   1967 (BBCTVE)   for sale only
Early Railway Scenes 1895–1900   (BFI)
Century of Steam (Ffestiniog, 1963–65) (colour)   (BFI)
100 Years Underground (story of LPTB)   1964 (BFT)
A Day for Remembering (Parade of LPTB stock)   1964 (BTF)

Road transport
Century of Buses (London's bus history) (colour)   1957 (BTF)
The Elephant will never Forget (London's last trams)   1953 (BTF)
Cycle Parade   c.1898 (BFI)
How a Motor Bicycle is Made   1912 (BFI)
The 'Sentinel' Steam-Wagon   c.1926 (BFI)
'Sentinel' Steam Lorries and Excavators   c.1930 2 reels (BFI)
Roads across Britain (historical record, showing different types of vehicle)   1939 2 reels
    (BFI)

Air transport
Airmen of Yesterday   1909 (BFI)
Balloon-making   1909 (BFI)
Aircraft   1916 (BFI)
The 'Porte' flying-boat   c.1917 (BFI)
Airship on a mooring mast   1917 (BFI)
British airships in the East   1917 (BFI)
Seaplane launching apparatus   1917 (BFI)
First flight of a 'Wren' monoplane   1923 (BFI)
The Imperial Airway   1924 (BFI)
Converted (safety of passenger flying)   c.1926 (BFI)
Imperial Airways   1924 (BAC/NFA)
Powered flight (history of aviation)   1953 (PFB)
Air Parade, 1909–1952 (history of aircraft development, made for the Festival of Britain)
    1952
History of the Helicopter   1951 (PFB)
Michael and the Flying Boats   1949 (EFVA)
Wings of Yesterday   undated (SS1)

Water transport
London–Birmingham by Canal   1947 (EFVA)
There go the boats (canal history and development)   1951 (BTF)
Indland Waterways (London–Birmingham)   1950 (BTF)
Canal Locks and Tunnels   1953 (BTF)

Manchester Ship Canal   *c.*1935 (BFI)
Thames Panorama   1899 (BFI)
The Port of London   1921 (BFI)
Barging through London   1924 (BFI)
Ocean Terminal (Southampton)   1952 (BTF)
Wonder Ship: the story of the *Queen Mary*   1936 2 reels (BFI)

Transport: general
Transport in England   1933 (BFI)
Our Transport Services (Glasgow)   *c.*1935 (BFI)
Early Transport Films 1893–1926   (BFI)

Key to sources of films

BBCTVE	BBC TV Enterprises, Television Centre, London W.12
BFI	British Film Institute, 81 Dean Street, London W.1
BTF	British Transport Films, Melbury House, Melbury Terrace, London N.W.1
Bowater	The Bowater Corporation Limited, Bowater House, Knightsbridge, London S.W.1
BAC	Business Archives Council, Industrial Films Sub-Committee, c/o T. Dalby, Hutchinson Benham Limited, 178–202 Great Portland Street, London W.1
CFL	Central Film Library, Government Building, Bromyard Avenue, Acton, London W.3
EFVA	Educational Foundation for Visual Aids, 35 Queen Anne Street, London W.1.
LAMS	London Association of Master Masons, 47 Bedford Square, London W.C.1
NCB	National Coal Board, Film Library, 68 Wardour Street, London W.1
NFBI	National Federation of Brick Industries, 36 Gordon Street, London W.C.1
PFB	Petroleum Films Bureau, 4 Brook Street, Hanover Square, London W.1
Rank	Rank Film Library, 127 Wardour Street, London W1V 4AD
SMBP	Shell Mex and BP Film Library, 25 The Burroughs, Hendon, London N.W.4
SSL	Sound Services Library, Kingston Road, London S.W.19

Bibliography

Much of the information needed by industrial archaeologists is to be found in periodicals and in the journals of professional societies. *The Transactions of the Newcomen Society for the History of Engineering and Technology* have been published annually since 1920 and cover a wide range of subjects of a technical nature. It is unfortunate that so few public libraries possess a set of these invaluable volumes. The *Journals* of the Institutes of Civil, Mechanical and Mining Engineers and of the Iron and Steel Institute contain valuable historical material, and so does *The Engineer* (1856 onwards) and *Engineering* (1866 onwards).

The local archaeological societies vary greatly in the coverage given by their journals to the history of industry and transport. Some, such as the *Transactions* of the Cumberland and Westmorland Archaeological Society, have shown a strong interest in publishing such articles; others, the majority, have concentrated much more heavily on prehistoric and medieval sites.

Within the past twenty years, the periodical field has been greatly enriched by the appearance of the publications of newly established historical societies operating within limited fields. The *Bulletin of the Historical Metallurgy Group* is of this type, and so are the *Bulletin of the Peak District Mines Historical Society* and the *Memoirs* (formerly *Transactions*) *of the Northern Cavern and Mines Research Society*. Some local industrial archaeology societies – Bristol and Wolverhampton are outstanding examples – produce annual journals of very high quality and most of the others rise to at least a quarterly newsletter, which usually includes notes and short articles of value to people with such specialised interests as mining, canals or iron foundries.

The quarterly *Journal of Industrial Archaeology*, which was founded in 1963, has given industrial archaeologists a regular opportunity to see their work in print and circulated not only in this country but in all the major industrial countries of the world. More topical information is provided by the *Newsletter* of the Association for Industrial Archaeology, which has its headquarters at Ironbridge.

Until 1973, the *Industrial Archaeologist's Guide*, published every two years by David and Charles, constituted a *vade-mecum* for those interested in the subject, with its details of museums, names and addresses of societies, sites accessible to the public and practical advice on techniques. Since its disappearance from the publishing scene there is nothing which does exactly the same job, although in due course, no doubt, a suitable replacement will appear.

Much useful material relating to industrial archaeology is to be found in more general periodicals. *Country Life* has a great deal related to the subject, especially in its correspondence section, which is, unfortunately, not indexed. The *Architects' Journal* and the *Architectural Review* often publish articles and notes which come within the field of industrial archaeology, with particular emphasis on the successful conversion of old industrial buildings. Of the national newspapers, the *Guardian* is the most likely to contain news of site and museum developments, and from time to time has a special feature article devoted to industrial archaeology.

Two publication from the Department of the Environment deal with what is described as 'the preservation of our building heritage in an age of change'. The first, *New Life for Old Buildings* (1971) consists of twenty-two case histories of historic buildings which have been adapted to new use. These include a granary at King's Lynn, converted into offices; a water-mill at Winchester, which is now flats; and the Corn Exchange at Sudbury, Suffolk, transformed into a branch of the County Library. *New Life for Historic Areas* (1972) deals with environmental improvement and adaptation. Two of the sites described are Widcombe Locks, Bath, and Ironbridge Gorge, Shropshire.

There are now several more or less general introductions to industrial archaeology, in addition to the present volume. The most straightforward is R. A. Buchanan's Pelican, *Industrial Archaeology* (1973), and in a similar price range there is Kenneth Hudson's *Our Industrial Heritage* (1975) and Arthur Raistrick's *Industrial Archaeology* (1972).

For all archaeologists, including those whose main concern is with industry and transport, one of the most rewarding and stimulating books is O. G. S. Crawford's *Archaeology in the Field* (1953). Dr Crawford's insistence on the need to regard archaeology as a broad, humane and historically continuous study is reinforced by Dr. W. G. Hoskins' great pioneering work, *Local History in England* (1959).

W. H. Chaloner and A. E. Musson, *Industry and Technology*, is a superbly illustrated but unfortunately out of print general history of technology. R. J. Forbes and E. J. Dijksterhuis, *A History of Science and Technology* 2 vols, (1963) is also helpful, especially the second volume, which deals with the eighteenth and nineteenth centuries. The standard, but now twenty years behind the times, works of reference remains the Oxford *History of Technology*, 5 vols. (1954–58), with its abbreviated *Short History of Technology* (1960), edited by T. K. Derry and T. I. Williams.

Lewis Mumford's classic *Technics and Civilisation*, first published in 1934 and seven times reprinted since then, traces the influence of technical change on the quality and aims of Western civilisation, and is as important and stimulating now as when it first appeared. The relationship between labour shortage and technical progress is well brought out by H. J. Habakkuk, *American and British Technology in the Nineteenth Century* (1962), and Kenneth Hudson, *The Archaeology of Industry* (1976), puts British industrial archaeology in its world setting.

J. P. M. Pannell's *The Techniques of Industrial Archaeology*, originally published in 1966, has been brought up to date and made even more useful by Neil Cossons (1974). The same author's *Illustrated History of Civil Engineering* (1964) presents a wide range of material in an attractive and reliable manner. Other books which deal with the development of technology in a way which is suited to the needs of the general reader are: A. P. Usher, *A*

History of Mechanical Inventions (1954); Aubrey F. Burstall, *A History of Mechanical Engineering* (1963); H. R. Schubert's *History of the British Iron and Steel Industry* (1957); W. H. G. Armytage, *A Social History of Engineering* (revised edition, 1966); and P. Dunsheath, *A History of Electrical Engineering* (1962).

The best short book on the Industrial Revolution is still T. R. Ashton, *The Industrial Revolution* (1948). It has an excellent, but now necessarily outdated bibliography. Professor Ashton has also revised Paul Mantoux's invaluable account of the beginnings of industrialisation, *The Industrial Revolution in the Eighteenth Century* (1961). This, too, has a very full and wide-ranging bibliography. A more recent book with a similar aim is S. D. Chapman and J. D. Chambers, *Beginnings of Industrial Britain*, which contains a survey of each major industry or group of industries. The Industrial Revolution is discussed from a purely technical point of view by A. E. Musson and E. H. Robinson, *Science and Technology in the Industrial Revolution* (1970) and by R. L. Hills, *Power in the Industrial Revolution* (1970). Dr. Hills' book, despite its title, is in fact concerned only with the development of machinery for spinning and weaving cotton, a theme which is also covered by G. Watkins' splendid 2-volume work, *The Textile Mill Engine* (1970 and 1971). *The Archaeology of the Industrial Revolution* (1971), edited by Brian Bracegirdle, has contributions from a number of leading specialists and carries the distinction of Mr. Bracegirdle's own superb colour photographs.

A reminder that our ancestors found aesthetic pleasure, as well as economic and technological pride in the Industrial Revolution is provided by Sir Arthur Elton's edition of F. D. Klingender's *Art and the Industrial Revolution* (1968).

J. M. Richards' *The Functional Tradition in Early Industrial Building* (1958), with Eric de Maré's unsurpassed black and white photographs, is an excellent record of a wide range of eighteenth and nineteenth century buildings illustrating the architects' ability to meet the demands for industrial and commercial premises which should look well and fulfil their purpose efficiently. There are frequent references to industrial buildings in Sir Nikolaus Pevsner's series, *The Buildings of England*. Workers' houses are the subject of two recent books, Stanley D. Chapman (ed.) *The History of Working-Class Housing* (1971) and J. N. Tann, *Working-Class Housing in Nineteenth Century Britain* (1971).

Dr. Norman Davey's *A History of Building Materials* traces changes in building techniques from biblical times onwards, and Kenneth Hudson, *A History of Building Materials* (1971) concentrates on what has happened since the sixteenth century. An important special field is covered by J. Gloag and D. Bridgwater, *A History of Cast Iron in Architecture* (1958).

David and Charles' series of regional books on industrial archaeology has now dealt with most of Britain, and their list also contains a number of works on specialised aspects of the subject. Dr. E. R. R. Green's *The Industrial Archaeology of County Down* (1964) published by H.M.S.O., before the first volumes of the David and Charles enterprise appeared, is a model of careful fieldwork and balanced description to which all subsequent industrial archaeologists must be indebted. Morgan Rees, *Mines, Mills and Furnaces: Industrial Archaeology in Wales* (1969) does a long-needed job for the Principality.

On particular industries, the following books are of special value:

Coal
Baron F. Duckham   *A History of the Scottish Coal Industry, 1700–1815*   1970
R. L. Galloway   *Annals of Coal Mining and the Coal Trade*   2 vols. 1898 and 1904

R. L. Galloway   *A History of Coal Mining in Great Britain*   1882
J. V. Nef   *The Rise of the British Coal Industry, 1500–1700*   2 vols., 1932
R. Smith   *Sea Coal for London*   1963

Other mining, quarrying
W. J. Arkell   *Oxford Stone*   1947
R. M. Barton   *History of the Cornish China-Clay Industry*   1966
A. C. Davis   *A Hundred Years of Portland Cement, 1824–1924*   1924
K. Hudson   *The Fashionable Stone: a history of the English building limestones*   1971
K. Hudson   *The History of English China Clays*   1969
Jean Lindsay   *A History of the North Wales Slate Industry*   1974
D. Purcell   *Cambridge Stone*   1967

Iron and steel
T. S. Ashton   *Iron and Steel in the Industrial Revolution*   1951
J. C. Carr and W. Taplin   *A History of the British Steel Industry*   1962
W. K. V. Gale   *Iron and Steel*   1969
W. E. Minchinton   *The British Tinplate Industry*   1957
A. Raistrick   *A Dynasty of Ironfounders: the Darbys and Coalbrookdale*   1953
E. Straker   *Wealden Iron*   1931

Non-ferrous metals
Robert T. Clough   *The Lead Smelting Mills of the Yorkshire Dales*   1962
H. Hamilton   *The English Brass and Copper Industries to 1800*   1967

Textiles, paper
S. J. Chapman   *The Lancashire Cotton Industry*   1904
D. C. Coleman   *The British Paper Industry, 1495–1860*   1958
G. W. Daniels   *The Early English Cotton Industry*   1920
W. English   *The Textile Industry*   1969
C. Gill   *The Rise of the Irish Linen Industry*   1925
H. Heaton   *The Yorkshire Woollen and Worsted Industries*   1920
E. Lipson   *The History of the English Woollen and Worsted Industries*   3rd ed. 1953
E. Lipson   *A Short History of Wool and its Manufacture*   1953
J. de L. Mann   *The Cloth Industry of the West of England, 1640–1880*   1971
K. G. Ponting   *The Woollen Industry of South West England*   1971
A. H. Shorter   *Paper Making in the British Isles*   1971

Glass
T. C. Barker   *Pilkington Brothers and the Glass Industry*   1960
W. B. Honey   *Glass*   1946
H. J. Powell   *Glass-making in England*   1923
S. E. Winbolt   *Wealdon Glass*   1933

Pottery
H. Owen   *The Staffordshire Potter*   1901
J. C. Wedgwood   *Staffordshire Pottery and its History*   1925

Chemicals
A. and N. L. Clow   *The Chemical Revolution*   1952
L. F. Haber   *The Chemical Industry during the Nineteenth Century*   1958
S. Miall   *A History of the British Chemical Industry, 1634–1928*   1931

Oil, rubber
P. H. Giddens   *The Birth of the Oil Industry*   1938
P. Schidrowitz and T. R. Dawson   *History of the Rubber Industry*   1952

Brewing
P. Mathias   *The Brewing Industry in England, 1700–1830*   1959

Animal, water and wind power
C. P. Skilton   *British Windmills and Watermills*   1947
R. Wailes   *The English Windmill*   1954
R. Wailes   *Tide Mills*   Part I, 1956; Part II 1957
P. N. Wilson   *Watermills: an Introduction*   1955

Steam power
D. B. Barton   *The Cornish Beam Engine*   1965
H. W. Dickinson   *A Short History of the Steam Engine*   1963
L. T. C. Rolt   *Thomas Newcomen: the Prehistory of the Steam Engine*   1963
L. T. C. Rolt   *James Watt*   1962
E. Vale   *The Harveys of Hale*   1966
G. Watkins   *The Stationary Steam Engine*   1963

Water transport
D. D. Gladwin   *The Canals of Britain*   1973
C. Hadfield   *British Canals, an illustrated history*   2nd ed., 1959
Robert Harris and C. Hadfield   *Canals and their Architecture*   1969
Eric de Maré   *The Canals of England*   1950
W. M. McCutcheon   *The Canals of the North of Ireland*   1965
L. T. C. Rolt   *The Inland Waterways of England*   1950

Roads
J. Copeland   *Roads and their Traffic, 1750–1850*   1968
Eric de Maré   *The Bridges of Britain*   1954
L. T. C. Rolt   *Thomas Telford*   1958
T. W. Wilkinson   *From Track to By-pass: a History of the English Road*   1934

Railways
B. Baxter   *Stone Blocks and Iron Rails (tramroads)*   1966
Terry Coleman   *The Railway Navvies*   1965
C. H. Ellis   *British Railway History*   2 vols., 1954, 1955
John R. Kellett   *The Impact of Railways on Victorian Cities*   1969
E. T. MacDermot   *History of the Great Western Railway*   revised by C. R. Clinker, 1963–64
C. F. D. Marshall   *A History of the Southern Railway*   1936
C. Meek   *The Railway Station: an Architectural History*   1957

R. K. Middlemas   *The Master Builders* (the four major nineteenth century railway
      contractors)   1963
L. T. C. Rolt   *George and Robert Stephenson: the railway revolution*   1960
L. T. C. Rolt   *Isambard Kingdom Brunel*   1957

Water, gas, electricity
D. Chandler and A. C. Lacey   *The Rise of the Gas Industry in Great Britain*   1949
W. T. O'Dea   *The Social History of Lighting*   1958
R. H. Parsons   *The Early Days of the Power Station Industry*   1940
F. W. Robins   *The Story of Water Supply*   1946

Gazetteer

A selection of industrial sites and monuments particularly worth visiting:

METALS

Blaenavon, Gwent   Blaenavon Ironworks. The ironworks, established in 1790, where Percy Gilchrist and Sidney Thomas carried out their experiments. Restored by the Department of the Environment, it contains five blast-furnaces, twelve workers' cottages, a cast-house and a water-balance tower. The cast-house contains an exhibition to show how the works was operated.

Coalbrookdale, Shropshire   Remains of the eighteenth century Darby ironworks, including the 1638 furnace where, in 1709, Abraham Darby first smelted iron with coke. Objects produced at the Coalbrookdale Works during the nineteenth century. Museum of iron-making and of the Coalbrookdale Company. Much of the area, including the Coalbrookdale site and museum, is now looked after by the Ironbridge Gorge Museum Trust, which also administers the Blists Hill Open-Air Industrial Museum and the Iron Bridge (1779).

Funtley, Hampshire   Site and surviving buildings of Henry Cort's pioneering iron-puddling works (1784). Part of the original furnace can still be seen, and there is interesting evidence of the ponds and watercourses built by Cort to provide a water-supply for his hammer and rolling mill.

Heage, Derbyshire   Morley Park Ironworks. Two cold-blast furnaces, for producing iron with coke, built in 1780 and 1818. The 36 ft. high furnaces are square-shaped and built into the hillside. They were last operated in the 1870s.

Redruth, Cornwall   Works of the Tolgus Tin Company. An operational tin-works, using nineteenth century methods and extracting tin from the waste of old mining operations. It has what is now probably the only set of Cornish stamps still operating anywhere in the world.

Sheffield, South Yorkshire Abbeydale industrial hamlet. Water-powered workshops, used in the eighteenth and nineteenth centuries for grinding cutlery.

Sticklepath, near Okehampton, Devon The Finch Foundry. Workshops where the Finch family made edge-tools from 1814 to 1960. The machinery, driven by three water-wheels, is all operational and includes two tilt hammers. A small museum illustrates the history of the business.

Taynuilt (near), Argyllshire Bonawe ironworks. A mid-eighteenth century charcoal works, the most complete surviving in Britain, preserved with its square stone-built furnace (1753), charcoal shed, storage shed for iron-ore and workers' housing (1795). On Loch Etive, near the works, is an eighteenth century jetty for the sloops which brought iron ore and supplies and took away pig-iron.

Wortley, near Sheffield, South Yorkshire Top Forge. An eighteenth century forge, which reached the peak of its prosperity in the nineteenth century, when it made wrought iron railway axles. The forge-hammer was water-powered. The buildings and machinery have been restored by the Sheffield Trades Historical Society.

Splitting and trimming roofing-slates at Dinorwic, *c*.1890

Bangor (near), Gwynedd   Dinorwic slate quarries and works. Formerly one of the most important slate-producing centres in Britain, Dinorwic ceased production in the 1950s. The quarry workshops, which are castle-sized, have been preserved by the National Museum of Wales, together with the original machinery, patterns and water-wheel (believed to be the third largest in Britain).

Barnsley (near), South Yorkshire   Elsecar atmospheric pumping engine, 1795, with later modifications. In regular operation until 1923. Now owned and maintained by the National Coal Board.

Camborne (near), Cornwall   East Pool beam winding-engine (built 1887, at Camborne) and engine house, restored and preserved by the Cornish Engines Preservation Society and now the responsibility of the National Trust. This is one of five engines owned by the Society, the earliest being the 1840 winding engine at Levant Mine, the oldest surviving engine in Cornwall.

Laxey, Isle of Man   The 'Lady Isabella' water-wheel (1854). Designed to pump water from the lead, zinc, copper and silver workings which were 2000 feet deep, the wheel was named after the Governor's wife, Lady Isabella Hope, who performed the commissioning ceremony. The largest water-wheel ever built in Britain, it is 72 ft. 6 ins. in diameter and developed 200 h.p. It needed an enormous quantity of water to drive it and the leats to bring this were three miles long. The workings were abandoned in 1929. Between 1965 and 1970 it was restored by the Manx Government and is now in working condition again.

Prestongrange Historical Site, East Lothian   Site museum of the ancient (since eleventh century) now-extinct local coal industry, centred on a Cornish pumping engine built by Harvey's of Hale, which operated from 1874 until 1954. The old colliery power-house contains an exhibition showing the history of mines and miners in the coalfield.

St. Austell (near), Cornwall   Wheal Betty china-clay works, now converted to a museum of the china-clay industry. The site is owned and maintained by English China Clays Ltd. and includes a group of the traditional pattern of settling tanks, part of a water-wheel driven rod-pumping system and the preserved ruins of one of the old type of clay drying plants and stores.

WIND AND WATERMILLS

Ballycopeland, County Down   Ballycopeland Windmill (*c*.1788). A tower mill, fully restored in 1958. With all its machinery complete and in working order, it is the best preserved windmill of its type, once common in northern England, Scotland and Ireland.

Birmingham (near), West Midlands   Sarehole Mill. This eighteenth century mill was leased by Matthew Boulton in 1755 and used by him to make small metal parts. It reverted to cornmilling in the mid-nineteenth century and continued in this function until 1919. It has been restored to working order and is now a museum of milling and grain production, and of English rural activities.

Brixton, London   Brixton Windmill, Blenheim Gardens. Tower mill (1816). Worked

Great Laxey Wheel, Isle of Man

by steam from 1860 onwards, the mill was bought by the LCC in 1945 and re-equipped with new sails and with machinery from a mill at Burgh-le-Marsh, Lincolnshire.

Cheddleton, Staffordshire North Mill (1756). The mill was built, probably by James Brindley, to grind flints, used as a whitening agent in the manufacture of pottery. Power was provided by two water-wheels.

East Linton, East Lothian   Preston Mill. The oldest watermill still working in Scotland. Both the building and machinery have been recently restored and since 1950 the mill has been the property of the National Trust of Scotland.

Faversham, Kent   Chart Gunpowder Mills (*c.*1760). A survival of a formerly extensive group of mills, which closed in 1934, Chart mills contain two pairs of mills, working in tandem off a large water-wheel. They have been restored by the Faversham Society.

Ivinghoe, Buckinghamshire   Pitstone Green Windmill. A post mill, rebuilt, but including timbers of the 1627 mill. National Trust property.

Leek, Staffordshire   Brindley Mill (1752), probably designed by James Brindley. Restored by the Brindley Mill Preservation Trust, the machinery and water-wheel are in good order.

Morden, London   Morden Snuff Mills. An early nineteenth century mill, driven by a large water-wheel, which is original. Owned by the National Trust.

Nether Aderley, Cheshire   Nether Aderley Corn Mill. A mill has been on the site since the fourteenth century, but the present building is sixteenth century. Two water-wheels, each driving its own set of machinery. The mill operated until 1930 and is now National Trust property.

Polegate, Sussex   Polegate Windmill (1817). A tower mill, which operated until 1943 and has all its machinery intact.

Skipton, North Yorkshire   High Corn Mill. Two water-wheels, one grinding corn, the other driving winnowers, hay choppers and other equipment.

Thornton Cleveleys, Lancashire   Marsh Mill (1794). Restored by the local council and open to the public.

Upminster, Essex   Upminster Windmill (1800). A weatherboarded smock mill, now restored, with a windshaft and sails from a post mill at Maldon.

WATER TRANSPORT

Bath (near), Avon   Claverton Pumping Station (1813). The pumps, used to lift water to the nine mile length of the Kennet and Avon Canal between Bath and Bradford-on-Avon, including seven locks taking the canal down to the Avon, are driven by two water-wheels. Designed by John Rennie, it was rebuilt in 1902–3 and restored 1969–73.

Buxworth, Derbyshire   Canal Basin (1793–97). This majestic basin on the Peak Forest Canal, has been cleared of trees and other rubbish, cleaned out to its original depth of 5 ft. 6 ins. and made water-tight once again by members of the Inland Waterways Protection Society – a five-year job.

Devizes, Wiltshire   Series of 29 locks (1810), designed by Rennie, carrying the Kennet and Avon Canal through and beyond Devizes. The second longest chain of locks in Britain, they are in very poor condition and constitute the main barrier to the Kennet and Avon Trust's aim of restoring and re-opening the whole of the Canal, from the Thames to the Avon.

Foxton, Leicestershire   Inclined plane (1900) on the Grand Union Canal. The largest and best preserved example in the country. Built to raise two narrow boats or one barge to a vertical height of 75 ft. Counter-balanced with a steam-driven winch.

Liverpool, Merseyside   Albert Dock (1845). Designed by Jesse Hartley and one of the finest surviving early dock installations in the country. Now under conversion to provide additional premises for Liverpool Polytechnic.

Llangollen (near), Clwyd   Pontcysylte Aqueduct (1795–1803), over the River Dee, by Telford. Cast-iron trough carried on nine 121 ft. high stone piers.

London   St. Katharine's Dock. Warehouses (1820s and 1830s) by Thomas Telford and Philip Hardwick. Some of the warehouses, converted into flats, now form part of a large redevelopment project, which includes the World Trade Centre and a new hotel.

Clifton Suspension Bridge, Bristol

Longton-on-Tern, Shropshire   Aqueduct (1795–96) by Telford, on the Shropshire Union Canal. Still standing, but now dry, this aqueduct used cast-iron for the canal trough.

Marlborough (near), Wiltshire   Crofton pumping station, now the property of the Kennet and Avon Trust. Built to supply water to the highest section of the Canal, it was originally equipped with two Boulton and Watt engines (1801 and 1812). The 1801 engine was replaced in 1845, but the 1812 engine is still operational and is believed to be the oldest working steam-engine in the world. Both engines are under steam once or twice a year, for the benefit of visitors, although since 1952 their normal duties have been carried out by electric pumps.

Portsmouth, Hampshire   Mid-eighteenth century storehouses and workshops at the Naval Dockyard. Some block-making machinery of the 1780s, probably the earliest example of machine-tools designed for mass-production, is still kept in its original workshop.

ROAD TRANSPORT

Bangor (near), Gwynedd   Menai Suspension Bridge (1826). Designed by Telford, it was the last link in the road from London to Holyhead. It has a main span of 579 ft. and the main piers are 153 ft. high. The bridge was unusually carefully designed and constructed. Each of the sixteen suspension chains was tested to 100 per cent in excess of the working load.

Bristol, Avon   Clifton Suspension Bridge. One of the most spectacular bridge sites in Britain. The bridge was begun in 1836, to Brunel's design, and completed, after delays due to shortage of money, in 1864. The chains were taken from Hungerford Bridge over the Thames, which was demolished in 1861.

Gloucester (near), Gloucestershire   Over Bridge. This stone bridge over the Severn is notable as being one of Telford's very few mistakes. There was a miscalculation over the foundations, which caused considerable settlement, but the bridge still carries trunk-road traffic. The arches are bevelled, so as to offer less resistance to the Severn floods.

Ironbridge, Shropshire   The Iron Bridge. The first iron bridge in the world, erected in 1779 and in regular use until 1934. Restored, with the abutments strengthened, 1971–74.

RAILWAY TRANSPORT

Bangor (near), Gwynedd   Britannia Tubular Bridge (1851). Robert Stephenson's railway bridge is 1513 ft. long. As originally built, the tracks were carried in two wrought-iron tubes. The pitch covering of these accidentally caught fire in 1970 and the damaged tubes have now been replaced by a reinforced concrete structure.

Birmingham, West Midlands   Portico and former offices of Curzon Street Station (1838), by Philip Hardwick. The original terminus of the London–Birmingham line. Used only for freight for many years and demolished in 1963.

Iron bridge at Coalport, spanning the River Severn

Bristol, Avon   Brunel's original Temple Meads Station (1841). Now used as a covered car-park, the train shed and office buildings are intact.

Chalk Farm, London   The Round House (1847). A locomotive shed, designed by Robert Stephenson. Now converted into a theatre and arts centre. The deep, brick-lined cutting at Chalk Farm is one of the most notable early achievements of the railway engineers and contractors.

Kilsby, Northamptonshire   Kilby Tunnel (1838), designed by Robert Stephenson. On the London to Birmingham Railway. The engineering problems caused by quicksand

Interior of Brunel's original terminus at Temple Meads, Bristol. The part of the trainshed beyond the signals and the number 13 is a later addition. Since this photograph was taken in 1964, the tracks have been removed and the building converted into a car-park

and flooding were immense. At one time thirteen pumping stations were in operation to drain the works. The tunnel has two huge ventilation shafts, 60 ft. in diameter and 100 ft. deep, with castellated towers.

London King's Cross Station (1852), by Lewis Cubitt. It was designed with two train sheds, one for arrival, the other for departure, linked by a brick colonnade. The roof-ribs of this straightforward building were originally of laminated wood, but they were replaced by iron in 1869 and 1886.

London Paddington Station (1854). The main interest is in its iron-arched interior, Victorian iron architecture at its best.

London St. Pancras Station (1874). Sir Gilbert Scott designed St. Pancras. High Victorian architecture at its grandest, as an expression of the wish of the Midland Railway to have a more splendid London terminus than any of the other companies.

Manchester Liverpool Road Station (1830). Considerably modified and added to as a goods station, it is the oldest railway building in Britain. The original terminus of

St. Pancras Station, London: station and hotel entrance

the Liverpool and Manchester Railway, it was superseded in 1836 by the first Lime Street.

Newcastle-upon-Tyne, Tyne & Wear High Level Bridge (1849), with road and railway on different levels. The architect was John Dobson, the engineer Robert Stephenson.

Newcastle-upon-Tyne, Tyne & Wear Railway Station. The train shed, also by Dobson and Stephenson, was completed in 1849, the façade in 1860. This was the earliest station roof in which round-arched iron ribs were used to form the main framework.

Saltash, Devon Royal Albert Bridge (1859), by Brunel. Two main spans of 465 ft. each. The zenith of wrought-iron as a constructional material.

South Queensferry, Midlothian Forth Bridge (1890). The first major steel bridge, it was a landmark in the development of bridge-building techniques.

Tanfield, County Durham Causey Arch (c.1780), the earliest surviving railway bridge in the world. Built to carry a coal tramroad from the pits to the coast.

AIR TRANSPORT

Cardington, Bedfordshire Airship hangars. These two hangars, both scheduled and preserved, are among the largest industrial monuments in Britain. The first was built in 1917 and extended from 106 ft. to 155 ft. in 1927, at the time of the construction of the R.100 and R.101. A second hangar, also of 155 ft., was added in 1927, the year of the R.101's maiden flight.

Croydon, Surrey Airport terminal building (1928). Now used as factory and offices. The old airfield is now an industrial estate and there is little glamour about the terminal itself, which road-widening has brought very close to the stream of traffic on the Gatwick Road.

Filton, Gloucestershire Brabazon Assembly Hall (1947). The structure is steel, but aluminium was used for the roof glazing-bars and for the enormous doors, which would hardly have been feasible in any other material. The thirty-two folding leaves weigh 200 tons and can be opened in two minutes.

WATER, GAS, ELECTRICITY

Blagdon, Avon Blagdon Pumping Station. Built in 1905 for the Bristol Waterworks Company, the station originally had four compound beam engines. Two were removed in the 1950s, when electric pumps were installed. The other two have been restored and preserved by the Company.

Fakenham, Norfolk Fakenham Gasworks (1852). Preserved as an industrial monument by the Department of the Environment, this charming survival of a small-town Victorian gasworks owes its continued existence to its compactness. Later nineteenth

Brabazon hangar, Filton, Bristol

century gas-producing plants and gas-holders were too large to make preservation possible.

Kew Bridge, London   Kew Bridge Waterworks. The finest collection of Cornish engines in the world. A Boulton and Watt engine (1820); an 1838 engine by Maudsley, Sons and Field, of Lambeth; an 1846 engine by Sandys, Caine and Vivian, of Hayle; an 1871 engine by Harveys, of Hayle. All are preserved by the Metropolitan Water Board.

Petworth, Sussex   Petworth House. Estate gas-works (1832). A remarkably complete survival, with retort house, exhauster house, steam and gas engines, and wet and dry purification plant.

Portsmouth (near), Hampshire   Eastney Sewage Pumping Station. Contains two compound beam engines (1886–87) by James Watt and Co. which worked until 1954. These engines, and their engine house, have been restored by Portsmouth City Museums, as the nucleus of an industrial and transport museum.

Sunderland, Tyne & Wear   Ryhope Pumping Station. Completed in 1868, the buildings are an outstanding example of Victorian industrial architecture, and the engines and equipment have a standard of finish which represents nineteenth century engineering design and construction at its best. It contains two beam engines (1868) by R. and C. Hawthorn, of Newcastle. The engines were last used in 1967, but have since been carefully restored and now occasionally run under steam.

MANUFACTURING

Bolton, Greater Manchester   Soho Foundry (1830). Founded by Benjamin Hick, this historic engineering business developed into Hick, Hargreaves and Co., which made its name especially for its works in the fields of railway and textile engineering. Parts of the original works still remain, surrounded by the modern factory buildings.

Bradford-on-Avon, Wiltshire   Former Spencer, Moulton rubber mill (1875). This square, flat-roofed mill, with its attractively recessed windows, is one of the most architecturally distinguished Victorian factory buildings. Now belonging to the Avon Rubber Group, the interior has been skilfully converted into office accommodation.

Bristol, Avon   'Puritan' soap-factory (1850), Broad Plain. The works belonged to Christopher Thomas and Co., and was the largest of the city's soap-factories. With its corner turrets and pinnacles, it was, and still is, a notable feature of the Bristol skyline. After the Second World War, it was taken over by Gardiner's, the builders' merchants, and is now used as the firm's warehouse and showroom.

Bristol, Avon   Tobacco warehouses. There are two groups of these bonded warehouses, which are among Bristol's most prominent landmarks. The first group (1905, 1908, 1919) are on Clift House Road and on the north side of the New Cut; they are brick-built. The second group, at Canon's Marsh, date from the 1920s and are of reinforced concrete.

Cromford, Derbyshire   Samuel Arkwright's cotton mills (1771–80). The first

Abandoned machinery in a nineteenth century ropewalk, Bridport, Dorset

successful water-powered cotton mills in the world. Converted to steam in the 1820s. The original 1771 mill can still be seen, together with the village which Arkwright built for his workers.

Dorchester, Dorset   Eldridge Pope's brewery (1870–72), with later additions and some rebuilding after a fire in 1922. In Victorian polychromatic style, using different colours of local brick.

Golcar, West Yorkshire   Pair of three-storey weavers' cottages (*c.*1800) in Cliffe Ash, now restored and used as a museum. These cottages are of the nineteenth century type, with the weaving-room occupying the top floor.

London   Whitbread's Chiswell Street Brewery (1773). The Porter Tun Room has been preserved. It has a clear span of 84 ft., second only to that of Westminster Hall.

Mossley, Greater Manchester   Buckton Vale Printworks (late nineteenth–early twentieth centuries, with some machinery and equipment of this period). Now run by the Calico Printers' Association. There are workers' cottages (1870s) which date from the previous ownership of a printworks on the site.

Newby Bridge, Westmorland Stott Park Bobbin Mill (1875). Carries on one of the traditional industries of the Lake District, making wooden bobbins for the Yorkshire and Lancashire woollen and cotton mills. A steam engine took over from the water-wheel in 1880 and worked until 1946, when electricity replaced steam. Both the steam-engine and the original mill-race are still there.

New Lanark, Lanarkshire Cotton mills, dating from 1795. Company housing (tenements) from 1810. Made famous by Robert Owen's experiments in industrial and social welfare.

St. Helen's, Merseyside Pilkington's Ravenhead Glassworks (1773). Two bays of the original casting-hall still survive, and in the walls are traces of what may have been annealing houses. This building has been restored by the Company.

Sheffield (near), South Yorkshire Catcliffe Glassworks. Conical glasshouse (1740), closed in 1887 and now restored and preserved as an industrial monument.

Styal, Cheshire Cotton mill (1784). The mill and the adjacent, slightly later industrial village, are now owned by the National Trust.

Stonehouse, Gloucestershire Stanley Mill (1813). A very beautiful cloth mill, built of brick and stone, with double iron pillars supporting the iron floor beams. The mill is fire-proof, the floors consisting of shallow brick arches resting on the beams, with stone flags laid on top of the arches.

Index

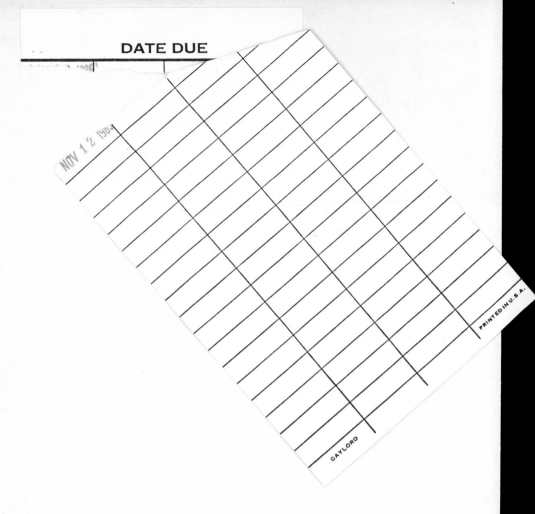